THE POSITION OF WOMEN IN THE VEDIC RITUAL

THE POSITION OF WOMEN IN THE VEDIC RITUAL

JATINDRA BIMAL CHAUDHURI

GYAN

Published by

GYAN

Gyan Publishing House
5, Ansari Road
Daryaganj, New Delhi-110002
Phone: 011-47034999, 9811692060
E-mail: books@gyanbooks.com

Distribution Network
gyanbooks.com
India, USA, Canada, UK, Australia, France

ISBN : 978-81-212-3909-7 (PB)
First Published, Calcutta, 1956

2nd Impression 2020

Printed at: Gyan Press, Delhi.

Pracyavani Research Series

THE
Position of Women in the Vedic Ritual

(Thesis approved for Ph.D. Degree by the University of London)

JATINDRA BIMAL CHAUDHURI

Secretary to Govt. Sanskrit Siksha Parishat, West Bengal; formerly, Principal, Govt. Sanskrit College, Calcutta and Head of the Department of Sanskrit, Presidency College, Calcutta.

SECOND EDITION

CALCUTTA

1956

Preface to the second edition

In the preface to the second edition of my work "The Position of Women in the Vedic Ritual," I have nothing more to add to what I said in the first edition.

The first edition was undertaken at a time when paper was scarce and many difficulties had to be faced due to the aftermath of the second World War. The work was well-received by the scholarly world and the first edition came to be exhausted within a few years of its publication. However, it is a matter of great regret that due to my preoccupation with other publications, the second edition could not be undertaken earlier.

It is indeed a matter of gratification that Women in Free India have made phenomenal progress in all spheres of life and culture within a short period. Hence it is but natural that a greater interest in the position of Indian Women throughout the Ages is being evinced to-day than ever before. It is indeed very striking that though there have been great upheavals—political, social, religious—in India with consequent repurcussions on Women in particular, Women of India have always been respected as the Highest emblems of Divinity, Purity, Sanctity and Sublimity. To an Indian, the Mother is the highest

Guru and has always been recognized as such in all ages from the Vedic down to to-day. The first and foremost Sermon of the Guru to the pupil during the Samāvartan is "मातृदेवो भव : revere thy Mother as thy God." Manu has rightly said :—

"सहस्रन्तु पितॄन् माता गौरवेणातिरिच्यते" ॥

And my humble thesis is nothing but a factual demonstration of this great and eternal doctrine of India.

Pracyavani, Vijayadasami
Calcutta, 1956.

J. B. C.

Preface to the first edition

The important subject of the Position of Women in Vedic India captured my imagination ever since I began my Vedic studies and as soon as I got an opportunity to take up Research work, I chose this fascinating subject. This was approved by the Board of Higher Sanskrit Studies, London University, on the recommendation of the Veteran Sanskrit Scholar Dr. L. D. Barnett, Curator, Oriental Section, British Museum, under the title "The Position of Women in Vedic Age" for the M. A. Degree of the University of London and along with my promotion to the Ph. D. Degree Course in course of a year, the subject was finally selected under the heading "The Position of Women in the Vedic Ritual" for the higher degree. This was approved for the Ph. D. Degree of the London University in 1934 on the recommendation of a Board of Examiners consisting of Prof. R. L. Turner, M. A. M. C. D. Lit., Head of the Dept. of Sanskrit, London University and Director of the School of Oriental and African Studies, London ; Dr. H. N. Randle M. A. D. Phil (oxon), Librarian, India office Library, London and Mr. C. A. Rylands, M. A., Senior Lecturer in Sanskrit, London University.

In addition to the printed Vedic works that were available both in the British Museum and India Office Library, many Mss. of Bhandarkar Oriental Research Institute Library, Banaras Sanskrit College, etc. were used.

My continued researches into the Position of Women in Sanskrit Literature have further confirmed my conclusions regarding the high position of Women in Ancient India. These researches have been published in seven volumes in my Series, "The Contribution of Women to Sanskrit Literature."

The present thesis is based entirely on original data collected from printed works and Mss. on various branches of Vedic Literature, viz, Saṃhitās, Brāhmaṇas, Āraṇyakas and Upaniṣads, and subsequent Literature such as the Sūtras, Epics, Purāṇas, Smṛtis, Prayogas and Paddhatis. Throughout my Thesis, I have tried to remove many misconceptions regarding the position of women during the Vedic Age, but in interpreting the texts and drawing conclusions from them, I have, all along strictly adhered to the letter and spirit of the original Texts and their authoritative commentaries.

Almost the whole of this work was published in the form of articles in well-known Research Journals, such as the Indian Historical Quarterly, New Indian Antiquary, etc. during the years 1939-1941. On account of this and my other important undertakings, such as the Contributions of Muslims to Sanskrit Literature, Contributions of Bengal to Smṛti Literature, Sanskrit Dūtakavya Literature, etc., the publication of the present work in book form was not immediately undertaken. Later on, the publication of this work was held up due to the World War. II.

Presidency College,
Calcutta
1945 J. B. C.

CONTENTS

Part I

Part II

* Mātṛdatta in his commentary on the Hiraṇkeśi- gṛhya-sūtra, Kirste's edition, p, 156, says,

बौध्यानि पलाशपर्णानि । तेषां विहारो विहरणं नानादेशेषु स्थापनं बौध्यविहारः कर्म नाम ।......अन्यो बौध्यानि विकीर्यन्ते यत्र स बौध्यविहार इति ॥"

Subject | Pages

DOMESTIC RITUAL

THE WIDOW IN THE VEDIC RITUAL

Chapter V

The Position of Women in the Vedic Ritual

CHAPTER I

THE DAUGHTER IN THE VEDIC RITUAL

The civilization of a country is best uuderstood by a thorough study of the Position of its Women. The woman in the various phases of her life as Daughter, Wife and Mother not only protects and invigorates the man to the best of her power but safeguards his interests even at her own cost. As soon as the manfolk begins to misjudge this latter magnanimity of woman as her weakness, a nation begins to sink slowly into the depth of degradation and misery. In the long history of Indian Civilization, our society has faced innumerable odds—constant invasion from outside, intermixture of heterogenous faiths and thoughts, ruthless persecution and so on—and certainly, changes there have been many with the consequence that, social conditions changed a good deal from period to period. Even then, ancient Indian Literature exhibits a uniform spirit of reverence for womanhood and Vedic Religion does not deny any right to women, not in the least the religious. Hindu Religion upholds the Vedas as the Highest authority and the view-points of the Smṛtis and Purāṇas contradicting those of the Vedas are simply to be ignored. This just attitude of the Hindu Society has saved it at all critical times. True there have been ups and downs in the position of Hindu Women, but they have never been shorn of their inherent goodness and greatness on account of oppression or excessive depression. Along with national regeneration from period to period, the liberties and possessions of women appear to vary and that is only natural; but even then, there is the constant attitude of very deep respect for women ingrained in Indian mind which is the direct outcome of the teachings of Vedic Religion. We must analyse this thoroughly in order that we may have a thorough grasp of the Position of women in Ancient and Modern India and this we shall do in the following sections of the work.

The Daughter is affection incarnate and it is as such that Vedic Literature depicts her. She has never been denied the rights her brother enjoys. A critical analysis will reveal that in the Vedic Ritual the Daughter is just as important as the son, if not more; as a matter of fact, in many places it would appear as though in ancient India the Daughter was more covetable for the parents than the son. Certain misconceptions took the upper hand in some parts of India during Mediaeval ages owing to the then degenerate conditions; the teachings of the Veda were really ignored though apparently the commentators intended to uphold them; nation as a whole was in a tottering state and no doubt, women also had to face all sorts of ordeals. Time is now ripe when Indians should look back to their glorious Vedic Age and allow the girls to enjoy the same Vedic Rights as our Holy Scriptures declare.

The Saṃskāras must all be performed for the Daughter as well as the Son and no discrimination ought to be made between them. The pseudo-Vedic attempts of a few scholars in Mediaeval India to prove the Daughter an unwelcome member of the family must be discarded as absolutely unvedic, unholy and suicidal as the early Vedic Ritual Literature uncompromisingly compels just the reverse conclusion. In subsequent ages, women have been denied the honour of the Puṃsavana and the privilege and dignity of the upanayana in particular. But this attitude is absolutely unvedic.

The Significance of the Vedic Rite Puṃsavana[1]. The Puṃsavana is an important Vedic rite, generally belived to be performed in order to have male children only.[2] But there is evidence to show that the puṃsavana is a rite performed with the object of averting any evil to the progeny and of having either a male or a female child as desired. According to the majority of Ritual authorities[2] this rite is

1. This section was published in Indian Historical Quaterly, Vol. XIV, 1931, pp. 831—835. 2. Cf. Monier-Williams, A Sanskrit—English Dictionary, Oxford Clarendon Press, 1899, p. 630, Column 2. 2. Cf. Pāraskaragṛhya-sūtra, (henceforth abbreviated as PārGS.) Bombay ed., 1918, p. 145 f., all commentators stick to the same principle; Saṃskāra-paddhati, Poona, 1924, p. 51, line 3; Baudhāyana-gṛhya-sūtra, (henceforth abbreviated as Baudh- GS.) Mysore University ed., p. 29.

to be performed on each occasion of the wife's pregnancy so that whenever the wife and the husband wish to have a daughter, they may use what is technically known as Ūha i.e. an alteration in the gender or other things as necessary in the sacred formulas, etc., just as they have the option to choose—if they want sons—whether they would have an heroic son or otherwise.[1] Both the Sīmantonnayana (the rite of parting the hair) and the Puṃsavana are really Garbha-saṃskāras, performed for removing the sin that might bring any evil to the embryo.[2] The word 'Puṃs' in the name of 'Puṃsavana' refers to both male and female and does not at all debar the use of 'Ūha whenever necessary.

That the first part 'Puṃs' of the compound 'Puṃsavana' does not stand for the male child alone is corroborated by the fact that nowhere in the Gṛhya-sūtras do the Sūtra-kāras intend to exclude daughters by the use of words in the masculine gender. The usual method is to speak about both males and females by the use of the masculine gender only; when the Sūtra-kāras have to say something particular about females, only tben do they use specifically the feminine gender. Thus when Laugākṣi in the Kāṭhaka-gṛhya-sūtra says, पुत्रे जाते नाम धीयते he does not mean to say that when a daughter is born, it is to be otherwise. In commenting

1. PārGS.. op. cit., p. 144, lines 7-8; for the Ūha used in this connection, see Saṃskāra-rantamālā, (henceforth abbreviated as Saṃs RM.) Poona, 1899, p. 813, II. 24-25.

2. Cf. PārGS., op. cit., p. 144, II. 9, 16. 29, etc. Saṃskāra-paddhati, op. cit., p. 51, I. 20; Saṃs RM., p. 813, II, 21f.

upon the sūtra, Ādityadarśana[1] expressly says that the daughter, too, should have the naming ceremoney. In the Jātakarman section of the Āśvalāyana-gṛhya-sūtra, an aphorism[2] makes the provision that when a 'Kumāra' is born, the child is to be treated with water mixed with gold. In commenting upon the sūtra, Haradatta[3] says that herein provision is made for a 'Kumārī' as well, as the gender is not intended to be stressed, 'liṅgasya avivakṣitatvāt.' Similarly is to be explained जातं कुमारमभिमन्त्रयते in the Baudh GS.[4] It will be seen that at the end of the section on Jātakarman, Baudhāyana points out the name given to a daughter should consist of an odd number of syllables[5] and makes the provision of blessing the child अमुष्मै स्वस्तीति । By the use of the masculine gender in "amuṣmai," Baudhāyana certainly does not mean that "svasti," i.e., benediction should not be uttered in case of the birth of a daughter of whom he speaks in the preceding aphorism. What he really

1. Op. cit., p. 137. 2. Trivandrum ed., 1923, p. 60. II, 17-18.

3. Āśvalāyana-gṛhya-sūtra, (henceforth abbreviated as ĀśvGS.) op. cit., p. 61, II. 1-2 "Liṅgasya avivakṣitatvāt kumāryā api prāpnoti." For his argument, see II. 2f. For similar examples where the gender is not intended to designate males only, cf. statements like svarga-kāmo yajeta : yaḥ svargakāmaḥ sa yajeta : one who, male or female, aspires to go to heaven, should sacrifice; see in this connection the Jaiminīya-mīmāṃsā-darśana. 6-1-7; see also Nyāya-mālā-vistara on the same 6-1-6 ff.; Karkācārya on the Kātyāyana-śrauta-sūtra, (abbreviated as KātŚS.) 1-1-7, Chowkhamba ed, 1908, p. 5; Yājñikadeva on the KātŚS., Berlin 1157, p. 8.

4. Op. cit., II. 1, 2, p. 33.

5. Op. cit, p. 35, I 17, अयुगक्षरं कुमार्याः ।

does is to revert to his general way of statement, uses the masculine gender to mean both males and females and concludes the section by prescribing the rule that the jāta-karman rites should be finished with the utterance of benediction for the child (boy or girl). The object (saṃkalpa) of the rite as stated in the Prayogas also shows that the word 'Puṃs' is not restricted to males alone. The rite is meant for removing the sin that may bring evil to the progeny. It is, most probably, owing to this fact that MānavaGS. omits the rite altogether, as it considers the saṃskāra called Sīmantonnayana, i. e., parting of the hair, quite sufficient for averting any evil to the embryo caused by the father or mother or both. That a girl should pound a herb for use during the Puṃsavana ceremony[1] also indicates that the sūtrakāras raise no objection to the birth of others of her sex, nay, more—they introduce a girl in particular, not a boy, because as shown by the analysis of the rites performed by, and for, the daughter—the daughter is for the parents the sum-total of purity, tenderness, affection, devotion and bliss.[2] If the meaning of the word 'Puṃs' be limited to males only and the Puṃsavana be a rite that must be performed, there remains no rite to be performed for the birth of a

1. Bhārdvāja-gṛhya-sūtra, (abbreviated as BhārGS.) Solomon's ed., London, 1913, 1, 22, p. 22, अथ पुंसवनं तृतीये मासि···न्यग्रोधावरोधाद्दत्वा नवस्नातया कुमार्या दृषत्पुत्रेण पेषयित्वा, etc.

2. It must be remembered that the introduction of a person or thing—a person in paticular—in Vedic rituals is significant.

daughter. But the fáct is that the birth of a daughter is most welcome. Parents perform Kāmya-śrāddhas on the second day of the moon in the hope of having a daughter.[1] Desirous of having a daughter, the husband touches all the fingers of the wife except the thumb during the marriage ceremony.[2] Longing for a daughter the bridegroom shows the bride after she has reached her new home[3] the Dhruva and other constellations.[4] The parents deem it a favour of god if they can have sons as well as daughters by their side during the performance of sacrifices.[5] The Ṛg-veda praises the father of many daughters.[6] The daughter claims her support from parents not for nothing, but for her devotion

1. Gobhila-pariśiṣṭa śrādha-kalpa, Bib. Ind., Calcutta, 1909, p. 186;Pār. G. S., op. cit., p. 538, I, 21, commentary of Gadādhara l.I.

2. ĀśvGS, Trivandrum ed., 193, I, 5, 3, p. 23, ll. Il-125 तिष्ठन् प्रत्यङ्मुखः प्राङ्मुख्या आसीनाया गृभ्णामि ते सौभगत्वाय हस्तमित्यङ्गुष्ठमेव गृह्णीयाद्यदि कामयेत पुमांस एव मे पुत्रा जायेरन्निति ; अङ्गुलीरेव स्त्रीकामः ; रोमान्ते हस्तं साङ्गुष्ठमुभयकामः। Commentary: पुत्रशब्दस्य स्त्र्यपत्येऽपि दर्शनात् पुमांस इत्युक्तम्। स्त्रीशब्दो दुहितृवाचि पुत्रसन्निधानात्। रोमान्ते रोमवतः प्रदेशादुपरि। उभयकामः पुत्रकामः स्त्रीकामश्च। Āpastamba-gṛhya-sūtra, (henceforth abbreviated as ĀpGS.), Madras, 1893, VI, 12. यदि कामयेत स्त्रीरेव जनयेयमित्यङ्गुलीरेव गृह्णीयात्। See also commentary.

3. This reflects a great anxiety for having daughters.

4, Kāṭhaka-gṛhya-sūtra. (abbreviatedKāṭh GS.), op. cit., XXV, 45, p. 114, ll. 1-2, जीवन्तीं ध्रुवं स्वस्त्यात्रेयं दर्शयत्यरुन्धतीं च। Devapāla's comm. जीवन्तीं कन्यामिच्छन् ध्रुवादिकं दर्शयेत्। 5. Rg-veda, VIII, 31, 8. पुत्रिणा ता कुमारिणा विश्वमायुर्व्यश्नुतः। उभा हिरण्यपेशसा। 6 VI, 75, 5. बह्वीनां पिता बहुरस्य पुत्रश्चिश्चा कृणोति समनावगत्य। इषुधिः सङ्काः पृतनाश्च सर्वाः पृष्ठे निनद्धो जयति प्रसूतः॥

to them.[1] They care for her as much as they do for their son; or it may be said—even more, as the father is found to worship the daughter (kumārī) as an emblem of Virginity, as an emblem of Purity, of Tenderness, Devotion, and what not.[2] Just as the Mātṛkā-pūjā is to take place at the beginning of all Vedic rituals, the Kumārī-pūjā is recommended to be performed at the end of all; and this latter worship, the Daughter-Worship, is impossible in the absence of a daughter as she is to be bodily present. The father wraps her up with new garments, entertains her with delicious dishes and walks round her. From her first year onwards, she is worshipped as different deities; if she is one year old, as Sandhyā; if two, Sarasvatī; and so on. Thus as she grows, the parents find in her different manifestations of the Supreme Soul,—blessing them in every possible way. The daughter is indeed the embodiment of all blessings for the parents and the family. In Sanskrit literature the word Puṃs does not exclusively mean males alone but is also found used in the sense of human beings in general. Thus, when Varāhamihira[3] says the earth has veins just as the

1 Rg-veda II. 17, 7. अमाजूरिव पित्रोः सचा सती समानादा सदसस्त्वामिये भगम् । कृधि प्रकेतमुप मास्या भर दद्धि भागं तन्वो येन मामहः ॥ Sāyaṇa in his commentary says:—पित्रोः सचा मातापितृभ्यां सह भवन्ती तयोः शुश्रूषणपरा... । 2. Tri-vedīya-kriyā-kāṇḍa-paddhati, Calcutta, 1887, p, 160. "......"कुमारीपूजनमहं करिष्य इति संकल्प्य कुमारीमानीय......पूजयेत् ॥"

3. Vizianagram Sanskrit Series ed., part II, 53, 1, also 85, 5. See also Bhāgavata-purāṇa, 8, 24, 41 for a similar use.

bodies of 'Puṃs' have, the word Puṃs conveys necessarily the sense of human beings, as women too have veins in their bodies. Hemacandra in his Abhidhāna-cintāmaṇi[1] gives "martya: one who is mortal," "bhū-spṛś:" one who touches (is born on) the earth," etc. as the synonyms of Puṃs. All these necessarily include the sense of women as well. In commenting upon a couplet quoted in the Bhāmatī which includes the word Puṃs in the genitive plural, Bhaṭṭa Gopīnātha in his treatise Upodghāta[2] says the word Puṃs means males as well as females. The Āśvalāyana-Śrautasūtra[3] too uses Puṃs in the same sense.

Thus the usual method of the Sūtra-kāras of including feminine in the masculine gender, the procedure of the rite itself, the importance of a daughter emphatically borne out by the whole range of Sanskrit literature, instances where the word Puṃs is found used in the sense of both males and females—all lead to the conclusion that the purpose of the Puṃsavana is to avert any evil to the progeny and to have any child—male or female—as the parents desire.

The Initiation of Women.[4] There is a general belief

1. Boehtlingk's ed., St. Petersburg, 1147.

2. निवृत्तिर्वा प्रवृत्तिर्वा नित्येन कृतकेन वा । पुंसां येनोपदिश्यते तच्छास्त्रमभिधीयते । Ānandāśrama Sanskrit Series, vol. 94, Poona 1924, p. 18. For grammatical support of our interpretation:, Pāṇini, 1-2. 66-67 Bāla-manoramā, Trichinopoly, (1110-22). p. 608, ll. 3f., Siddhānta-kaumudī, 939-33.

3. Bib. Indica ed., 1874, p. 203, sūtras 3, 2, 12ff.

4. This whole section was pub. in IHQ. March, 1939.

that women are not entitled to be initiated for Vedic studies. Such a belief is absolutely wrong. The Gṛhya Sūtras say in connection with the initiation ceremony of the Brāhmaṇa "अष्टमवर्षे ब्राह्मणमुपनयेत्"[1] or "सप्तमवर्षे ब्राह्मणस्योपनयनम्"[2] or "गर्भाष्टमे ब्राह्मणमुपनयेत्"[3] or exactly similar things[4] meaning that the Brāhmaṇa should be initiated in the 7th or 8th year after he was conceived or born; they make similar rules for the Kṣatriyas and Vaiśyas too—only extending the age-limit for them. Here by Brāhmaṇa, Kṣatriya and Vaiśya the Sūtra-kāras mean that both the boy and the girl of these castes are to be initiated. As in the case of स्वर्गकामः[5] in "स्वर्गकामो यजेत", here also the gender is not intended to designate the Masculine alone. By a rule like this "ब्राह्मणो न हन्तव्यः i.e. the Brāhmaṇa should not be murdered" it is meant that the ब्राह्मणी also should not be murdered. Similarly by saying "मरणधर्मा मानवः or man is mortal", we mean that the woman is also mortal.

1. AsvGS. I, 19, 1, p. 64, Bom. ed.
2. KathGS. 41, 1, p. 159.
3. VārGS. V, p.
4. GobhGS. II, 10; Khādira, II, 5, 1, p. 70; Gobhila-gṛhya-karmaprakāśikā, p. 84; JaimGS., 1, 1, 1; ApGS. 10, 1; the Mān GS, mentions no limit but begins 'उपनयनप्रभृति व्रतचारी; One should observe vows from initiation." ParGS. 11, 2, 1, p. 196 Bom. ed., SanGS. 1, p. 13. Benares edn. p. 47. Compare also ĀśvGK. 16, 1, p. a75; Śaunaka-kārikā, f. 31a; Āśv. Yā. Pad., India Office Ms. Bühler 15, fol. 24b; Reṇukārya f. 12b; Baudhāyana-gṛhya-paddhati, f. 74a.
5. See KatSS. 1, 1, 7 "स्त्री चाविशेषात्" and the commentaries of कर्काचार्य and याज्ञिकदेव on it; pp. 5 & 8 of the Chowkhamba ed., and Weber's ed., respectively.

Hārīta[1] says women are of two types: those who speak about Brahman and those who soon become wives (i.e. those who do not grow old in their parents' house). Of them, the first type has (the right to) initiation, establishment of fire, Vedic studies, and observance of begging alms in their own houses; the second is initiated and (soon after) married. Yama[2] as quoted in the Kūrmapurāṇa, says that in ancient times the tying of the girdle is prescribed for girls; so also the teaching of the Vedas, and the utterance of the Sāvitrī. Nobody except her father, uncle or brother should teach her. The vow of begging alms is prescribed for her within (the limit of) her house. She should dispense with the deer skin, the bark and the wearing of matted locks. Here Yama seems to refer to the existence of the custom not only in ancient times, but also in his own days, the construction being पुराकल्पे (यथैष्यत) तथा (अधुनाऽपि) इष्यते. The word तथा is significantly put by Yama by way of a comparison between the old time and his own time. So he makes the rule for his own time that nobody other than the girl's father, uncle or brother should teach her, she should beg in her house only (and not elsewhere) and she should not wear deer-skin,

1. द्वि-विधाः स्त्रियो ब्रह्मवादिन्यः सद्योवध्वश्च। तत्र ब्रह्मवादिनीनामुपनयनमग्नीन्धनं वेदाध्ययनं स्व-गृहे भिक्षाचर्या चेति; Saṃskāra-ratna-mālā, Poona, 1899, vol. I, p. 165, l. 6-7.

2. पुरा-कल्पे कुमारीणां मौञ्जी-बन्धनमिष्यते। अध्यापनञ्च वेदानां सावित्रीवाचनन्तथा॥ पिता पितृव्यो भ्राता वा नैनामध्यापयेत् परः। स्व-गृहे चैव कन्याया भैक्ष-चर्या विधीयते॥ वर्जयेदजिनञ्चीरं जटाधारणमेव च॥

bark and matted locks. If Yama had intended to say that, unlike in ancient times in his own time the girl should not be initiated, he would have surely said something like this:—पुरा-कल्पे कुमारीणां मोञ्जो-वन्धमिष्यते । इह कल्पे तासामेवं न कुर्यान्मतिमान् क्वचित् ॥ As he continues with a series of verbs, all in the present tense—one in Laṭ and two in Liṅ, it is only reasonable to think that he prescribes the rules for his own days as was the case in ancient times too.

Without being initiated ceremonially, nobody is entitled to utter holy mantras. But the woman is found to utter sacred formulas in various sacrifices, gṛhya as well as śrauta. In the Sākamedha, the third four-monthly sacrifice, the girl uses the Tryambaka Mantra.[1] Mahīdhara[2] in his commentary Veda-dīpa says the unmarried girls of the sacrificer should walk round the fire three times along with the other males, the sons of the sacrificer and others while uttering the Tryambaka Mantra for Tryambaka's blessing. According to the Śatapatha Brāhmaṇa[3] the priests and the sacrificer go round the altar thrice from right to left—smiting the left thigh; but the maidens go from left to right—smiting the right thigh. While doing so, the maidens utter the formula: "We worship Tryambaka, the fragrant bestower of husbands. Even as a gourd is severed from its stem, so

1. VājSamh III, 60b, "त्र्यम्बकं यजामहे सुगन्धिं पतिवेदनम् । उर्वारुकमिव बन्धनादितो मुक्षीय मामुतः" ॥ 2. P. 92, Weber's edition of the White Yajurveda. 3. II, 6. 2, 13f. p. 197, Weber's edition; for Sāyaṇa, see op. cit., p. 218.

may I be severed from this world, not from thence."[1] Kātyāyana[2] says "कुमार्य्यश्चोत्तरेण उभयत्र पतिकामा भगकामा वा : the unmarried girls (of the sacrificer) too (should go round the fire), the latter[3] while uttering part of the mantra, in both the directions (पितृवद्देववच्च परिक्रमणे : in going round both in the direction of the manes i. e. the left, and in the direction of the gods, i. e., the right) either with the object of having husbands or fortune." Yājñikadeva[4] in the Paddhati says, "वचनात् कुमार्या अपि मन्त्रपाठ : i. e. the maiden too is to utter the sacred formula as it is so prescribed." Satyāṣāḍha[5] also says that if the daughter of the sacrificer longs for marriage, she should take the reverse course (to the one taken by the males) along with the utterance of the Tryambaka formula.[6]

In the Varuṇa-praghāsas, the second four-monthly sacrifice, after Haviṣ is placed on the north and south altars, the Pratiprasthātṛ—while leading the wife to the fire for the Karambha-pātra oblation—asks her if she has any lover or lovers. After her declaration[7] she utters the for-

1. They want to be severed from this world i.e. their father's house and be permanent in their husbands' families. Cf. Mahīdhara also. They like to leave their father's gotra as well.

2. Śrauta-sūtra, 5, 10, 17, Weber,s ed., p. 361.

3. The former one i. e., Vāj Sam., III, 60 a, being used by the males. 4. P. 536, Weber's ed., of W. YV. 5. Śrauta-sūtra, 5, 5., p. 489, vol. II. 6. The B. YV. schools have a different reading उर्वारुकमिव बन्धनान् मृत्योर्मुक्षीय मा पतेः ।

7. For details and references, see our section on "The Wife in

mula[1] "प्रघासिनो हवामहे मरुतः etc.: we invoke the Maruts, the voracious consumers," etc.[2] Then either the wife or the wife and husband both lift up the Karambha vessels on the winnowing baskets, place them on the head and offer oblations in the Dakṣiṇāgni with the formula यद्ग्रामे etc.; which in the village, etc.".[3] On her way back, the wife recites the formula "अक्रं कर्म etc.: having performed the work etc."[4]

In the agniṣṭoma too, the wife, entering by the south door, anoints the axles of the Soma-cart with the remnant of the clarified butter left after the Sāvitrī-homa along with the utterance of the formula, "देव श्रुतौ etc."[5]

There are several such instances where the wife or wives use sacred formulas. The Purāṇas and the Smṛtis as well furnish examples as to the right of women to utter the holy mantras. The Skanda-purāṇa[6] says that the wife should sacrifice with the sacred formulas in the rituals in accordance with the regulations; so, in the funeral rite too, she, according to the sacred law, is entitled to utter the sacred mantras.

the Cāturmāsya Sacrifice" below under "The Wife in the Vedic Ritual," 1. Vaj-Saṃh., III, 44; for Mahīdhara see Webers' ed., vol. I, p. 83; Karka, op. cit-, vol. III, p. 473, on KatSS. 5, 5, 10.

2. See also other YVSs. 3. Vaj-Saṃh,, III,45. 4. Op, cit., 47.

5. Vāj-Saṃh, 5, 17, The mantra has, however, variant readings in the different Saṃhitās and Sūtras. Cf. Mait-Saṃhitā 1, 2. 9; Kat-Saṃh., II, 10; Śat-Brā, III 5, 3. 13-14; MānSS, 2, 2, 2, 15; KātSS, 8, 3. 32.

6. Ed., by Pañcānana Tarkaratna, Calcutta, 1911, vol. IV, p. 2326; also quoted in the श्राद्धमयूख p, 22.

The Kāladarśa, as quoted in the Śrāddha-mayūkha[1] of Nīlakaṇṭha Mīmāṃsaka Bhaṭṭa, quotes the following lines from the same source to show that women are not entitled to utter the sacred formulas in the funeral and śrāddha rites: सर्वाभावे स्त्रियः कुर्युः स्वभर्तॄणाममन्त्रकम् : in the absence of all others, the स्त्रियः i.e. the women should offer to the bhartṛs i.e. the maintainers without mantras." Unfortunately we cannot trace the line in the Calcutta edition of the Skanda-purāṇa. The line, however, occurs in the Mārkaṇḍeya-purāṇa.[2] We read herein like this:—a सर्वाभावे स्त्रियः कुर्युः स्व-भर्तॄणाममन्त्रकम् । b तदभावे च नृपतिः कारयेत् स्व-कुटुम्बिनाम् ॥ c तज्जातीयैर्नरैः सम्यग् दाहाद्याः सकलाः क्रियाः । and preceding these lines are—i पात्र-त्रये प्रेत-पात्रं अर्घ्यञ्चैव प्रसेचयेत् । ये समाना इति जपन् पूर्ववच्छेषमाचरेत ॥ j स्त्रीणामप्येवमेवैतदेकोद्दिष्टमुदाहृतम् । मृताहनि यथान्यायं नृणां यद्वदिहोदितम ॥ But Raghunandana[3] takes the stanzas in the following order; a. b. i. j. to run concurrently and argues that "apy evam" in j. means "amantrakam" as in a. and so "स्त्रीणां मन्त्रनिषेधोऽपि तत्सम्प्रदानकश्राद्ध एवावगम्यतेः the prohibition (of the use) of mantra applies to those cases only where the women offer the Śrāddha". We cannot find out in any of the printed editions or manuscripts available in the India Office Library the order followed by Raghunandana. Moreover, the word "स्त्रियः" in *a* above does not

1. Ed., by Gharpure in the Collection of Hindu Law Books, vol. XVIII, p. 22. 1, 24-25.
2. Dr. K. M. Banerjee's ed. in the Bib. Ind., p. 189.
3. श्राद्ध-तत्त्व, p. 508, Calcutta, 1909-10.

mean "Wife", but any and every woman maintained by the deceased. In the Śrāddha-viveka, after enumerating the long list of those who are entitled to perform the Śrāddhas, the author says "तदभावे यथाकथञ्चित् परिगृहीताः स्त्रियः—these failing, any and every woman taken hold of by any means would do." These are the women meant in line *a* above and not the wife. The claim of the wife (Patnī) to perform the funeral and Śrāddha for her husband follows immediately after the son, i.e. the son failing, the wife is to do so. Saṅkha, Kātyāyana, Śrāddha-viveka, Śrāddha-mayūkha, Śrāddha-kriyā-kaumudī and all other authorities are unanimous on the point. So by "स्त्रियः" in "सर्वाभावे स्त्रियः कुर्युः", the wife can by no means be meant. The words "apy evam" in line *j* in the order we find mean that the mantras "ये समानाः", etc. are to be uttered and that the rites following should be the same as mentioned before. The Kalpa-taru says that "स्त्रीणामप्येवम्" etc. means: "यादृशेन सम्बन्धेन पितृव्यत्वादिना पुरुषाणामेकादशाहादि श्राद्धं, तादृशेन च सम्बन्धेन स्त्रीणामेतत् कर्तव्यमिति"। Here it is evident that the women also utter the mantra in the Śrāddha. After having said that the Ekoddiṣṭa and Sapiṇḍīkaraṇa should be offered with mantras, Yājñavalkya[1] says "This Sapiṇḍīkaraṇa as well as Ekoddiṣṭa should be offered to the woman also". Yājñavalkya has suggested no distinction whatsoever. The Chandoga-pariśiṣṭa[2]

1. ÙnaSamh, ed., by Pañcānana Tarkaratna, Calcutta 1903, p. 161, l. II. śl. 254. 2. मातुः सपिण्डीकरणं पितामह्या सहोदितं। यथोक्तेनैव कल्पेन etc.

also says that the Sapiṇḍīkaraṇa of the mother is said to be observed with the grandmother (on the father's side) in accordance with the rites as mentioned. Here also no distinction whatsoever is suggested. The Śrāddha-kriyā-kaumudī[1] also-comments on the couplet स्त्रीणाममन्त्रकं श्राद्धम् etc. thus: स्त्रीणाममन्त्रकं श्राद्धमिति वचनात् स्त्रीणां सकल-श्राद्ध एव सकल-मन्त्रपाठो नास्तीति वदन्ति। तन्मन्दं वचनस्यामूलत्वात् सकलसंग्रहेष्वदृष्टत्वात्। etc, Here he thinks the couplet "Strīṇāṃ amantrakaṃ' śrāddham," etc. is baseless (an interpolation) as it is not found' in all the Saṃgrahas and the view that the woman is not entitled to perform the Srāddha with mantras is not tenable. The Brahma-purāṇa[2] also says distinctly that women should offer the Śrāddha with mantras. Śaṅkhā[3] says that the daughter too after her saṃskāra should, like the boy, observe the Aśauca, perform the funeral rite, offer Piṇḍas and celebrate the Ekoddiṣṭa for her father. Here too no distinction has been suggested and accordingly the mantras are to be uttered by the daughter too. The reason why the "स्त्रियः" in line *a* above who are really "यथाकथञ्चित् परिगृहीताः स्त्रियः" in the language of the Srāddha-viveka-kāra should not utter the mantras is, therefore, not that the woman, because of her sex, is not entitled to utter the mantra in the Śrāddha-

1. S. of Govindānanda, Bib. Ind. Cal., 1904, p. 377, ll. 19-78, l. 1f. 2. स्त्रीभिश्च अवरवर्णैश्च श्राद्धं विप्रानुशासनात्। मन्त्रवत् विधि-पूर्वं तु वह्निपाक-विवर्जितम्॥ 3. दुहिता पुत्रवत् कुर्यात् माता-पित्रोस्तु संस्कृता। अशौचमुदकं पिण्डमेकोद्दिष्टं सदा तयोः॥ as quoted in श्राद्धमयूख p. 23; the श्राद्धक्रियाकौमुदी puts the verse under the name of Bhāradvāja.

ha, but because these women somehow picked out in the absence of all others need not utter the mantras. Such women will perform the Śrāddha somehow, and nobody would like them to perform the Śrāddhas in all the details. If the mantras are cut out, the oblations are also necessarily cut out and the ceremonies too become reduced by almost two-thirds. This is the reason why the यथाकथञ्चित् परिगृहीताः स्त्रियः thould not utter the mantras.

The Nṛsiṃha-tāpanīya Upaniṣad says सावित्रीं प्रणवं यजुः स्त्रीशूद्रयोर्नेच्छन्ति : (some) do not recommend (the utterance of) the Sāvitrī, Praṇava and Yajuṣ for the woman and the śūdra."[1] Baudhāyana[2] says, "अमन्त्रा हि स्त्रियो मताः—some say, women are not entitled to utter the mantra." The words "नेच्छन्ति" and 'मताः" in the above texts show that the authorities themselves do not think that women are not entitled to utter the mantras though there are a few schools who think otherwise. Moreover, the authority of the Smṛti cannot be reckoned as valid against that of the Śruti. Thus, Vedavyāsa[3] says that where Śruti, Smṛti and Purāṇa differ (in opinion), the Śruti should be considered as the authority; of the (latter two) Smṛti precedes (over the Purāṇa). So, the schools whom Baudhāyana mentions need not be taken into serious consideration. The opinion of the school quoted by

1. P. 10 of Ānandāśrama edition (vol. 30), 1. 6. 7. 2. As quoted in श्राद्धतत्त्व, Hṛṣikeśa Śāstrin's ed., Calcutta, 1909-10, p. 411, l. 4. 3. श्रुति-स्मृति-पुराणानां विरोधो यत्र दृश्यते । तत्र श्रौतं प्रमाणं स्यात्त-योर्द्वैधे स्मृतिर्वरा ॥ SmṛSam Poona, 1905, p. 367, l. 7 (verse 4).

the Nṛsiṃha-tāpanīya Upaniṣad is to be ignored not only because the Upaniṣad itself considers it ignorable, but also because the opinion of the majority should prevail when the authorities differ among themselves. Our copious Śruti evidence shows that the opinion of the opponent school cannot prevail.

In the Piṇḍa-pitṛ-yajña[1] and other Śrāddhas[2] the middle cake[3] given to the manes is to be eaten by the wife (Patnī). The husband gives her the cake saying that she should eat it as it represents the juice of the annual herbs growing in waters; as a result she should become pregnant with a human embryo. The wife too[4] eats the cake with the prescribed mantra. If the house-holder has many wives, he divides the cake amongst them all and all of them should eat their respective portions along with the utterance of the above sacred formula. The author of the Vaijayantī as mentioned in the Saṃskāra-ratna-mālā[5] says this eating of the cake is not optional but obligatory whenever the Śrāddha is celebrated. According to him, therefore, the utterance of this mantra is not an occasional but a regular right of the wife: if the eating of the cake is a regular (nitya) right, the utterance of the mantra must also be her regular right during the observance

1. See Saṃs R. M. Poona, 1899, p. 983, ll. 9f. 2. श्राद्धमञ्जरी, Poona, 1909, p. 37. 3. If there are 6 cakes, the wife should eat both the middle पिण्डषट्के मध्यमयोर्द्वयोः प्राशनम्, श्राद्धमञ्जरी, p. 37. 4. If the wife, however is not in a fit stage, she should not eat the cake. 5. Poona. 1899, p. 983, l. 13.

of all the Śrāddhas. It does not seem, however, that the eating of the middle cake or both the cakes is compulsory. The Śrāddha-mayūkha[1] says it is only optional and not obligatory. Manu uses the word "Sutārthinī: desirous of a son" while prescribing the eating of the cake by the wife. Devaṇṇa-bhaṭṭa in the Śrāddha-kāṇḍa[2] says if she is desirous of a son or a daughter, the wife should eat the cake. Yama also says the wife desirous of an issue should do so. The Vāyu-purāṇa puts the word "Prajārthinī: longing for a son or a daughter" as an adjective to the wife and mentions the sacred formula "आधत्त पितरो गर्भम्" which, it assures, is सन्तानवर्धनः (capable of) increasing (the number of) sons or daughters." Anyhow, the fact remains that whenever the wife eats the middle cake she as a rule utters the mantra. It is her right and no authority has ever intended to deprive her of this.

Āśvalāyana[3] says in his Gṛhyasūtra that from the time of marriage onwards the house-holder himself, the wife, the son, the unmarried girl, or a disciple, should offer regular oblations to the Gṛhya fire. GārgyaNārāyaṇa[4] and Haradatta[5] also cite the opinion of some schools according to whom the wife and the unmarried daughter are

1. Ed. by J. R. Gharpure,
Collection of Hindu Law Books, vol, XVIII, मध्यमपिण्डप्राशनं केवलमेव न नित्यम्। 2. स्मृतिचन्द्रिका vol. IV, p. 402. 3. 1, 7, 1, पाणिग्रहणादि गृह्यं परिचरेत् स्वयं पत्न्यपि वा पुत्रः कुमार्यन्तेवासी वा। 4. P. 33, l. 3, Bombay ed, of ĀśvGS., 5 ĀsvGS Trivandrum ed., p. 133. l. 21.

entitled to offer the oblation without any reservation. Khādira[1] says, "Some say the wife should sacrifice; the wife is the house and the fire belongs to the house." Gobhila[2] also says the wife should verily offer the morning and evening oblation to the domestic fire for the same reason. According to the Prayogaratna[3] too, the wife, the unmarried daughter, the son, or the disciple, should offer the sacrifice in accordance with the above-mentioned order. The Smṛty-artha-sāra[4] also holds that the sacrifice offered by the wife, the daughter, etc. is to be considered just the same as offered by the sacrificer though the wife and the daughter should offer without the besprinkling (पर्युक्षण). So the wife and the unmarried daughter are entitled to offer the oblation along with the utterance of the mantras unquestionably, together with the Om at the beginning and end of each mantra.[5] The connection between the domestic fire and the wife is so close that the fasting in case of its extinction devolves on the wife.[6]

1. Ed. by A. Mahādeva Śāstrin, Mysore Govt. Or. Lib. Series, no. 41, 1, 5, 17-18, p. 40. पत्नी जुहुयादित्येके। गृहाः पत्नी गृह्योऽग्निरेष इति। The definition of गृह्य, acc. to खादिर 1.5.1,—"यस्मिन्नग्नौ पाणिं गृह्णीयात् स गृह्यः"। Also cp. "न गृहं गृहमित्याहुर्गृहिणी गृहमुच्यते"। 2. 1, 3, 15, p. 95, Bib. Ind "कामं गृह्येऽग्नौ पत्नी जुहुयात् सायंप्रातर्होमौ, गृहाः पत्नी, गृह्य एषोऽग्निर्भवतीति" 3. Bombay edition.

4. एतैरेव हुतं यच्च हुतं स्वयमेव तु, p. 34 (Ā.S.S., vol. 70).

5. Upodghāta, Poona, 1924, p. 47, l. 12-13. सर्वमन्त्राणामाद्यन्ते च प्रणवो वक्तव्यः। 6. Āśv GS. 1. 7. 3 यदि तूपशाम्येत् पत्न्युपवसेदित्येके।

Tarkālaṅkāra in his commentary on Gobhila,[1] however, thinks that the wife should be given, on this account, so much education as would suffice for this, because "without studies she cannot sacrifice, nor does the Sūtra say that she should offer silently." Anyway, this much confession is sufficient to show that the wife is entitled to the Initiation ceremony so that she may be entitled to read at all, not to speak of uttering the Vedic mantras.

Pāraskara[2] says that the wife should, if she is desirous of conception, offer the first oblation in the evening as well as in the morning along with the utterance of the prescribed mantra wherein she should utter the "Svāhā" again.[3] All the commentators, Karka,[4] Jayarāma. Harihara, Gadādhara and Viśvanātha agree that the wife should worship the fire with the first oblation in the morning as well as in the evening with the above mantra. The mantra

1. 1, 5, 15, 1. 10 f., Bib. Ind. ed. न खल्वनधीत्य शक्नोति पत्नी होतुम्। न च तूष्णीमित्याह वचनम्। 2. ParGS. 1, 9, 3-5. p. 110, Bom. ed., 1918, "...पुनः स्वाहेति पूर्वां गर्भकामा"। 3. This "Again" means that she should first offer the oblation with the mantra "Agnaye svāhā Prajāpataye svāhā" in the evening and "Sūryāya svāhā prajāpataye svāhā" in the morning, and then should offer another oblation with this mantra together with "Svāhā."

4. For the commentaries, see pp. 110; Jayarāma, 1. 3-4, p. III; Harihara, 1. 34 f. 'अत्र पूर्वां गर्भकामा'इत्यस्य कोऽर्थः ? किं नित्ययोर्द्वयोराहुत्योः प्रथमा पूर्वशब्देन विवक्षिता उत ताभ्यां पूर्वापूर्वं होतव्या एव। किं तावत् प्राप्तम्? अन्यैव इति, मन्त्रान्तरेण देवतान्तर-होम-विधानान्मन्त्रस्य देवतायाश्च गुणत्वेन कर्म-भेदकत्वात्।" Gadādhara, 1. 6f. p. 114; Viśvanātha, 1. 9f., p. 115.

prescribed for her is a Homa-mantra ending with "Svāhā: Hail"; as she is to offer the first oblation with this, it is she who is to utter the Praṇava also. Without the upanayana, the wife can never do so.

Āśvalāyana[1] in connection with his section on Nāmakaraṇa says: 1. नाम च अस्मै दद्युः। 2. घोषवदाद्यन्तरन्तस्थमभिनिष्ठानान्तं द्व्यक्षरम्। 3. चतुरक्षरं वा। 4. द्व्यक्षरं प्रतिष्ठा-कामश्चतुरक्षरं ब्रह्म-वर्चस-कामः। 5. युग्मानि त्वेव पुंसाम्। 6. अयुग्मानि स्त्रीणाम्। 7. अभिवादनीयञ्च समीक्षेत तन्मातापितरौ विद्येतामा उपनयनात्। In the commentary upon the Sūtra marked 5 by us, Haradatta says that because of the mention of "Tu" and "Eva" in the Sūtra all that is said in the above Sūtras (2-4) is not sufficient; and it is prescribed here that the names for males should consist of even syllables. The names of females should consist of an odd number of syllables. Āśvalāyana thus finishes what he has to say about the सांव्यवहारिक नाम and proceeds, without making any more distinction, to say about the abhivādanīya name of the child (male or female)[2]—"(He) should find out a name to be used (by the child) at the time when the child bows down to her[3] (during the upanayana); the parents should keep the

1. I, 15, 4 f, p. 55, Bom. 2nd, ed.; 1, 13, 4 f, p. 62, Trivandrum ed. 2. सांव्यवहारिकं नाम कृत्वा अभिवादनीयञ्च कार्यमित्याह अभिवादनीयञ्च etc. Gārgyanārāyaṇa, p. 56. एवं तावत् संव्यवहारार्थस्य नाम्नः करणमुक्तम्। अथ अभिवादनीयस्य नाम्नः करणमाह अभिवादनीयञ्च etc., Haradatta, p. 63.

3. Āśvalāyana does not repeat this rule in the section on Upanayana as this rule has been mentioned here.

name concealed (to themselves) till the child's Initiation.[1]" Kumārila Bhaṭṭa[2] also holds the same view when he says "Nāma abhivādanīyaṃ tu pitror hṛdyā upanītitaḥ: But the name for the child's abhivādana the parents should keep secret till the upanayana.[3]" Āpastamba (1.15.8) also holds an identical opinion. Śāṅkhāyana and Kauṣītaki (1.24) also mention this secret name, an earlier reference to which is found in the Bṛh. Up.(vi.4.26)—with ceremonial details. The consensus of opinion is that this secret name must be given. This name reserved for use during the initiation ceremony for the girl has no meaning if the girl is not allowed to bow down to the Guru at the proper time.[4]

Gobhila[5] says exrpressly that the bride should wear the sacred thread when the bridegroom leads her to the altar—"प्रावृतां यज्ञोपवीतिनीमभ्युदानयन् जपेत् सीमोऽददाद् गन्धर्वायेति"[6] Leading her forward who is clothed in the proper way and wears the

1. See Nārāyaṇa and Haradatta, p. 56 and 63 respectively of the Bombay and Trivandaum editions. Their interpretation completely agrees with our translation.

2. Gṛhya-kārikā, pp. 253-326 of the Bombay ed. of Aśv GS. 2nd ed., 1.9.3, p. 273. For the use of the Abhivādanīya name during the upanayana see 1, 13, 23, p. 276.

3. MānGS. 1. 18. 2, BhārGS. 1. 26. HiranGS. 2. 4.—10 15 and VārGS. mention two names, one to be known to the parents and the preceptor, and the other an ordinary name (cf. Tait Samh. vi. 3. I. 3). 4. For the Sāmavedic Sūtras, see Khā GS. 2. 2. 31; Gobh. 2. 7. 15 and Jaimini 1. 8. This view of Āśvalāyana is corroborated by the ManGS. I, XVIII, p. 83, l. 1-4, Baroda ed.; cf. आश्वलायन op. cit., l. 14-15. 5. 2, 1, 19. 6. Ṛ̣V. X. 85. 41; AV. XIV. 2. 4.

sacrificial cord (over the left shoulder), he should murmur the verse "Soma gave her to the Gandharva, etc." Prāvṛtā here means evidently प्र प्रकर्षेण आवृता वेषपरिहिता यज्ञोपवीतिनो यज्ञोपवीतविशिष्टा i.e. she who has worn the dress properly and the sacred thread. In the Adhikāra Sūtra, Gobhila himself as well as Kātyāyana[1] say that one must always wear the sacred thread. So the repetition of yajñopavīta here means that for ceremonial purpose the bride should change her former yajñopavīta and wear a new one.

Candrakānta Tarkālaṅkāra, however, thinks otherwise. He gives us two alternative explanations.[2] Firstly, he says the word yajñopavītinīm in the passage means यज्ञोपवीतिनीमिव यज्ञोपवीतकृतोत्तरीयाम् The bride is prāvṛtā kṛtottarīyā. How is she Prāvṛtā? : like a yajñopavitinī, like one who has worn the upper garment in the form of a sacred thread." Secondly, "Prāvṛtām" means प्रकर्षेणाच्छादितां स्मृत्युक्तरीत्या परिहिताधरीयवसनाम् and "yajñopavītinīm" means यज्ञोपवीतत्वात् परिहितोत्तरवसनाम् i.e. the bride who has worn her lower garments in the manner prescribed in the Smṛti and worn her upper garments in the fashion of a yajñopavīta. The learned commentator also says the word yajñopavīta may be used in the sense of the uttarīya for showing which way the uttarīya is to be worn. These explanations are not tenable,

1. GobhGS. 1, 1, 2, यज्ञोपवीतिनाऽचान्तोदकेन कृत्यम् p. 8; Karmapradipa, Bib. Ind., vol. 178, p. 11. 1. 1, 'सदोपवीतिना भाव्यं सदा बद्धशिखेन च। विशिखो व्युपवीतश्च यत् करोति न तत् कृतम्॥"

2. For the Text, see GobhGS. Bib. Ind., p. 308.

Tarkālaṅkāra quotes the Smṛti to show how the bride should be properly dressed: "She should not show the navel, the virtuous wife should wear the clothes down to the heels and should not keep the breasts uncovered." According to his second explanation "Prāvṛta" means "she who has worn the lower garment" and "Yajñopavītinī" means "she who has worn the upper garment in the form of a sacred thread." The explanation that he gives does not follow the direction he mentions. If "Prāvṛtā" does not mean "One wearing both upper and lower garments" but "One wearing the lower garment" only, the breasts remain uncovered. The uttarīyavasana used in the form of a sacred thread cannot cover her breasts.[1] The commentator in commenting upon Gobh. 1.1.2. says on p. 17 "तदिदं यज्ञ-सूत्र-द्वयमुत्तरीयञ्च खल्विह कर्म-मात्र-शेषतया विधित्सितं विन्यासविशेषस्तु उत्तरीयस्येव यज्ञसूत्रस्यापि तत्र तत्र तत्तद्वाक्यादवगन्तव्यः। This pair of sacred threads and the upper garment are here mentioned as a rule as requisite for every ritual; but the particular manner of wearing it—as of the upper garment, so of the sacred thread—is to be known from those particular passages in those particular places". For this reason the word yajñopavīta cannot be used in the sense of the uttarīya. It is declared in the Smṛti:—[2] यज्ञोपवीते द्वे धार्ये

1. For the right manner of wearing the yajñopavita, see Karmapradipa, ch. I, verse 2: त्रिवृदूर्ध्ववृतं कार्यं तन्तुत्रयमधोवृतम्। त्रिवृत्तच्चोपवीतं स्यात्तस्यैको ग्रन्थिरिष्यते ॥ GobhGS. p. 64, l. 12f. 2. KarmaKP. Bombay, 1921 f. 51; cf. Smṛtyarthasāra. p, 5. 1. 10; GobhGS. p. 65.

श्रौत-स्मार्तेषु कर्मसु । तृतीयश्चोत्तरोयार्थं वस्त्रालाभे तदिष्यते ॥ "Two sacred threads are to be worn in the Śrauta and Smārta sacrifices; a third one also should be worn for an upper garment: this is prescribed if a cloth is not availble." Here it is said that a third sacred thread is to be used if an uttarīya is not available . If the uttarīya is not wanting, the third thread is not to be used. Here the word yajñopavīta is not certainly used in the sense of uttarīya, but it is said that yajñopavīta is to be substituted for the uttarīya. A substitute for a thing can never be the thing itself. Nor is it reasonable to think that beacause two different things are worn in the same manner, Gobhila has nsed one word for the other. Why should he? The uttarīya is as well-known as the yajñopavīta. What reason is there that the word uttarīya would be dropped at will and the word "yajñopavīta" be substituted for it? The learned commentator quotes in p. 65 the Nigama-pariśiṣṭa "वाससा यज्ञोपवीतानि कुरुते, तदभावे त्रिवृता सूत्रेण"[1] in which, he thinks, the word "yajñopovīta" means an upper garment (uttarīya). To follow the commentator, the sacrificer is to wear three upper garments which is nowhere prescribed in the Ritual literature. Again, three uttarīyas to be made of a cloth is an anomaly, for, in order to wear it properly, one is to wear the cloth wound round nine times on one's shoulder sideways. Two, and sometimes three of these, are to be worn. Nobody wants the sacrificer to carry a heap of clothes round about him. The real meaning

1. See KarmaKP. f. 50; GobhGS., Bib. Ind., p. 65.

of the passage is what is expressed in the couplet above. The cloth, not a sacred thread but an accompaniment of the two threads normally used, is considered as making the number of threads three. We come across a similar use in the following passage: "Yajamānapañcamā ṛtvija iḍāṃ bhakṣayanti:[1] the priests with yajamāna as the fifth drink the iḍā.' Here, too, similarly, the "Upavīta', means two sacred threads with the garment as the third, i.e. the "Upavītāni" three in number together with the garment which is not an 'upavīta' as in the above case the yajamāna is not a priest. So it is here by no means said, as our commentator thinks, that the 'yajñopavīta' is 'uttarīya.'

In a sacrifice to be performed even by the widow, she should wear the sacred cord on the right or left shoulder as prescribed[2] and should herself offer the annual or other śrāddhas to her husband, father-in-law, etc.[3] When she performs an ekoddiṣṭa śrāddha for a son, daughter, etc. she should herself do all the initial ceremonial necessaries up to the initial resolution (Saṃkalpa) and may then give permission to a priest to perform the śrāddha on her behalf.[4]

1. Very frequently used in the S-Ss; also cf. uses like वेदानध्यापयामास महाभारतपञ्चमान्। 2. श्राद्धमञ्जरी, ed. by Vapu Mahadeva Kelkar, Ānandāśrama Sanskrit Series, Poona, p. 117.

3. स्वभर्तृ-प्रभृति-त्रिभ्यः स्वपितृभ्यस्तथैव च। विधवा कारयेच्छ्राद्धं यथाकालमतन्द्रिता ॥ SmrSam, Poona, 1905; also quoted in श्राद्धमञ्जरी, Poona, 1909, p. 115. 4. कश्चिद् ब्राह्मणमृत्विक्त्वेन परिकल्प्य तं ब्रूयात् 'ममाज्ञया त्वमिदममुकश्राद्धाख्यं कर्म कुर्विति।" She may herself perform it if she likes, see l. 20, p. 117, op. cit.

In course of the ceremony she wears the sacred cord on the right or left shoulder accordingly as the priest does.[1] This is the case when she gives a priest permission to perform the rite for her; no wonder she will do the same in course of performing the rite herself. If she is not entitled to be initiated for the vedic studies and wear the sacred cord, she cannot wear the sacred thread during the sacrifice. In the section on Adhikāra-sūtra prescribing general rules (to be observed in all the rites), Gobhila[2] says that the ceremony should be performed by one wearing the sacrificial thread on one's left shoulder (as a rule) and having sipped water. In other places we have shown that the woman is entitled to perform the sacrifices. Without following the general rule, how can she perform the sacrifice properly? Even in modern usage there is some relic of the woman's wearing the sacred thread. Now-a-days the bride is made to wear during the marriage the sacred thread of the bridegroom. This is a rite observed by women.[3] Women, owing to their conservative nature,[4] always stick to things of time immemorial. Āpastamba and others pay their due respect to these Stry-ācāras when they recommend them to be observed as their prescribed rules.[5] So it is certain that by

1. ऋत्विक्-कर्म-काले तद्-यज्ञोपवीतित्वे ऽनुज्ञायाऽपि यज्ञोपवीतिता कर्तव्या। तत्प्राचीनावीतित्वे तया प्राचीनावीतिता कर्तव्या।

2. यज्ञोपवीतिनाऽऽचान्तोदकेन कृत्यम् Gobh GS. 1. 1. 2.

3. Stry-ācāra. 4. Buckle, Fraser's Magazine, April, 1858; Mason, Women in Primitive Culture, p. 273.

5. ĀpGS. 2, 15; here he recommends that the ceremonies that

"Yajñopavītinī" Gobhila means a bride who has worn the sacrificial thread and not one who has worn the upper garment in the form of a "Yajñopavīta". Gobhila here means that the bride should be properly dressed with the lower garment (adharīya) as well as upper (uttarīya), and should wear a pair of new sacred threads; then the husband should lead her, hand in hand, to the marriage alter, while uttering the sacred formula "Soma gave to Gandharva," etc. Though in the section on general rules (Adhikāra-sūtras) it has been prescribed that the sacred thread should be always worn while sacrificing,[1] the repetition of "Yajñopavīta" would here mean that a pair of new sacred threads are to be worn during the marriage ceremony.

Kātyāyana says in the Karma-pradīpa[2] that in accordance with the seniority in caste and age, the honest wives should separately stir the fire. In stirring the fire the husband should not appoint a śūdrā, an uncontrollable or a vicious wife.[3] The strongest of them who is the best of them as

are required by custom should be learnt from women; cf. ĀpDS. 11, 6, 15, 9; 11, 11, 29, 11-12: ĀśvGS. 1, 14, 8: etc.

1. Whenever the word "Yajñopavīta" is repeated in the Sūtras, there is always a special sense behind it; see Śrīdatta, Snāna-prakaraṇa in Ācārādarśa f. 22, a-b. "Yajñopavīti", etc. Harihara, स्नानसूत्रभाष्य, Benares edition of ParGS. pp. 55⁸-559: कात्यायनस्मृत. etc. 2. 1, 8, 6 f, Bib. Ind., vol. I. नैकयापि विना कार्यमाधानं भार्यया द्विजैः। अकृतं तद्विजानीयात् सर्वा नान्वारभन्ति यत्॥ वर्णज्येष्ठेन बह्वीभिः सवर्णाभिश्च जन्मतः कार्यमग्निच्युतैराभिः साध्वीभिर्मन्थनं पृथक्॥ 1. 8. 5. 6

3. नात्र शूद्रां नियुञ्जीत न द्रोहद्वेषकारिणीम्। नाव्रतस्थां नान्येन पुंसा च सह सङ्गताम्॥ Op. cit 1. 8. 7.

it were and certainly, the best of all those initiated (i.e. the most learned)[1] should stir the fire last of all with all her heart's content. This shows that Initiation for studies was a condition, not only necessary, but essential, for having preferential treatment in the religious, and consequently, in household affairs too.

In the Rāmāyaṇa,[2] queen Kauśalyā and in the Mahābhārata,[3] Sāvitrī and Ambā offer oblations along with sacred formulas.

In his section "Strī-saṃakāras" in the Madana-pārijāta,[4] Madana Pāla quotes Kātyāyana[5] to show that if any purificatory rite (saṃskāra) before the initiation ceremony is left unobserved, it should be performed with the offering of oblations. If the time for initiation expires, according to Madana, sacrifices for recovering the rights forfeited (Vrātya-stomas) and other expiations are to be observed. As Madana deals with these things in his section on Strī-saṃskāra, it is clear that women are entitled to be initiated.

The brilliant record of their Vedic education also shows that women are entitled to be inititated for Vedic studies. The Ṛg-veda furnishes us with a long list of seers composing or discoursing on sacred texts (Brahmavādinīs). Accord-

1 ततः श्रक्तवमा पश्चादासामन्यतमाऽपि या। उपेतानां चान्यतमा समेन्देदग्निं निकामतः॥ 1. 8. 8 p. 116, 1, 2

2. II, 20 14 ff.

3. III. 296; V. 186.

4. p. 362. Bib. Ind.

5. कात्यायनसंहिता forming part of the UnavSamh, ed. by P. Tarkaratna, p. 330, देवतानां विपर्यासे जुहोतिषु कथं भवेत्, etc.

ing to the Bṛhaddevatā,[1] they form three groups: (1) those that praised the deities; they are all strictly speaking, vedic seers; (2) those who conversed with seers and deities; (3) those who sang of the evolutionary forms of self: these latter two groups may also be called seers in that the hymns or the Ṛks were revealed through them. In the first group are घोषा,[2] गोधा,[3] विश्ववारा,[4] अपाला,[5] उपनिषद्,[6] निषद्,[7] ब्रह्मजाया,[8] named जुहु, sister of अगस्त्य[9] and अदिति.[10] इन्द्राणी,[11] इन्द्रमाता,[12] सरमा,[13] रोमशा,[14] उर्वशी,[15] लोपामुद्रा,[16] नदी,[17] यमी[18] and शाश्वती नारी[19] form the second group. श्री,[20] लाक्षा[21] सार्पराज्ञी,[22] वाच्,[23] श्रद्धा,[24] मेधा,[25] दक्षिणा,[26] रात्रि[27] and सूर्या सावित्री[28] come within the third group.[29]

Yājñavalkya teaches his wives Gārgī and Maitreyī the most abstruse philosophical doctrine of Soul.[30] Gārgī

1. Compare आर्षानुक्रमणी X, 102; बृहद्देवता II, 84.
2. RV. X.39,40. 3. X. 134. 6.7. 4. V. 28.
5. VIII. 91 6. and 7. Seers of the Khila beginning वा धारयन्तु मधुनो घृतस्य 8. X. 109; Cf. Ārsā., X. 51.
9. X. 60. 6; Cf. Ārṣā., X. 24, 10. Some Rks of IV. 18.
11. X 86 (several stanzas) and 145. 12. X. 153; Cf. Ārṣā., X. 72. 13. Several Ṛks of X. 108. 14. I. 126. 7.
15. Several stanzas of X. 95 16. I. 179. 1.2.
17. Several Ṛks of III, 33. 18. X, 10 and 154.
19. VIII. I. 34; Cf सर्वानुक्रमणी on ṚV. VIII, 1.
20. Supposed seer of Khila after V.V. 87 (Śrī-sūkta).
21. Seer of Khila below VII, 51. 22. X, 89.
23. X. 125 24. X. 151. 25. Medhā-sūkta, Khila after X, 151. 26. X. 107. 27. X. 127. 28. X. 85.
29. For a critical appreciation of the hymus by these Women Seers, see Sanskrit Poetesses, Part A, p. lxxix-lxxxix.
30. Bṛh Upan II, 4. 1-14 and 4.5. 1-15.

Vācaknavī is venerated as the champion of all the learned Brāhmaṇas present in the court of Janaka to ask Yājñavalkya, the most learned sage of his age, a series of questions in order to ascertain if they should debate with Yājñavalkya or not.[1] This time she asks him two questions which he manages to answer. On a subsequent occasion[2] she takes up the question of the old water cosmology. Yājñavalkya is, however, compelled to dissuade her from asking any further question. Umā Haimavatī tells Agni and Vāyu of the one Supreme Soul.[3] The A V. in extolling the Brahmacarya says that by Vedic studentship a girl wins a young husband.[4] The Vedic literature contains a long list of the names of female teachers of Philosophy and the Sāṇkhāyana[5] and Āśvalāyana[6] gṛhya-sūtras mention the names of Gārgī Vācaknavī, Vaḍavā Prāthitheyī and Sulabhā Maitreyī in the list of Ṛṣis. The Aitareya[7] and Kauṣītaki[8] Brāhmaṇas quote the authoritative opinion of a "Kumārī Gandharva-gṛhītā: maiden seized by a Gandharva" that the Agnihotra Ritual which was once performed on both days is now performed on alternate days only. Paṭañcala Kāpya's wife[9] and daughter[10] were also Gandharva-gṛhītās. Students from all over the country visited them for knowledge. Kāpya himself learnt many things from his wife. The extensive use of matrony-

1. Bṛh. Up., III, 3. 2. Op. cit., III, 6. 3. Talavakāra Upaniṣad, IV, I f. 4. Atharva-veda, XI. 5. 18, ब्रह्मचर्येण कन्या युवानं विन्दते पतिम्। 5 IV. 10. 6. III, 4, 4. 7. V. 29. 8. II, 9. 9. Brh Upan, III, 7, 1. 10. Op. cit., III, 3, 1.

mics also may partly be due to the wide reputation of the learning of the mothers, some of whom were most probably teachers. Kātyāyana recognises the established position and honour of women teachers in his Sūtras (Vā. 2477) "Acār-yād aṇatvam ca" and (Vā. 125) "Mātulopādhyāyayor ānug vā."[1] Because of the honour shown to the learned women, the parents perform some special ceremony for having a learned daughter.[2] They boil rice mixed with sesamum, eat it with butter and make themselves worthy of giving birth to a learned daughter. Ātreyī goes from North India to the South to learn the Vedānta from Agastya and others.[3] Ubha-yabhāratī[4] mediates in the controversy between her husband Maṇḍana Miśra and Śaṅkarācārya who represent the Vedic learning in their age.[5] Even in the RV., women are found exhorted for addressing popular assemblies (vidathas)[6] and certainly some of them were good orators.

In the Vedic ritual women have a recognised position for their songs and aptitude in music. Most probably these

1. Bāla-manoramā, vol. I. p, 379-80; for Bāl. itself, p. 379, l. 31 f.—80, l. 9 f. 2. Paṇḍitā duhitā; Bṛhad-āraṇyaka Upaniṣad, VI. 4. 17. 3. Bhavabhūti, Uttara-carita, act II. अस्मिन्नेव अगस्त्य-प्रमुखाः प्रदेशे भूयांस उद्गीथविदो वसन्ति । तेषामधिगन्तुं निगमान्त-विद्यां वाल्मीकि-प्रमुखादिह पर्यटामि ॥ 4. Most probably because of her vast learning she is also known as "Sarasvatī." 5. For studies in general, cf. Mahā-nirvāṇa VIII, 47; कन्याप्येवं पालनीया शिक्षणीया चातियत्नतः i.e. the daughter should be brought up with as much care and given as much education as the son. 6. RV.x. 85. 26-27

were parts of their Sāma-vedic learning. The ṚV bears testimony to women's songs on ceremonial occasions.[1] Women are more willing to have singers rather than Brahma-vādins. Women love men who can sing.[2] In the Ma āvrata, wives sing and play various sorts of instruments.[3] The Satyāṣāḍha-śrauta-sūtra[4] mentions in this connection the name of the following instruments, viz., Apaghāṭalikā, Tālukavīṇā, Kāṇḍavīṇā, Pichorā, and Alāvu-kapiśiṣṇa; the Sāṅkhāyana-śrauta-sūtra,[5] Ghatakarkarī, Avaghāṭarıkā. Kāṇ-ḍa-vīṇā, Pichorā, etc; the Laṭyāyana-śrauta-sūtra[6] also gives a similar list. The Aitareya-Āraṇyaka[7] simply refers to the fact, but does not give any detail. According to Lāṭyā-yana, the wives should sit to the west of the Udgātṛ and each wife should alternately play lutes.[8] They must not play one particular instrument called Ghāṭarī slowly[9]. As every part of the ritual must be perfectly performed, it may be fairly assumed that the wives were expected to be expert musicians and singers. The aptitude of women in dancing is also exhibitted in the RV.[10]

In one Pravādana karma mentioned in the Vārāhagṛhya-sūtra[11] in connection with the marriage ceremony the face of

1. RV.ix. 66. 8. समुत्वा, etc; ix.56. 3, अभि त्वा योषणो दश, etc.

2. Sarasvaty-anuvāka; 20, KathGS. Appendix, IV, p. 303.

3. Tait. Śaṃh., VI. 1.6.5; Mait Samh. 111. 7, 3, etc; Śat. Brāh., 111,2,4,9. 4. XVI, 6, 21, vol. VI. p. 382. 5. XVII, 3, 12; for the way how to play these instruments, see the Ś. and G. sūtras; also LātSS. IV, 6f. 6. IV. 2, 1-8. 7. V. 1.5.

8. LātSS. IV, 2,5. 9. Op. cit., Sūtra 17. 10. e.g. 1.9.2,4, अविपेशांसि वपते, etc. 11. Prof. Raghu Vira's edition. pp. 34-35.

the bride is anointed with hands smeared with ghee for making her dear to her husband, brother-in-law etc. and then she plays the various instruments and drums which have been consecrated beforehand for the purpose; she prays to the Dundubhi and Gomukha for excellent children and particularly for charming daughters who, growing up under the same roof and friendly with Indrāṇī, would play together, and also to Prajāpati for children and welfare.

The references to Viśpalā's being provided with a leg of iron in Khela's battle would show that women were trained in the Military art as well.[1] Being chased by Mudgalānī her husband's enemy took to heels.[2] There were many fighting women in the non-Aryan fold as well.[3]

No better honour could be shown to the learning of women than by depicting the deity of learning as a goddess. Vāc and Sarasvatī represent the highest recognition and respect the Hindu sages could ever show to women.

From our above arguments the conclusion follows that the girl is entitled to have the Upanayana, wear the sacrificial thread and utter the mantras together with the praṇava.

The Daughter in other Vedic Rituals than Saṃskāras[4]. The daughter after her Saṃskāra is entitled to perform the śrāddha rites for her parents. She cannot, however,

1. RV. i. 116. 15, चरित्रं हि वरिवाच्छेदि, etc. RV. 1. 112. 10; RV. 1. 118. 8 and x.39. 8 2. RV. x. 102. 2. For other instances, see RV. 5, 61; 80. 6; 3. RV. 5.30.9; 1. 32.9. vii. 78.5; 8.33.19, etc. 4. This section was mostly published in New Indian antiquary, Vol. IV, No. 2, May, 1941, pp. 77-85.

in any case, precede in her claim over her brother. The Śrāddha-mayūkha thinks as the wife precedes the daughter in her claim over the property, the former should precede in the śrāddhas toö.[1] Govindānanda, author of the Śrāddha-kriyā-kaumudī also holds the same view.[2] He also thinks that the unmarried daughter will have the right to perform the śrāddha in precedence over the married one as the Gotra of the letter has beeu changed'[3] If the daughter is rendered a Putrikā, she precedes over her mother in her claim.[4] *Ś*ūlapāṅi,[5] however, thinks that in case of absence of the 13 kinds of son, the son of the Putrikā will be the proper person. As the Putrikā is really a substitute for the son, most probably Śūlapāṇi means if the Putrikā is dead, her son should observe the rites.

Govindānanda[6] specifically says that the daughter will have the right and not her father, to perform the funeral and śrāddha rites for her mother provided she is brotherless.

Just like the son, the daughter also is not entitled to be married within one year of her father or mother's death,as the Vṛddhiśrāddha cannot be performed for her.[7]

1. P. 20, l. 1. The Srāddha-vivekakāra, (f. 22a) however, mentions a long list of persons after whom the daughter is to have her claim. 2. Op. cit., p. 462. 3. P. 465, l. 15f: Tad-abhāve sahodarā ity atra duhitrabhāve'pi boddhavyam. Patnī-duhitaraś caiva iti Yājñavalkyena patny- anantaraṃ duhitur dhanādhikāra-pratipādanāt tasya copakāravyāpyatvāt piṇḍa-dānādikañcopakāraḥ. 4. P. 22. l.13. 5. Śrāddhaviveka f. 22a. 6. Śrāddha-kriyā-kaumudī, p. 464; also p. 469. 7. Op. cit., p 358, l. If; also p. 468, कन्यासंस्कारे

So far as the Agnisaṃskāra is concerned, the daughter has the same right as the son.[1] If the child does not exceed two years, it is not, as a rule,[2] entitled to have the Agnisaṃskāra i.e., to be cremated. Covered with an unwashed garment adorned with flowers and scented,[3] it is put in a pit. No water-libation is to be offered.[4]

If a daughter under two dies, the parents become impure for one day or three days only.[5] According to some authorities, if she dies before the Cūḍākaraṇa, the Aśauca (Impurity) passes away immediately;[6] if after Cūḍākaraṇa, and

कन्यादानाधिकारिणया जनन्याऽपि स्वकन्याविवाहे वृद्धिश्राद्धं कर्तव्यमेव। वाचस्पतिमिश्राणामपि मतमेतत्। 1. Pār GS. III, 10, 5, p. 361 Bom. According to Āpastamba (Dh. S. II, 6, 15. 7) the child is buried if it is below one. The paraents as well as those who bury it take a bath (and are purified). 2. If the parents or other relatives so desire, the child may be cremated; see Karka, Bom Ed. of PārGS. p. 363, 1.4; Jayarāma, op. ait. p. 366, l.5; Śrāddhaviveka, f. 22b. 3. ParGS. p. 377, l.8; VaikhGs V. p. 82.

4. According to the Śrāddhavivekakāra, the girl after two is entitled to the Pūrvakriyā till her marriage. Her father or brother should offer this. By Pūrvakriyā, he means all the rites beginning from the cremation down to the end of the Aśauca, तत्र दाह मारभ्याशौचान्तदिनपर्यन्ता क्रिया पूर्वा। In case she is cremated, the water-libations must be offered For the offering of water-libation and the Aśauca, see also Vaśiṣṭha, IV, 9-10; Viśiṣṭha cites the opinion of some who think the child should be cremated after the appearing of the teeth. Cf. Gautama, XIV, 34; Viṣṇu XXII, 27-28.

5. PārGS, III, 10, 2-4. Similarly, in case of the son too.

6. See Karka, PārGS, Bom. ed. p. 363, 1. 1-2 Jayarāma, op. cit., p. 366, 1. 2. For divergent opinions, see Kullukabhaṭṭa on Manu, VIII, 72, p. 192, Nirṇayasāgara ed.

before marriage, it continues for three days.[1] For the death of a married daughter, the parents need not observe any impurity. But if she dies in their house, they observe Aśauca for three nights.[2]

As the Vedic Authority is to supersede the Authority of the Smṛti, the daughter has the right to marry in her adult age at her discretion the person whom she loves most. Adult marriage seems to have been the rule even down to the Sūtra period. Against Prof. JOLLY,[3] Dr. Bhandarkar[4] maintains that the passages in question, viz., GobhGS., III, 46, HirGS., 1,12,2 and Gṛhyāsaṃgraha II, 17, do not go in support of the marriage of a "Nagnikā". The Jaim GS.[5] expressly says the bride should be "Anagnikā: not one who has not menstruated, i.e., she should have puberty". The Vār GS.[6] says, the bride should be not only anagnikā, but "Aspṛṣṭamaithunā: having no sexual experience"; the latter adjective signifies that the girl is married at an age when she is able to have had previous sexual experience. Bloomfield also accepts the reading anagnikā in ZDMG[7]. Paṇḍit Satyavrata Sāmaśramin accepts in his edition of the Gṛhyāsaṃgraha the reading "Anagnikā."[8] Mahāmahopādhyāya C. Tarkālaṅkāra in 1908 quotes the verse Gṛhyāsaṃgraha

1. See Karka and Jayarāma. 2. Viṣṇu, XXII, 33. 34.

3. ZDMG, XLVI, 313f; XLVII, 610f. 4. Op. cit XLVII, 143f. 5. P. 19, l. 11. For our interpretation of Anagnikā cf. Amara-kośa नग्निकाऽनागतार्तवा p. 125, 17, 6. P. II, Baroda Ed.

7. XXXV, p. 572. 8. P. 10-11 जषा Ser, I vol. 10.

II. 17. in his edition of Gobh GS.[1] with the nagnikā reading while the same learned author recants his old faith in his later publication (1910) of the Gṛhyā-saṃgraha[2] itself and supports the Anagnikā reading.

The two verses RV. X. 85, 40.41—AV. XIV. 2, 3.4 are found in various Gṛhya-sūtra.[9] Here it is said that Soma, Gandharva and Agni are the three previous husbands of the women and her human husband is the fourth one. Gobhilaputra says in his Gṛhyā-saṃgraha[3] that along with the indications of youth Soma begins to enjoy the woman, Gandharva with the development of breasts, and Agni after puberty. Now, if the human husband is to marry after Agni has enjoyed her as his wife, Agni being the third husband, he is to marry her after her puberty.

The Vrata of the fourth night[4] is to be celebrated for solemnizing the marriage itself as without it the wife cannot

1. Vol. II. p. 83. 8. P. 72. But this annotation तु in the sense of अपि is uncalled for and wrong. नग्निकां तु वदेत् कन्यां यावन्नर्तुमती भवेत् । ऋतुमती त्वनग्निका तां प्रयच्छत्त्वनग्निकाम ।

2. सोमस्य जाया प्रथम गन्धर्वस्ते परः पतिः । तृतीयोऽग्निष्टे पतिस्तुरीयस्ते मनुष्यजाः ॥ सोमोऽददद् गन्धर्वाय गन्धर्वोऽददद्ग्नये । रयिं च पुत्रश्चादादग्निर्मह्यमथो इमाम् । PārGS. 1. 4. 16; HirGS. 1. 202; MānGS. 1. 10a.

3. II.19. The Text of this verse, तस्माद्व्यञ्जनोपेतामरजामपयोधराम्। अभुक्ताश्चैव सोमाद्यैः कन्यकान्तु प्रशस्यते is corrupt. Candrākānta Tarkālaṁkāra's justification of प्रशस्यते can hardly be supported. Moreover, it contradicts the Vedic Text and must, therefore, be rejected.

4. GobhGS. II, 5; KhāGS., 1. 4. 12.GS 1, 23, II; 24 and 25; ApGS., 8.8 seq; BhārGS., 1, 19; PārGS. 1, II, 13; SānGS., 1, 18, 19.

be one with her husband in Piṇḍa, Gotra and Sūtaka.[1] This vrata sanctifies the female body for all purposes and makes the wife same flesh and blood, heart and soul with her husband.[2] If the husband and the wife observe penance for one year, they are sometimes given the assurance of having a Ṛṣi son;[3] if they cannot restrain themselves, they may have sexual enjoyment after 5, 3, or 1 month or even after 12, or 6, or 3 days, or 1 day at least. As the authorities prescribe that they may enjoy sexually even after a day, the girl must be physically fit for such enjoyment. So in the Sūtra period the girl cannot be married before puberty. With the lowering of the agelimit in later times which came down and down so much that even conception-marriage became a matter of great religious concern, the law-givers stick to the principle of the solemnization of the marriage by means of this vrata, but they speak no more of the vrata to take place within one year or after a few days, the reasons for which are obvious. Even those early law-givers who, unlike Manu, Parāśara and Nārada, think that widows should not be re-married even when they suffer from five forms of distress, admit that an akṣarayoni (having no experience of sexual intercourse) widow should, however, be re-married. While there was no scope in olden times for any such distinction, the later device was made as a concession to popular feelings, specially because Law-givers as well as their follow-

1. See GobhGS., Bib. ed. 2. cf. the mantras PārGS. 3. AsvGS; see the Commentaries of Gārgya Nārāyaṇa and Haradatta.

ers were still immensely guided by the influence of the Sūtrakāras.

Again, the marriage ritual in the Gṛhya-sūtras has no place in it for the girl's father after the Kanyādāna rite. The subsequent rite is entirely an affair of the husband and wife. The mutual promises and assurances of love protection and obedience[1] presuppose a much greater, capacity in both than can be attributed to them even in their adolescent period. The proper performance of the ritual requires that the wife must understand the mantras she utters;[2] this also presupposes a reasonably advanced age. The Mantra-Brāhmaṇa[3] expressly says the girl should be given in marriage only when she longs for a husband.

The Kāma-sūtra and Epics also uphold the discretionary power of the maiden in choosing her husband. The former[4] expressly says that the Gandharva, i.e., the Love-form of marriage is the best of all the eight; and it mentions various ways by which the maiden should capture the heart of her lover and the lover that of his lady-love. The

1. The wife: VārGS. Raghuvira's Ed., p. 36, 1.8 ff; p. 43, 1.2f, etc.; KāthGS., p. 20, 1.1f, part. 1.14f; p. 109, 1.8f, 16 f, etc., p. 113, 1.15 f; p III 1.4 ff; etc.

2. The Upodghāta of Bhaṭṭoji Gopinātha Dīkṣita. p. 44. 1.24. मन्त्रार्थ-ज्ञान पूर्वकमेव कर्मकर्तव्यताकथनम्, also 1.27; Vyāsa, as quoted in the same, मन्त्रार्थमनुसन्धाय जपहोमादिकाः क्रियाः ।

3. 2, 1. 1. For the forms of marriage that obtained in Vedic India and particularly, for ·love-marriages, see Introduction to my edition of the Sambandha-viveka of Śūlapāṇi, Vol. I of my series Contribution of Bengal to Smṛti Literature. 4. Kāmasūtra p. 232.

Svayaṃvara[1] form of marriage of the Epics is well-known. Manu[2] also recognises the Gandharva marriage, the voluntary union of a maiden and her lover, as dharmya, sanctioned by Religion. He also recognises the discretionary power of the bride when he says that the consent of the maiden would be necessary[3] if she were to be given in marraige to the younger brother of the person who had paid the nuptial fee. The Vedic Saṃhitās. too, show that there was no parental control in this respect, though the parents helped the girl to the best of their power in finding out her husband.[4] Here the maiden is found anxious to leave her father's gotra and family for ever and be permanent in her husband's family. If successful in love-matters, the younger sister marries before her elder sister even; if unsuccessful, daughters grow old in the parental abode.[5] In order that the maiden may get the husband she wants to have, the AV. gives a series of love-charms which pass under the name of Strī-kṛtya hymns.[6] Rival lovers and lady-loves perform malicious rites to win the hearts of the desired.[7] There is a magical rite in the AV.[8] in which

1. For absolute Love-marriages, cf. those of Damayantī, Sāvitrī etc. This, however, differs from the Svayaṃvara of the Smṛti in which the choice of husbands is conferred upon the girl if she is not married till three years after puberty; cf. Manu, IX, 90, etc.

2. III, 25; cf. III. 32.

3. IX 97 यदि कन्यानुमन्येत

4. The parents take part in the rites which the girls perform for a happy ending of their love affairs; cf, AV. II, 36; VI, 60, etc.

5. RV. I, 117, 7; II. 17, 7, etc.; cf. AV. XVIII, 8. 47.

6. AV. II, 30, 2-3, etc.

7. AV. II, 30, 2-3, etc.

8. AV. VI. 138; VII. 90.; I. 14. 11. VII. 37.

the bride binds the lover with her hair; this symbolically means that the lover will be truly hers and hers alone. Various domestic rites[1] are also prescribed by the AV. to be performed by the maiden; these are calculated to help her in love-affairs. While the maiden, anxious for having her lover, takes recourse to various love-charms and other domestic rites, the parents perform for her good the rites[2] named Rākāholākā, Kumārīyajña and the Saṭoddharaṇa. As to the interpretation of Rākāholākā, Devapāla[3] cites different opinions; however the rite is celebrated in the morning for the happiness of the maiden in order that the marriage of the maiden may draw nigh. Brahmadarśana[4] says Holākā is a famous rite in the Central Provinces as well as in Kāśmīra, wherein a fire is kindled near the gate of the house; after the ājyabhāgānta, the main oblation is offered with the Mantra 'yāste Rākā' etc. The Kumārīyajña[5] also is celebrated for the happiness of the maiden in the place where she dresses herself. After the ājyabhāgānta, the sacrifice is offered with the Mantra "Indrāṇīm āsu nāriṣu"; etc. The Saṭoddharaṇa[6] is performed for a betrothed girl during the Sīmantonnayana ceremony of a pregnant wife. The symbolic meaning of the rite is, therefore, nothing but praying for similar fortune of the girl also.

In this rite the hair of the maiden is parted in a charm-

1. AV. II 36; VI, 30; VI. 82 etc. 2. These rites have not been mentioned by any other Sūtrakāra than Laugākṣi.

3. KāṭhGS., p, 287, l. 23f. 4. KāṭhGS., p. 288, l.6.

5. Op. cit., l.9-13. 6. KāṭhGS, p. 133, l. 11-21.

ing manner and anoined with cosmetics and adorned with sarvoṣadhi (a mixture of different herbs) and saffron. Ādityadarśana says[1] herein the plating of the hair should be ceremonially performed with mantras; during the Anavalobhana[2] (the rite for preventing disturbances that bring on danger to the embryo) which is to take place together with the Sīmantonnayana of the same pregnant wife, the hair of the maiden should be parted in a charming manner, but this parting should be hardly seen. Thus every tender care is taken that the maiden may get a suitable husband and be happy in marriage while she herself prays to Agni and other gods to win the heart of her lover or if she has none, to hava a suitable husband.

Just as the mother is the highest object of veneration and the wife is of love, so the daughter is of affection[3] and tenderness. A pretty girl is symbolic of good luck.[4] Eight girls represent eight objects of good luck during the consecration ceremonies of kings or crown-princes.[5] At times sixteen of them participate in similar ceremonies.[6] The goddess of Fortune and Beauty resides in their bodies.[7] Even a sight of her averts evil.[8]

Parents get the daughter after much longing and penance as the self of Blessing,[9] and it is only natural that they

1. KāṭhGS., p. 133, l. 20-21. 2. Cf. ĀśoGS., I, 13, 1.
3. Manu, IV, 135 "Duhitā kṛpaṇaṃ param"; Ait. Brā. VII, 13. 4. MBh. vii. 82. 22. 5. Ram. ii. 14. 36
6. Rām vi. 128. 38 and 62. 7. Viṣṇu, 99. 14
8. cp: MBh ix. 56. 24f. 9. MBh. xiii. 87. 10; xiii. 104. 151, iii. 83. 190; xiii. 83 51.

would rear her up with as much care as the son.[1] The supposition of Schrader[2] and others[3] that the depositing of the cooking vessels during the final bath (Avabhṛtha) after Somayāga refers to the adherence of Vedic people to famale infanticide is not tenable. In the Soma sacrifice the cooking vessels are considered as females and the wooden vessels named vāyavyas as males. Now, the Taittirīya,[4] Maitrāyaṇī[5] and Kāṭhaka saṃhitās[6] make similar remarks that as the sacrificer and his retinue carry vāyavya vessels depositing the sthālīpātras in the bathing place, the daughter is deposited after birth while son is lifted up. The difficulty arises in connection with the right interpretation of the word Parāsyanti. In his article inZDMG, Boethlingk says "As 'As' with prepositions is used not only to imply 'to throw', but also to mean 'to place, to lay', we may very well translate "Parāsyanti" by 'put aside', perhaps among others also by 'hand (the child) over immediately to the person waiting for the child'.[7] As

1. कन्याप्येवं पालनीया शिक्षणीया चातियत्नतः। Mahā-nirvāṇa-tantra. MBh. xiii. 83. 15 116 12

2. Schrader, Reallexicon der ind. Altertumskunde, p. 52-53.

3. Weber, Ind. St. IX, 48; Zimmer, Alt. Leben, p. 319f; cf. also Kaegi, Der Ṛgveda VI, 49; Ludwig, RV. VI, 142; Pischel, Vedische Studien, 2, 48. 4. VI. 5. 10. 3 5. IV. 6. 4 (85, 3). यत् स्थालीं निघ्नन्ति न दारुमयं तस्मात् पुमान् दायादः स्त्र्यदायादाऽथ यत् स्थालीं परास्यन्ति न दारुमयं तस्मात् स्त्रियं जातां परास्यन्ति न पुमांसम्; the last sentence in 4, 7, 9 (p. 104, 20) also. 6. XXVII, 9: same statement as before. 7. For the original in German, see ZDMG, vol. 44, p. 495.

against 'Parā-as' meaning 'to expose', the same scholar publishes the fragment of a letter from Prof. Roth who regrets, on his reading Delbrueck's Die indische Verwandschaftsnamen, that the seed of this error was planted by him in the Dictionary under As with Parā.[1] Boehtlingk also says that Delbrueck was pleased with, and had nothing to say against, his article.[2] Jolly also accepts the view of Boehtlingk in his excellent work "Recht und Sitte"[3]. The Vedic Index[4] also accepts Boehtlingk's view. Schrader,[5] however, is not satisfied with the explanation of Boehtlingk, and thinks that in common with other Aryan people ancient Indians also practised female infanticide. Boehtlingk[6] is justly sympathetic when he says "It hurt me to attribute to the ancient Indians such a piece of barbarism," but gives us sound reason later on. "Then I thought the matter in itself was very improbable, because without a girl the highest blessing of an Indian, viz. the begetting of a son, could not be achieved. As the lifting up of a boy after his birth is to be considered as an expression of joy, so is it easy to presume by Parāsyanti a corresponding expression of disagreeable surprise". There is no doubt that the verb "parāsyanti" and "ud haranti" express contraries. Āśvalāyana[7] uses the verb "ud hṛ" in the sense of "lifting up" when he says "noddharet prathamaṃ pātram", etc; 'Yadā vā tu uddhṛtaṃ

1. Op. cit., p. 1. 2. Op. cit., p, 1. 3. P. 78, 1, 18-21. 4. Vol. I 5. Reallexicon der ind. Alterumskunde, p. 153, 6. ZDMG, vol. 44, p. 7. See Trivandrum Edition. 1,8 and 10.

pātram", etc; here, too, this verb in the passages in question means the same. The text in the Taittirīya clearly says the boy is lifted up (ut pumāṃsaṃ haranti) and therefore as a contrary action the girl would be deposited, be kept on the ground and not thrown away; this is only in keeping with the comparison given—the Soma vessels are lifted up and as a contrary action the cooking vessels are allowed to stay on the ground and evidently are not thrown away. These sacrificial utensils are held as pure and are the last objects in the possession of the sacrificer to be thrown off.

The passage in the Maitrāyaṇī-saṃhitā seems to have been quoted by Yāska in his Nirukta.[1] Durga[2] in his Ṛjvartha says expressly अथ यत् स्थालीं परास्यन्ति हवनकर्मणो न तया जुह्वति न दारुमयं परास्यन्ति हवनकर्मणो दारुमयेनैव जुह्वति तस्मात् स्त्रियं जातां परास्यन्ति परस्मै प्रयच्छन्ति न पुमांसम् i.e. so as the cooking vessel is deposited, in the offering of oblations no offering is made with it and the wooden vessel is not deposited, in the offering of oblatians offerings are made with the wooden vessel only,—the daughter born is given away to others and not the son. Skandasvāmin[3] also gives a similar interpretation. Sāyaṇa also understands by स्त्रियं परास्यन्ति वरकुले परित्यजन्ति. The learned commentators do all think that the daughter is given away and evidently, given away to her husband's family and this act is symbolically performed after the birth of the daughter by handing her over to a

1. See p. 60, Sarup's edition; III, 4. 2. Durga's commentary on Niruktā, Bom. Ed., p. 255, 13, 5. 3. Commentary, ed. by L. Sarup. p. 128, 1.

third person. In their opinion, female infanticide is out of the question. This Parāsana simply shows much anxiety, even from her birth, of the parents to do the best service to their daughter—to make her happy in marriage and nothing more than that. This simply shows that the parents were saddened at heart at the remembrance of the painful day when they would be compelled to be robbed of their beloved treasure by the bridegroom as Bāṇabhaṭṭa has so beautifully put it in both the Harṣa-carita and the Kādambarī. The question of her future happiness also weighed heavily with them. Viṣṇusarman has excellently given vent to this parental worry in his Mitrabheda, 28. 6— पुत्रीति जाता महतीह चिन्ता कस्मै प्रदेयेति महान्वितर्कः। दत्ता सुखं प्राप्स्यति वा न वेति कन्यापितृत्वं खलु नाम कष्टम् ॥ The Kathāsaritsāgara is the unequivocal champion of the cause of women[1] and when it states—शोककन्दः क्व कन्या हि क्वानन्दः कायवान् सुतः (28. 6.), it simply repeats the above idea. Kālidāsa expresses this sentiment of parents, probably, most beautifully:—अर्थो हि कन्या परकीय एव तामद्य संप्रेष्य परिग्रहीतुः। जातो ममायं विशदः प्रकामं प्रत्यर्पितन्यास इवान्तरात्मा ॥

It will also be seen in this connection that at the time and in the place where these Texts were composed females, probably, exceeded the males in number. The Maitrāyaṇī[2] qualifies the Parāsana of the daughter with the statement "Striya eva atiricyante". The Tait. Samh. says one man can very well have two wives but not one woman two

1 E. g. 28. 47 ff. 2. MSaṃh 4. 6. 4 (p. 84, l.4); 4, 7, 9 (p 104).

husbands. How could the females supersede the males in number if female infanticide had been the custom?

Schrader's[2] remark that the Greeks also practised exposition is distinctly opposed to the theory of Cook,[3] who fights out his cause to show that the current idea as to exposition is "totally unfounded." Schrader[4] again gives us an analogy in favour of his theory that the old were also exposed. Analogy is no valid proof. Moreover, the reference in AV. XVIII. 2.34 is to the dead men, and not to the old; as regards Praskaṇva on whom Parṣadvana took pity (RV. VIII, 51, 2. Vālakhilya III, 2) it is only to be supposed that Praskaṇva was expelled for some crime or other and in his exile he grew old and decrepit. The exposure of the old is quite incompatible with the repeatedly mentioned wish of the Vedic people to live the full extent of life (i.e. 100 years).

The Nirukta[5] holds that the excellent Vedic Mantra "You are produced from each and every limb, you are born from the heart; verily, you are the Self named son; so may you live hundred years" is applicable equally to both the

1. VI, p. 6. 4; यदेकस्मिन् यूपे द्वे रशने (स्त्रौ) परिव्ययति तस्मादेको द्वे जाये विन्दते; यन्नैकां रशनां द्वयोर्यूपयोः परिव्ययति, तस्मान्नैको द्वौ विन्दते। 2. Reallexicon, p. 153. 3. Zeus, Vol, 2, p. 1229.

4. Cf. his article "Alte Laute", p. 39, where he refers to Zimmer, Alt, Leben, p. 328. 5. II, 4; p. 60, Sarup's edition. The Nirukta quotes this verse in connection with Female Inheritance. This mantra is recited by every Vedic school during the Jātakarma and the Proṣyāgatakarma. अङ्गादङ्गात् स तोऽसि हृदयादधिजायसे। त्वं वै पुत्रनामासि स जीव शरदां शतम्॥

children and no distinction is to be made whatsoever. Durga[1] in his Ṛjvartha says as the same rite is observed for the daughter as well as the son and they both are born from each and every limb and the heart, no distinction is to be made, i.e., they are equal. Manu[2] says the son is equal to one's self and the daughter is equal to the son and repeats the same view emphatically when he says the son's son and the daughter's son have no difference[3] with respect to worldly matters as well as to sacred religious observances and no distinction is to be made between them as the daughter's son is equally fit to save the grand-father (and therefore, the grand-mother too) in the other world like the son's son.[4] Bhīṣma also declares the son is just the same as the daughter —they are both one's very self.[5] In xiii. 47. 25f., the Mahābhārata again declares the daughter equal to the son. The Law Literature also advocates the same opinion specially stating that both are born of the same limbs and have reasonably the same rights over paternal property.[6]

1. Bhadkamkar's Ed., vol. I. p. 254, l.5-7. तथैव सति यथैव पुमान् अङ्गादङ्गात् सम्भवति हृदयाच्चाभिजायते तथैव दुहितापीत्यविशेष उपपद्यते ॥ 2. IX, 130; यथैवात्मा तथा पुत्र: पुत्रेण दुहिता समा p. 362, 1.18, Nirṇaya-sāgara Ed. 3. IX, 133, op. cit., p. 263, l.4; cf. Yajn. II, 128. 4. Manu, IX, 139; p. 364, l. 10-11. 5. MBh. XIII. 45. 11. 6. Cp. no distinction between son's sons and daughter's sons; Manu IX. 13 and Visṇu XV. 47. पौत्रदौहित्रयोर्लोके विशेषो नोपपद्यते। दौहित्रोऽपि ह्यमुत्रं तं सन्तारयति पौत्रवत् See also Nārada, xiii. 50; Bṛhaspati, xv. 55f; Yājnavalkya 2. 135f.; Visṇu xvii. 7f; the daughter and the son are born of the same limbs and therefore, equal.

Thus we see that the daughter has in no way a less honoured or responsible position than the son in Vedic Ritual. The parents long to get her and perform all the Saṃskāras for her as for the son. She has the same rights as the son to wear family locks, to have the upanayana, to utter the Vedic mantras together with the Praṇava and to perform all the rites in relation to her parents. The son, has, no doubt, precedence over her in several rituals, particularly the Antyeṣṭi, but this is because she is to care more for her husband's family than her parents' and cannot be supposed to have as much privilege as the son. Moreover, she belongs to the gotra of her husband after the Caturthī-karma for which privilege and honour she prays to Agni and performs various domestic rites, the Mother-Instinct being supreme in her. This principle is pronounced remarkably in the fact that the younger sister has precedence over her if the former is unmarried. In case of her death before marriage, the same rights are performed as for the son; but if she is married, her own people do everything for her; still the ceremonial shows that her parental connection is also much cared for. In matrimonial affairs she is as free as the son and has the same rights as he. Nowhere does the Vedic Ritual ignore her importance. On the contrary, the unmarried daughter—Purity, Affection and Bliss embodied—seems to be more important than the son with regard to the welfare of the parents. Anyway, the hypothesis enunciated by Manu and other authorities meaning "Putreṇa duhitā samā" remains true and declares the glory of the Creator who does not make any distinction between His sons and daughters.

It is quite in keeping with the above spirit of the Vedic Religion that the Vedic seers as well as the Smārtas offer the daughter a substantial share, if not an equal share, with her brother in the property of the father.

A daughter (having brother) in her unmarried state is found claiming her share in her father's estate during the the early Vedic period.[1] According to some school as quoted in the Nirukta,[2] the daughter is entitled to half the property of her father, her brother being entitled to the other half. Yāska in this counection quotes as the authority of this school[3] the well known Vedic verse as quoted above[4] as well as another verse refering to the opinion of Manu.[5] Even at a later period the same spirit prevails in as much as Śukra in his Smṛti advocates that if the father divides his property during his life-time, he should do so amongst his sons, wife, daughters and daughters' sons. He should give the daughters half the property, of which one half should go again to her children.[6] If the property is

1. 2. 17. 7, अमाजूरिव पित्रोः सचा सती समानादा सदसस्त्वामिये भगम्। कृधि प्रकेतमुप मास्या भर दद्धि भागं तन्वो येन मामहः॥

2. Nirukta, 3. 4. 3. अविशेषेण मिथुनाः पुत्रा दायादा इति, तदेतदृक्-श्लोकाभ्यामुक्तम्। 4. अङ्गादङ्गात् सं.तोऽसि. etc.

5. अविशेषेण पुत्राणां दायो भवति धर्मतः। मिथुनानां विसर्गादौ मनुः स्वायम्भुवोऽब्रवीत्॥ 6. Śukra-Smṛti, 4. 5.299:—समानभागा वै कार्याः पुत्राः स्वस्य च वै स्त्रियः। स्वभागार्धहरा कन्या दौहित्रस्तु तदर्धभाक्॥

not divided during the life time of the father and is, therefore, subsequently subdivided among the inheritors after his demise, the brothers should get less than half, as the mother gets one-fourth of the property and more than that goes to the sister.[1] Viṣṇu[2] and Nārada[3] also uphold this view with the amendation that only unmarried daughters are entited to their fathers' shares. Even in later times the law-givers[4] ordained one-fourth share for the daughter, as her brothers must spend this for her marriage.

Again, in the Vedic period, a daughter without a brother could be adopted as a Putrikā in which case she practically became a son. That is why Vaśiṣtha[5] mentions the "Putrikā" as the third in the list of inheritors in his Dharma-śāstra. A Putrikā is met with in subsequent times as well. Jayāpīḍa's wife Kalyāṇadevī was looked upon as the Putrikā of her father. As the daughter could be substituted as son, an adopted son during the Vedic age was hardly a necessity. From the religious point of view as well, the son of a daughter is as good as that of a

1. Op. cit. 300:—मृताधिपे तु पुत्राद्या उक्त-भागहराः स्मृताः । मात्र दद्याच्चतुर्थांशं भगिन्यै मातुरधिकम् ॥

2. 17. 4. मातरः पुत्रभागानुसारेण भागहारिण्यः । अनूढा दुहितरश्च ।

3. 13. 3. ज्येष्ठायांशोऽधिको देयः कनिष्ठायावरः स्मृतः । समांशभाजः शेषाः स्युरप्रत्ता भगिनी तथा ॥

4. Yājñāvalkya 2. 124 असंस्कृतास्तु संस्कार्या भ्रातृभि. पूर्वसंस्कृतैः । भगिन्यश्च निजादंशाद्दत्वांशं तु तुरीयकम् ॥ See also Manu 9. 118; Smṛti-candrikā, Vyavahāra-kāṇḍa, p. 625.

5. 17. 15

son as both can perform all the obsequial ceremonies for their grand-father with equal right and credit.[1] The Ṛgveda[2] bears a record of the inheritance of a daughter without brother; this principle has been adhered to in the Mahābhārata[3] as well as several Smṛtis[4] and the Artha-Śāstra of Kauṭalya.[5]

The MBh. (xii. 33. 45) declares outright that the daughters will be entitled to become rulers if there be no sons.

We have seen before that women were the seers of the hymns of the Ṛgveda[6] and were Brahmavādinīs; as late as

1. Śaṅkha:—पौत्र दौहित्रयोर्लोके विशेषो नोपपद्यते। दौहित्रोऽपि ह्यमुत्रं तं सन्तारयति पौत्रवत् 2. 1, 124. 7—अभ्रातेव पुंस एति प्रतीची गर्तारुगिव सनये धनानाम्। 3. 13. 80. 11—यथैवात्मा तथा पुत्रः पुत्रेण दुहिता समा। तस्यामात्मनि तिष्ठन्त्यां कथमन्यो धनं हरेत्॥ दुहिताऽन्यत्र जाताद्धि पुत्रादपि विशिष्यते॥

4. Yājñavalkya, 2. 135; Bṛhaspati, 2.5.55; Nārada, 13. 50. Vaśiṣṭha 15. 7; Gautama 5. 28. 21; Manu IX. 185; daughter altogether excluded, Āpastamba, 2. 14. 2-4: the claim of the daughter is rather thwarted back, 6. 3-5.

6. घोषा गोधा विश्ववारा अपालोपनिषन्निषत्। ब्रह्मजाया जुहूर्नाम अगस्त्यस्य स्वसाऽदितिः॥ इन्द्राणी चेन्द्रमाता च सरमा रोमशोर्वशी। लोपामुद्रा च नद्यश्च यमी नारी च शाश्वती॥ श्रीर्लक्ष्मीः सार्पराज्ञी वाक् श्रद्धा मेधा च दक्षिणा। रात्री सूर्या च सावित्री ब्रह्मवादिन्य ईरिताः। नवकः प्रथमस्तासां वर्गं तुष्टाव देवताः॥ ऋषिभिर्देवताभिश्च समूदे मध्यमो गणः॥ आत्मनो भाववृत्तानि जगौ वर्गस्तथोत्तमः। उत्तमस्य तु वर्गस्य य ऋषिः सैव देवता॥ आत्मानमस्तौद्वर्गस्तु देवतां यस्तथोत्तमः। तस्मादात्मस्तवेषु स्याद्य ऋषिः सैव देवता॥ संवादेष्वाह वाक्यं यः स तु तस्मिन् भवेदृषिः। यस्तेनोच्येत वाक्येन देवता ततः सा भवेत्। Bṛhad-devatā, 2, 82-88.

the Upaniṣadic period women scholars proved equal to the sages of outstanding fame like Yājñavalkya in public debates.[1] Women of this age e.g. Maitreyī, wife of Yājñavalkya —quite in keeping with their Vedic learning, aptly declared that they cared for nothing else than the Highest knowledge.[2] Women are born students of theology; the two daughters of Dākṣāyaṇa are typical examples.[3] The keen interest of women in theology is also manifest from the Therīgāthā where they are found sworn to attain Nirvāṇa at any cost.[4] The Mahābhāṣya shows that women attained fame as Mīmāṃsakas or theologians as well; the lady specialists of the Kāśakṛtsna came to be known as Kāśakṛtsnās.[5] The Mahābhāṣya specifically mentions the group of women grammari-

1. Bṛhad-āraṇyaka, 3.6.

2. मैत्रेयीति होवाच याज्ञवल्क्य उद्यास्यन् वा अरेऽहमस्मात् स्थानादस्मि हन्त तेऽनया कात्यायन्याऽन्तं करवाणीति। सा होवाच मैत्रेयी यन्नु म इयं भगो: सर्वा पृथिवी वित्तेन पूर्णा स्यात् कथं तेनामृता स्यामिति। नेति होवाच याज्ञवल्क्य:···सा होवाच मैत्रेयी येनाहं नामृता स्यां किमहं तेन कुर्यां यदेव भगवान् वेद तदेव मे ब्रूहीति। Bṛh. up 2. 4. 1-14 and 4. 5. 1-15.

3. Bhāgavata-purāṇa, 4. 1. 64. 3. For an account of these Buddhist Poetesses, see Sanskrit Poetesses, Part I, Vol. II of my Series Contribution of Women to Sanskrit Literature,

4. Mahābhāṣya IV. 1. 14; 3. 155.

5. एवमपि काशकृत्स्निना प्रोक्ता मीमांसा—काशकृत्स्नी, काशकृत्स्नीमधीते—काशकृत्स्ना ब्राह्मणी, अत्र प्राप्नोति॥ महाभाष्य, Vol. 4, p.44; see also लघुशब्देन्दुशेखर, Vol. I, p. 550, अतएव काशकृत्स्निना प्रोक्तां मीमांसामधीते "काशकृत्स्ना ब्राह्मणी" इत्यत्रापि न ङीप्। काशकृत्स्नि was a well-known grammarian as well; cp. इन्द्रश्चन्द्र: काशकृत्स्नापिशलि: शाकटायन:। पाणिन्यमरजैनेन्द्रा जयन्त्यष्टौ हि शाब्दिका:॥

ans called Āpisalās.[1] The Grammar also records the proficiency of women scholars in the Kaṭha and Ṛg-veda; they were known as Kaṭhīs and Bahvṛcīs.[2] Ubhayabhāratī was a champion scholar in theology.[3] Sulabhā was so learned that she could teach even Janaka.[4] She could not be married as no male was her equal; she was, therefore, initiated to the utmost bounds of knowledge and became a lonely ascetic.[5] Women were not only themselves good singers and dancers as is evidently seen from the Patnī-sāmans or wives' songs which were compulsory in Vedic Rituals[6] but they were also

1. Vārtika—पूर्वसूत्रनिर्देशो वाऽपिशलमधीते इति Mahābhāsya—आपिशलमधीते ब्राह्मणी—आपिशला ब्राह्मणी। अणन्तादितीकारो मा भूदिति॥ महाभाष्य Vol. 4, p. 43, 4. 1, 1. See also लघुशब्देन्दुशेखर, Vol. I, p. 551, "एवञ्च 'आपिशला' इत्यादावप्यस्यैव व्यावर्त्यम्" For reference to आपिशलि, see Pāṇini's sūtra, वा सुप्यापिशलेः 16-1-92.

2. सिद्धान्तकौमुदी, p. 128, पूर्वार्ध 518, under Sūtra जातेरस्त्रीविषयादयोपधात्—Pānini 4. 1. 63...गोत्रं च चरणैः सह। कठी, बह्वृची। After commenting upon the word बह्वृची, ज्ञानेन्द्रसरस्वती makes a significant remark here—'यद्यपि स्त्रीणामध्ययनं प्रतिषिद्धं, न तथापि पुराकल्पे तदासीत्, तदाह यम; etc. 128. see also p. 591, part I of the लघुशब्देन्दुशेखर।

3. शङ्करदिग्विजय, viii. 51, विधाय भार्यां विदुषीं, etc.

4. MBh. XII. 320.

5. Verse 183. The Jain Literature records that Jayantī, daughter of King Sahasrānīka of Kauśāmbi, did not marry as she wanted to be wedded to Religion and Philosophy; Bhagavatī Sūtra, Gujrati edition, Vol. III. p. 257.

6. The dance of women was a normal and pleasant affair in certain rituals; e.g. the wedding ceremony. Four or eight women, certainly maidens of the family, had to dance in it. (ŚānkGS. 1. 11. 5) They sang (gāthās) in weddings and other Vedic rituals;

connoisseurs of these arts. Thus, by singing and dancing, gods are said to have won over the goddess of speech and disappointed the demons who did not know the art of winning over women.

Even in subsequent ages women have not contributed a little to the various branches of Indian learning.[1] If the country would have provided all the facilities to women as in the Vedic ages throughout the long history of Indian Civilization, the fate of the country would have been quite otherwise. In all ages we could have expected many Ghoṣās, Viśvavārās, Śīlā Bhaṭṭārikās, Prāṇamañjarīs, Lakṣmīdevīs and so on. Asahāya, commentator of the Nāradasmṛti, has rightly remarked that the inferiority of women (in subsequent ages) is due to the suppression of their educational facilities —शास्त्राध्ययनानधिकारित्वाच्छास्त्रमात्रोपजीविधर्माधर्मज्ञानाभावाद्-स्वातन्त्र्यम् । When one looks at the long series of the works of women that have survived the ravages of time[1], one cannot but sigh very long for the travesty of fate India dragged

the Patnī-sāmans or wives' song had a recognized position. The Śat Brā. XIV. 3. 1. 35. says explicitly—पत्नीकर्मैव तेऽत्र कुर्वन्ति यदुद्गातारः। Even in the postvedic period, much importance is attached to the skill of woman in Music and Art. Of the 64 arts described in the Kāma-Sūtra, the most important are Music and Dance (1.5.16). Heroines in Sanskrit dramas are very clever in singing. The Kathāsaritsāgara specifically states that society girls used to dance before a select audience. The Kāma—sūtra (U. 1) shows that girls used to go to dramatic concerts, etc. with their elders or lovers.

1. For a long list of these learned women scholars and seers, see the volumes published in my Series No. I, The Contribution of Women to Sanskrit Literature.

herself into by minimising the position of her women and curtailing their educational facilities.

A question at once arises: What are the causes that led to the deterioration in the position of women?

Because of the development of the caste-system (a solitary reference to which is found in the Puruṣa-sūkta of the Ṛg-veda) throughout the Vedic and postvedic periods till it reached the most astonishing complications in the Smṛtis, the social and personal freedom of women had to be curtailed. After all, love knows no law and the women in the Upaniṣadic period even were very learned. A learned woman falling in love with somebody of the prohibited caste could not but marry him and co-education did not play an insignificant part in it.[1] In early periods of the development of the caste-system, social leaders used to frighten such learned ladies with tortures in hell, not only for herself but also for her agnates and cognates inclusive of her parents. In spite of these social regulations learned women, to whom their love meant their whole existence, did not, certainly, go by the ideal superimposed upon them. And necessarily, the patrons of religion, who were dwarfed in divinity only by an earthly existence, had to stifle them to a staggering death by slowly tightening the rope of violent injunctions.

1. Thus, Ātreyī was a class-mate of Lava and Kuśa, vide Uttara-Rāma-carita, Act II; Kāmandakī was a class-mate of Bhūrivasu and Devarāta. In big hermitages, venerable sages certainly used to teach the male and female students together. Again, girl-students often resided with the family of a teacher the same number of years as the boys; cf. Ambā's residence with the Śaikhāvatyas.

Scholars have reasonably suspected that the joint family system is a later development. There is no trace of it in the early Vedic period Formerly, sons as well as daughters left the parents after marriage; but now when the joint family system developed, only daughters had to leave their parents after marriage. Sons, as members of the family, contributed to its welfare or suffered the same fate as the family might be driven to. Daughters had not to bother about the parent's family after the full-fledged development of the joint family system. So the daughter was considered a lesser necessity.

The increasing difficulties of giving the daughters in marriage owing to the development of rigorous caste-system and joint-family system brought about economic difficulties not known before. Economic cause played no insignificant part in determining the position of women in subsequent ages. In ancient India, there was no reason for the excessive worry of parents; no fear of unwanted life-long miseries on account of interminable widowhood, no anxiety for obligatory marriage within a limited number of years, nothing of the sort. A woman's life was as free as that of a man. The passages that breathe of anxieties on the part of parents simply show that the daughters, as natural, were objects of great care and affection.[1] Matters, however, became quite different in subsequent ages.

1. Janaka's anxiety for Sitā; Rāmāyaṇa, II. 119. 35-36; Cf. Kaṇva's anxiety for Śakuntalā in the Abhijñānaśakuntala.

CHAPTER II

The Chief Wife In The Vedic Ritual

The first wife only is the patnī in the fullest sense of the term. She is the dharmapatnı while even the second wife (and naturally all other wives) is meant for sexual satisfaction only: a second wife is entitled to no unseen (adṛṣṭa) religious merit.[1] A man having several wives is required to observe his religious duties with first wife only; preference is however, sometimes given to the savarṇā wife so much so that even though she may be the youngest, he will observe religious duties with her and in case the savarṇā, be she the youngest, is not present or unable to attend, the claim would devolve upon one coming from the class immediately lower. A Śūdrā wife is always to be excluded by a Brāhmaṇa.[2] According to Manu[3] it is the first wife who is to attend personally and help the husband in his daily religious rites; he cannot show preference to other wives in these matters for fear of being a Caṇḍāla Brāhmaṇa. The Karmakāṇḍa-pradīpa[4] also says that only the first wife has the adhikāra. Disparagement of marriages other than the first is expressed in the fact that during the second and following marriages, the polygamist is to marry a pitcher (kumbha)[5] or some such thing. According to Yājñavalkya, too, the religious rites should be performed with the first wife of the same caste,

1. Dakṣa-saṃhitā. Iv, 14, Smṛ. Sam. p. 79, I 19 (Una Sam. IV, 15, p. 428 प्रथमा धर्मपत्नी च द्वितीया रतिवर्धिनी। दृष्टमेव फलं तत्र नादृष्टमुपजायते॥ 2. Viṣṇu XXVI, 1-4, Una. Sam. p. 66, II. 8 f. 3. Manu IX, 85-86. 4. F. 149b, I. 9 f. 5. Op. cit., p. 150 f.

not with others.[1] Rites observed for the highest religious merit or salvation are to be observed with the first wife.[2] Highest results (such as obtaining heaven, etc.) may be achieved only if the rite is performed along with the first wife.[3] The wife first married is to be considered as the eldest, not the one who is the oldest of the lot;[4] the Śat. Br.[5] says she is the consecrated consort.

Even though other wives are allowed to join in the sacrifice, it is the first wife who performs all the important rites. In the Darśapūrṇamāseṣṭi she trims the fire,[6] husks and pounds the rice.[7] After the Patnīsannahana (girding with the yoktrapāśa) and Gārhapatyopasthāna the wives are required to sit to the north of the Gārhapatya; the Mukhyapatnī occupies the seat exactly to the north, i.e. the best seat while other wives take their seats somewhere to the north of the

1. Yājñ. I, 88. सत्यामन्यां सवर्णायां धर्मकार्यं न कारयेत। सवर्णासु विधौ धर्मे ज्येष्ठया न विनेतरा:॥ cf. Śāṅ. ŚS. vol. II. p. 54, II. 4-5.

2. Sat. ŚS. vol. I. p. 160, I. 21. परार्थानि etc."

3. Op. cit., I, 22 "सकृत्कृतं etc"

4. Sat. ŚS. vol. III. p. 695, I 3 ज्येष्ठत्वं विवाह-कृतं न तु वयस्कृतम्।

5. VI. 5, 3, 1; p. 541. I. 6, Weber's Ed.

6. Āp. ŚS. I, 6, 12; vol. I p. 23.

7. Of course, there is provision here that she might be replaced by a Śūdrā in pounding. However, no strict regularity seems to be observed in husking or pounding. See Sat. ŚS., p. 132, II. 17 f.; Āp. ŚS., I, 21, 9. According to Āp. ŚS., op. cit., a Śūdra is to pound if the rice is to be pounded again; "Anena punaspeṣaṇe dāsyā niyamo varṇyate." If for some reason or other the wife could not be present the Agnidhra or some other priest might do this for the wife; Sat. ŚS. p. 132, I. 23; Āp. ŚS., I, 20, 13; 70.

Gārhapatya, no doubt, but at a distance from the first wife.[1] After the Patnīsaṃyāja the chief is to eat the Iḍā[2] If simultaneously God-speed is to be wished now for the husband and the wife, it should be desired for the chief wife[3] only. Towards the close of the sacriffce the kuśa grass is removed from the lap of the wife and the cord with which she was girded is loosened; according to the Śāṅkhāyana school,[4] only the first wife is to observe these rites. During the utterance of the Saṃpatnīya it is the first wife who is to touch the husband as this act is meant for "Parārtha or Supreme Bliss."[5]

In the Agnyādhāna and the Agnihotra only the first wife, so long as she is living, is entitled to participate. The newly-married couple establish the sacred fires and observe the Agnihotra in the same fire till the end of the life of one of them. If the first wife is dead, the widower may marry and establish the fires again. But in no case, after the Agnyādhāna, should the first wife be deprived of her right of participating in the Agnihotra, even if she be deficient in religious performance or in procreation. On account of her

1. Sat ŚS., Vol. 1 p. 161, 1. 7. यथाप्रदेशं मुख्यपत्न्युपवेशनं समीप इतरासां तामेव दिशमवलम्ब्य व्यवधानेन etc. 2. Baudh. ŚS., p. 30, II. 16.

3. Cf. Śat. Br., I, 9, 2, 14; Weber's Ed,, p. 90. II. 14.

4. I, 15, 10; see Comm. on the same, vol. II. p. 54. According to other authorities, however, all the wives are to observe those rites as they do not think these are meant for Parārtha; Sat. ŚS,, Vol. I, p. 228 pratipatni vedādānāditi gamyate.

5. Sat. ŚS., Vol. I, p. 223, II. 23-24 "Parārthāny ekena iti," etc.

assistance in the kindling of the fires she has been for her life associated with and given to the service of these fires.[1] The fires are inseparable from her; so long as she is in the house, they are there; when she goes with her husband to a foreign place, they move with her.[2] So long as the husband lives without his wife and consequently, without the fires, be it even in the next village, it is nothing but living in a foreign land but when the wife and her constant companions, the Fires, go with him, even the most distant land will not be considered as such (pravāsa).[3] If in any case the wife does not go with him, he must go without the fires and when he comes back he offers oblations to them but in order that they may be thoroughly pleased, he is to please the wife with his look.[4]

Before the Agnihotra actually begins, the wife cleanses the surrounding areas of the fires;[5] from the beginning to the end of the sacrifice she remains sitting to the south or the south-east of the Gārhapatya fire.[6] There can be

1 Ap., II, 5, 11, 13f; see the Scholiaft in particular; Manu V, 167-168; Yaāj. I, 89. 2. Cf. Sat. SS. vol. I, p. 161.

3. Op. cit., vol. I, p. 358, I. 2; op. cit., vol. II. p. 541, 1. 16.

4. Op. cit., vol. II, p. 534, I. 27.

5. Āp. SS., vol. I, p. 322, I. 20, Scholiast on 6, 3. 1.

6. Āp. SS., VI, 5, 2, vol. I, p. 328, II. 15-17. cf. Śān. SS., 2, 7. "Behind the Gārhapatya".

no substitute for the first wife in the Agnihotra; nevertheless, she must be present or be considered as virtually present in her shed.[1] Whenever the husband offers oblation, he does so for both of them.[2] Towards the end of the sacrifice water-libations are offered to the Sarpadevajana, Bhūta and Mahat with either three ladlefuls of water or in three portions from the same ladleful;[3] the sacrificer then takes another ladleful of water or offers with the remaining portion of the water. Of this water he pours half on Earth and the other half he pours into the hands of the wife. In case of her absence from the sacrifice on account of unavoidable circumstances the whole quantity of the fourth ladleful or of the fourth portion of the same ladleful according to Bhāradvāja, is to be twice poured, upon the seat of the wife or the Earth. In no case should this water be poured into the hands of any other wife.[5] The object of this pouring is to pray for domestic bliss and

1 Compare the remark of the Scholiast on *Āp. ŚS.*, VI, 5, 1, vol. I, p. 328. ll. 12-13.

2 *Śat. ŚS.*, vol. II, p. 529. "Vratabhṛd ahaṃ nāv ubhayor vratam cariṣyāmi, etc." The same spirit is remarkably seen in the Vājapeya, too; cf. "Patni! svargaṃ rohāvaḥ, etc."

3 *Śāṅ. ŚS.*, 2, 10, 5 "Traidhaṃ karoti"; *Śat. ŚS.*, vol. I, p. 354. *Āp. ŚS.*, VI, 12. 4-5; vol. I, pp. 343-44. The W.Y.V. ritual, however, does not refer to this rite; cf. p. 304, Chow. Ed., Sūtras 341-42.

4 Scholiast on *Śat., ŚS op. cit.*

5 *Śat. ŚS.*, vol. I, p. 354, ll. 20 f. "न च यजमानपत्नीसंस्कारोऽयं द्वितीयादिश्रुतेरश्रवणादत एव न प्रतिपत्ति विभज्य निनयनं...सर्वग्रहणाच्च प्रतिपत्त्यावृत्तिनिरासार्थम्"; similarly, Scholiast on Śāṅkhāyana 2, 10, 6, "Ekavacanañ ca vivakṣitam, etc."

triumph for and by the wife;[6] no other wife than the first is ever entitled to be the mistress of the house.

At the end of the evening oblation the wife together with her husband should observe silence and fast till darkness has set in.[7]

As in the Vaiśvadeva, so in the Varuṇapraghāsas, it is the first wife who should husk the barley, and deposit the husk for the Avabhṛtha.[8] She should make the Karambhapātras out of the barley-powder which she should herself make of unfried barley.[9] Some schools, however, empower her to husk the barley on the previous day, fry them a bit on the Anvahāryapacana, pound them and make Karambhapātras out of the powder.[10] As a rule, the Adhvaryu and the Pratiprasthātṛ make a ram and a ewe respectively with their sex marks made prominent.[11] But according to the Vājasaneya Ritual[12] the wife should, after having made the Karambhapātras, make the ram and the ewe, too, of the barley similarly fried and powdered. These rites should be observed by the chief wife alone as these are by no means Strīsaṃskāras; moreover, in making the ram and

6 Cf. the Mantra "Gṛhebhyas tvā gṛhān jinva", *B*, *YV*.; "Saṃ tvā sṛjāmi prajayā dhanena" iti, *RV*.

7 *Āśv*. *SS*., III, 12, 9, *Bib*. *Ind*., p. 50 and 25a.

8 Scholiast on *Āp*. *SS*., VIII, 5, 40, vol. II, p. 28:

9 According to several authorities the husband also participates in this; e.g. *Sat SS*., p. 463, I. 16-21.

10 *Āp*. *SS*., VIII, 6, 3, vol II, p. 29; Scholiast, II. 10 f.

11 *Baudh*. *SS*., I, p. 136, II, 1-16; *Sat SS*., p. 462, II. 28-31.

12 As quoted in *Āp*. *SS*., VIII, 6, 4, vol. II, pp. 29-30; cf. *Baudh*. *SS*., vol. I, p. 133, I. 12, also quoted by the Scholiast on *Āp*., *op*. *cit*.

the ewe, she is really a substitute of the priests, which other wives cannot be supposed to be. These are Parārthaka rites and as such, only the chief wife should observe them.

After the rite of the declaration of paramours, the wife invokes the Maruts[13] when she is led by the Pratiprasthātṛ. She is offered the Karambhapātras[14] in a winnowing basket which she places on her head. Both the sacrificer and the wife[15] now pass between the altars and seat themselves in front of the Dakṣiṇa fire with their faces towards the west. The wife gives these dishes to the sacrificer which he in his turn places on his head.[16] The husband utters the Anuvākyā.[17] Then both the husband and the wife offer oblations to the Maruts[18] to expiate their sins which they have incurred either in village or the wild, in company or corporeal sense, etc., the dedicatory formula[19] being

13 *Tait. Saṃh.*, 1, 8, 3, 6; *Vāj. Saṃh.*, III, 44, etc.; *Mān. ŚS.*, 1, 7, 4, 12, p. 55.

14 According to Baudhāyana these dishes should have been given round the fire; *Baudh. ŚS.*, p. 136, ll. 19, "Abhiparyagnikṛtāni."

15 The wife goes out by the south door, *Baudh. ŚS.*, p. 137, ll. 1-2.

16 *Baudh. ŚS.*, *op. cit.*, ll. 6-7.

17 *Tait. Saṃh.*, 1, 6, 53, cf. 1, 8, 3 (c); *Vāj. Saṃh.*, III, 46; *Baudh. ŚS.*, p. 136 l. 8.

18 "Praghāsasya Marut devatā", *Sat. ŚS.*, vol II, p. 465, ll. 24-25.

19 *Vāj. Saṃh.*, III, 47; *Kap. Saṃh.*, 1, 7, p. 35, ll. 21-22; etc., *Sat. ŚS.*, vol. II, p. 465, ll. 21 f. The adhvaryu may perform this for them while they keep on touching him, ll. 26-27 (*Sat. ŚS.*) *Baudh ŚS.*, vol. I, p. 137, l. 10; *Mān. ŚS.*, 1, 7, 4, 15, p. 55; *Āp. ŚS.*, VIII, 6, 24.

pronounced by both. According to Kātyāyana[20] the mistress alone is entitled to observe this rite. The husband and the (chief) wife now offer thanks to priests and praise their bounteous nature in having kindly undertaken and performed the sacrifice with a delightful voice.[21]

In the Avabhṛtha it is the chief wife who should wash the back of the sacrificer and he should, in his turn, wash her back too.[22] They offer their drenched garments to whomsoever they like.[23] The chief wife joins the priests and the sacrificer in the Sun-worship, and in adding fresh fuel to the Āhavanīya fire.[24]

In the Sākamedha the chief wife cooks the sacrificial food on the Southern Fire and participates later on with all others in eating it.[25] In the Traimbaka oblation after the sacrificer and priests, etc., and the maidens have walked round the fires, she lays fuel on and worships the Gārhapatya.[26]

In the animal sacrifice the chief wife anoints the surface of the sacrificial post while the sacrificer anoints the top of it. She rubs all over the post in order to impart to it lustre without omitting to rub any part of it.[27]

20 V, 5, II.

21 *Sat. Brā.*, II, 5, 2, 29; *Mān. SS.*, 1, 7, 4, 16; *Āp. SS.*, VIII, 6, 25; *Sat. SS.*, p. 465, l. 28.

22 *Āp. SS.*, VIII. 8. 16.

23 *Āp. SS.*, VIII. 8. 17.

24 Scholiast on *Āp. SS.*, VIII, 8, 18, "Sarvam etat samānaṃ patnyāḥ."

25 *Āp. SS.*, VIII; 10, 10, vol. II, p. 53; *Sat. SS.*, vol. II, p. 473, ll. 5-6 Scholiast "Patnīstrīkumārā iti Vaikhānasaḥ".

26 *Sat. SS.*, vol. II, p. 469, l. 28.

27 *Baudh. SS.*, vol. I, p. 114, ll. 6-7.

The prime duty of the wife in this sacrifice is to wipe the organs of the animal so that its soul (literally, the lives here) may rest in peace,[28] and this is done by the chief wife.[29] Before she proceeds, she, with a water-jar in her hands, worships the Sun.[30] During her advance towards the cātvāla the Pratiprasthātṛ prays for offspring and increase of wealth. Then she propitiates and takes water from the cātvāla. She also recites mantras for propitiating the sacrifice and then wipes each organ of the animal with appropriate mantras.[31] According to some, she pours the water on the organs and the Adhvaryu wipes them or he pours water and she wipes them. After cleansing the victim, she purifies herself at the pit along with the utterance of a mantra.[32]

28 प्राणाप्यायन—"आप्याययति तत्स्थानमभिलक्ष्य अपः प्रक्षिपति ; प्रक्षिप्तोदकस्थानाभिमर्शनम् आप्यायनम्" Scholiast on Satyāṣāḍha, vol. II, p. 424, ll. 21 f.

29 Scholiast on Satyāṣāḍha, *op. cit.*, Parārthāny ekena kriyerann iti mukhyā eva abhiṣecànam āpyāyanaṃ karoti; similarly, Scholiast on Āpastamba (1. 8. 17), vol I, p. 436, ll. 17-19.

30 *Baudh.* S., vol. I, p. 118, ll. 7-8; *Mān. SS.*, 1, 8, 4, 1; *Sat. SS.*, vol. II. p. 424, ll. 6 f. "Pūrṇapātradhārañam ekasyā eva āpyāyanasthatvāt."

31 *Tait. Saṃh.*, 1, 3, 9; *Kat Saṃh.*, III. 6; *Kap. Saṃh.*, II. 13, (pp. 21-22); *Mait. Saṃh.*, 1, 2, 16; *Vāj. Saṃh.*, VI. 14-16; *Āp SS.*, VII, 18, 17, vol. I, p. 436, ll. 21 f.; *Sat. SS.*, vol II, p. 424; *Man. SS.*, 1, 8, 4, p. 68; *Baudh. SS.*, vol. I, p. 118, ll. 12 f. It remains doubtful who, the sacrificer and the Adhvaryu or the sacrificer and the wife, should use, *Vāj. Saṃh.*, VI, 15-16. For the reasons why the wife should wipe the organs, see *Sat.* Brā., III, 6, 2, 5.

32 *Vāj. Saṃh.*, VI, 17; *AV.*, VII, 89, 3; *Kāt. SS.*, Chow. ed., p. 398, *Sūtra* 146; *Sat. SS.*, vol II, p. 424, II. 16 f.

After the Patnīsamyāja she offers the killer the front leg and the Adhvaryu some front piece.[33] During the iḍā-bhakṣaṇa the sacrificer first gives the iḍā to her and she hands it over to the Adhvaryu or some other priest.[34] The sacrifice ending, while all others worship the Āhavanīya, she adds fresh fuel to and worships the Gārhapatya.[35]

In the Agniṣṭoma after the offering called Hiraṇyavatī the sacrificer steps into the seven foot-prints of the cow. The wife together with the other wives, the sacrificer and the priests sit round the seventh foot-print wherein a piece of gold is laid. After due offerings the Adhvaryu takes one-third portion of the dust from there and hands it over to the sacrificer with the blessings for the latter's wealth. The sacrificer gives it to the chief wife[36] so that she may have wealth ; while it is being given to her she prays that she may not be deprived of wealth. She preserves the dust in her own residence or

33 *Sat. SS.*, *op. cit.* p. 443, ll. 1.

34 *Āp. SS.*, VII, 27, 12, vol. I, p. 463.

35 *Sat. SS.*, *op. cit.*, p. 444, II. 11-12; cf. *Āp. SS.*, VII, 27, 16, vol. I, p. 464, according to which she is to have a wash, worship the Sun and the *Āhavanīya*.

36 Scholiast on *Āp. SS.*, X, 23, "पत्न्यनेकत्वेऽपि महिष्याः प्रयच्छति निधानार्थत्वात्" similarly, Scholiast on *Sat. SS.*, vol. III, p. 629, ll. 11-12 "निधानार्थत्वादसंस्कारकर्मत्वाच्च" *Baudh. SS.*, p. 170, l. 5. According to the Scholiast on *Kāt. SS.*, sūtras 176-177, p. 449, Chow. ed., the adhvaryu gives her the dust and the Neṣṭṛ makes her recite the Mantra; *Sat. Brā.*, III, 3, 1, 12; *Tait. Saṃh.*, VI, 1, 8, 5; etc. etc.

in one of the three sheds, viz. Prāgvaṃśa-Sālā, Patnī-śālā and Vāhya-śālā.[37]

It seems only the first wife should hold on to the cart from behind;[38] because this is no Patnī-saṃskāra. By this rite the chief wife, as the household gear and as the approver of her husband's gift[39] honours the king Soma as a very worthy guest when he is brought forward on a car. While she does so, the Adhvaryu offers the water libations to the guest Soma. Or she may herself with her own hands make the offering or while the priest offers, she may present to the guest the Vaiṣṇava Navakapāla with her own hands.[40]

It is the chief wife who anoints the axles of the Soma-carts;[41] the object is to have children with heroic deeds.[42] While the Advaryu walks out of the hall by the front door with clarified butter taken a second time in four lad-

37 *Sat. SS.*, vol. III, p. 630, ll. 10 f., specially, the Scholiast; *Ap. SS.* X, 23, 10.

38 *Ap. SS.*, X, 30, 5; *Sat. SS.*, p. 652, ll. 8-11; *Baudh. SS.*, VI, 16, vol. I, p. 174, ll. 14-15. "अप: प्रणीयातिथ्यं निर्वपत्यन्वारब्धायां पत्न्याम्" *Kāt. SS.*, Chow. ed., sūtra 2, vol. I, p. 463.

39 *Cf. Tait. Saṃh.*, VI, 2, 1.

40 *Ap. SS.*, X, 30, 5-6, vol. II, p. 288, ll. 9 f.; Scholiast "यदि पत्न्या हस्तेन निर्वापस्तदा हस्तोऽग्निहोत्रहवणीधर्मान् लभते" *Sat. SS.*, vol. III, p. 652, ll. 23; 653, ll.11.

41 Scholiast on *Sat. SS.*, vol. III, p. 695, ll. 28 f. "Mukhyā eva anakti; Scholiast on *Ap. SS.*, XI, 6, 4, vol. II, p. 309 'पत्न्यनेकत्वेऽपि मुख्या उपानक्ति अक्षसंस्कारत्वात्' *Baudh. SS.*, VI, 24, vol. I, p. 184, ll. 12 f.; *Kāt. SS.* VIII, 82 f.; p, 480, ll. 5 ff., Chow. ed.

42 Cf. the Mantra "No vīro jāyatām, etc."

lings, the sacrificer's wife is led by the South.[43] The Adhvaryu lays down a piece of gold in the right wheel of the southern cart and makes offerings; he pours the residue of clarified butter into her folded palms. According to Baudhāyana,[44] she mixes half of the dust of the third footprint with it. Then she anoints the right axle of the southern cart with her right hand.[45] According to Āpastamba[46] she may anoint this axle twice. Now, in order that she may anoint the axle of the northern car, she is made to walk round by the back of the Gārhapatya fire to the wheel-tracks on the north side. This time, the assistant of the Adhvaryu observes the same rites as the Adhvaryu in the previous case, and pours the residue of clarified butter after his offerings, into her folded palms. According to Baudhāyana she mixes up the remaining dust with it. She anoints and prays for her desired ends.[47] According to Kātyāyana[48] she should anoint both the axles simultaneously with both the hands.

During the second pressing she approves of the gifts

43 *Śat. Brā.* III, 5, 3, 13ff., *Kāt. ŚS.*, Chow. Ed., vol. I, p. 840, ll. 6 f. "Dakṣiṇayā dvārā, etc." According to *Baudh. ŚS.*, vol. I, p. 164, l. 12: "Pūrvayā dvārā."

44 *Baudh. ŚS.*, vol. I, p. 184, l. 16, "Atha eteṣāṃ padapāṃsūnām, etc." Cf. *Śat. ŚS.*, vol. III, p. 695, l. 8 "Dvidhāvibhaktasya ekāṃśena."

45 Scholiast on *Śat. ŚS.*, *op. cit.*, l. 21.

46 *ŚS.*, XI, 6, 5, vol. II, p. 309; see also Sūtra 8 "Sakṛd vā;" cf. Scholiast.

47 *Vāj. Saṃ.*, V, 17 "Parāg devaśrutau, etc."

48 *ŚS.*, vol. I, p. 480, ll. 6-11 "......Pāṇibhyāṃ...yugapat..."

given by her husband to the priests and others.[49] In the third pressing, after all the rites up to the filling of the pots have been performed, the chief wife[50] churns the Soma in the shed for Agnīdhra; then she enters into the Soma-cart by the western door and stays there.[51] She and the sacrificer then carry the purified Soma in the Pūtabhṛt covered by the purifying Kuśa (Pavitra).[52] According to the scholiast on Kātyāyana,[53] she, touched from behind by all other wives, looks at it and addresses Āditya for children, wealth and sinless living.

As the personal attendant of her husband in religious affairs, it is the chief wife who should wash the back of her husband during the final bath (Avabhṛthà).[54] When she comes back to her own shed she worships the Gārhapatya by laying on the Udumbara fuel which she cleanses beforehand in front of the cow-shed.

Towards the end of the Udanīyeṣṭi, she burns theKuśa-grasses used therein in the Prāgvaṃśa.[55]

49 *Kāt. SS.*, X, 2, 38, Weber's Ed., p. 802; Chow. Ed., p. 570, Sūtra 62; cf. Commentary in Weber.

50 Scholiast on *Sat. SS.*, vol. IV, p. 919, ll. 9-10 "पत्नीबहुत्वे मुख्यैव मथनं पूतभृत्यवनयनश्च करोति, न तु सर्वाः" The Mantra used in this connection: "अस्मे देवासो वपुषे चिकित्सदिति"

51 *Kāt. SS.*, Chow. Ed., p. 574, ll. 4-5; Weber's Ed., X, 4, 3, p. 807; *Sat. SS.*, *op. cit.*

52 *Sat. SS.*, *op. cit.*

53 *SS.*, X, 5, 4, Weber's Ed., p. 810, ll. 3 f.; Chow. Ed., p. 577, Sūtra 105. The Mantra: *Vāj. Saṃh.*, VIII, 5.

54 *Sat. SS.*, vol. IV, p. 947, ll 14 f. For the ūha, see Commentary.

55 *Sat. SS.*, vol. IV, p. 954, ll. 22 g.

According to certain Śākhās of the *W.YV.*, she puts a log of wood on the Gārhapatya fire without the utterance of any mantra[56] in the Pravargya sacrifice.

In the Agnicayana the first wife makes the Ukhā, the fire-pan to which she prays for offspring; increase of wealth, cattle, horses and also for making the fellows of the sacrificer subject to him.[57] She also makes from clay Āṣāḍhā, the invincible brick, and marks it with three lines.[58]

In the Vājapeya, the garland of gold which forms the fee should be worn by the chief wife only, as this is a rite producing highest results. The fee would pave the way of the wife as well as of the sacrificer to Heaven.[59] After twelve Āpti and Kḷpti offerings have been offered on the Āhavanīya fire for procuring for the sacrificer all that the twelve months of the year and the six seasons can bestow, the Neṣṭṛ or the Pratiprasthātṛ makes the chief wife wear garments of Darbha grass or Caṇḍātaka or Dṛhara[60] while the sacrificer wears silken garment.[61]

56 Scholiast Devayajvan on *Kāt. ŚS.*, XXVI, 7, 40, Weber's Ed., p. 1108; Chow. Ed., p. 1042.

57 *Vāj. Saṃh.*, II, 58; *Mait. Saṃ.*, 2, 7, 6; *Kāṭ. Saṃ.*, 1, 6, 5; *Āp. ŚS.*, XVI, 4, 5; vol. III, p. 5; *Sat. ŚS.*, vol. 5, p. 14, ll. 7 f., etc.

58 *Sat. ŚS.*, vol. V, p. 15, ll. 21-13; *Śat. Brā.*, IV, 5, 3, 1, 4; p. 541, ll. 4-6, Weber' Ed.

59 *Kāt. ŚS.*, XIV, 5, 36, Weber's Ed., p. 868.

60 *Kāt. ŚS.*, XIV, 5, 3, Weber's Ed., p. 866.

61 *Sat. ŚS.*, vol. V, p. 144, l. 2; "Paridhatte" has been explained by the commentators as "Paridhāpayati." For the Mantra she utters: *Vāj. Saṃ.*, 10, 8; *Tait. Saṃ.*, I, 7, 9, 1, etc.

The Neṣṭṛ then leads her to the post against which a ladder having seventeen stairs has been put. The sacrificer now gets ready to mount the post and enquires about her willingness to accompany him.[62] She replies in the affirmative. Thrice the sacrificer asks and thrice she replies.[63] The sacrificer now wishes that he should mount for both of them to which she readily consents. She may herself mount the post if she likes[64]. In this case she should pray similarly as the sacrificer for the success of life by sacrifice and such other things.[65] Most probably she should stretch her arms, too, to show that she has mounted the top just as the sacrificer does and express herself the joy of approaching the gods and of being capable of becoming immortal and the offspring of Prajāpati. She should also look down to the ground and pray for offspring and increase of wealth.[66] If she does not accompany her husband, she is looked at by him from above after he has reached the top.[67] If she accompanies him, he helps her in descending from the post.[68] It is the

62 *Vāj. Saṃ.*, (Kānva rec.) 10, 4, 3; *Tait. Saṃ.*, I, 7, 9, 1; *Sat. Brā.*, 5, 2, 1, 10; *Tait. Brā.*, I, 3, 7, 2; *Kāt. SS.*, XIV, 5, 6; *Āp. SS.*, XVIII, 5, 9; *Sat. SS.*, vol. V, p. 144, ll. 9 f.; *Baudh. SS.*, XI, 11, vol. II, p. 80, ll. 2 f., etc.; cf. Hill., Ritlit. p. 142, ll. 31 f.

63 *Sat SS.*, *op. cit.*, I. 11 "Evaṃ tri."

64 *Op. cit.*, I. 17 "Ubhau vā."

65 For the Mantras, see *Tait. Saṃh.*, I, 7, 9, 1; *Vāj. Saṃ.*, IX, 21 (cf. XXII, 32) ;*Kāṭ. Saṃ.*, XIV, 1; *Mait. Saṃ.*, I, 11, 3; *Sat. Brā.*, V, 2, 1, 4; *Āp. SS.*, XVIII 5, 13

66 *Tait. Saṃ.*, I, 7, 9 f.

67 *Sat. SS.*, vol. V, p. 145, I. 9 "Patnīm iti bhāṣyakṛt."

68 *Baudh. SS.*, vol. II, p. 80, I. 9.

chief wife who should observe the above rites as it is she who is to propitiate the sacrifice;[69] it is she only who makes the sacrificer complete by addition of one-half of his own self;[70] and as he is to achieve heavenly bliss together with her only.[71] She and her husband are one Soul divided into two bodies, not only on this mortal land, but also in heaven—to participate in worldly affairs, in sacrificial matters, in earthly blessings as well as in divine joy.

In the Piṇḍapitṛyajña the eldest wife stands on the black deer-skin with her face towards the south-east and husks the paddy in a wooden mortar. She must not sit. She removes the husk by means of a winnowing basket, but does not separate the husked from those which are still not done. She husks them only once.[72]

Now, to come to the chief queen. The Mahiṣī is the consecrated consort; all other wives are meant for sexual pleasure only.[73] In the Politico-religious ceremonies, viz. the Aśvamedha, Rājasūya, Puruṣamedha and Rāḍ-yajña, she, properly speaking, performs all the important rites while the "Bhoginī" queens are allowed to participate therein as mere companions of the chief queen as it were; the part that they play therein is insignificant.

69 *Sat. SS.*, p. 285, II 5 f.;

70 *Op. cit.*, V, 2, 1, 10.

71 *Op. cit.*

72 *Sat. SS.*, p. 285, I. 5 f.; *Ap. SS.*, I, 8, 10-11, vol. I, pp. 26-27; *SSS.*, IV, 3, 7, vol. I. p. 35; Scholiast, *op. cit.*, vol. II, p. 170, I, 11; *Asv. SS.*, (*ASS*) II, 6, 7, p. 68, II. 13-15.

73 *Amarakoṣa*, p. 124, I. 10 "Kṛtābhiṣekā mahiṣī bhoginyo'nyā nṛpa-strīyaḥ."

At the beginning of the Horse-sacrifice which occurs on the eighth or ninth of the month of Phālguna, the chief queen and the king prepare themselves for ritual observance in the regular way as they do in other sacrifices. They cook for themselves food for breaking fast mixed with clarified butter as well as milk and eat it (in the afternoon) and wash their mouths in a golden bowl.[74] Then they keep silent and perform Agnihotra in due time. According to Baudhāyana all the queens are allowed to wear silver ornaments[75] for the occasion; but the chief queen wears several ornaments in addition which signifies her power over man in general.[76] According to Kātyāyana all the wives should wear golden ornaments.[77] But the distinctive position of the chief queen is seen in the fact that the one hundred maidens that accompany her must be either daughters[78] or wives[79] of kings; while the maidens of the Vāvātā are to be daughters or wives of subordinate Chiefs, or of the Ugras;[80] those of Parivṛkti, daughters or wives of Charioteers, and those of Pārāgalī, daughters or wives of Revenue Collectors. In the evening they all enter the hall of sacrificial fires by the southern door.[81] After the

74 *Baudh. SS.*, XV, 2, p. 206, ll. 7 f.; note particularly "Ubhau' in line 9. Cf. *Āp. SS.*, XX, I, 10 f., vol. III, p. 142.

75 *Op. cit.* XV, 3, p. 206, ll. 13-14

76 *Op. cit.*, I. 9.

77 XX, I, 12, Weber, u. 961.

78 *Kāt. SS.*, XX, 1, 13, Weber, p. 961.

79 According to *Baudh. SS.*, cf. p. 228, II. 14 f.; *Āp. SS.*, XX, 15, vol. III, p. 159, I. 8.

80 *Sat. SS.*, vol. 5, p. 237, I. 24 "Ugrāṇām rājadāsabhūtānām śataṃ Vāvātāyāḥ."

81 Commentary on *Kāt. SS.*, Chow. Ed. p. 829. Sūtra 17.

Agnihotra the Vāvātā avails herself of the coveted fortune of getting the king on her lap with his head towards the north;[82] this simply signifies the justification of her name "Vāvātā: the favourite" and nothing important so far as the supermundane bliss is concerned. The queens together with the maidens most probably help the king in keeping awake throughout the night. In other sacrifices as well as in this it is the chief queen who needs to keep awake along with the sacrifices and not all.

On the return of the horses on the second Soma-pressing day they are all bathed. Now the first three queens are to anoint the sacrificial horses and entwine pearls or coins into its mane and tail.[83] The order of anointing and entwining does not seem to be strictly observed.[84] The chief queen anoints the fore-parts, the favourite queen the middle and a discarded wife the hind-part. Again, the chief queen takes recourse to the Gāyatrī metre, the most important of all metres; the second, the Triṣṭubh; Parivṛkti, the Jagatī. The stuff that the chief queen uses for anointing is clarified butter mixed with the sap of the sacred Pūtu-dru tree; that the Vāvātā uses is clarified butter mixed with the ordinary thing bdellium[85] and that the Parivṛkti uses is Ghee mixed

82 *Op. cit.*, Sūtra 18.

83 Pālāgalī, a Śūdrā by birth, cannot observe these rites, cf. *Sat. Brā.*, XIII, 2, 6, 7. Anointing and entwining: *Kāth. Saṃh.*, III, 12, 18, 19; *Vāj. Saṃh.*, XIII, 5-8; *Tait. Brā.*, III, 9, 4, 1-8; *Sat. Brā.*, XIII, 2, 6, 1-6; *Āp. SS.*, XX, 15, 6 f.; Kāt. SS., XX, 5, 10 f.; *Baudh. SS.*, XV, 24, vol. II.

84 Cf. Baudhāyana and Āpastamba.

85 Gaulgulava, known in Bengal as Guggul.

with the sap of the Mustā plants that grows anywhere and everywhere. The companions that they have are the same as before. The varied rank of these maidens at once brings out the respective position of the queens. Again, during the entwining of pearls the chief queen adorns the parts in front of the place where the yoke rests with golden pearls; the Vāvātā below that and the buttocks with silver ones; the Parivṛkti below the buttocks with any and every pearl that may come from the sea.[86]

After the wild animals are released, the horse is killed, most probably, by stifling in robes. Then the Unnetṛ or Pratiprasthātṛ[87] or Adhvaryu[88] leads them up from their ordinary place near the Gārhapatya to the victim. They carry in their hands jars of water.[89] According to Satyāṣāḍha only the chief queen should be led by the Pratiprasthātṛ; so, other wives are to follow her.[90] In order to make amends for the slaughtering of the victim and to invoke the divine helpers to help the chief queen in the most important rite that follows,[91] they walk round the victim nine times while fanning him with the flutter of

86 According to *B.YV.* ritual, each of them uses 100 pearls; *Āp. ŚS.*, XX, 15, vol. III, p. 159, l. 11; *Baudh. ŚS.*, vol. II, p. 228, ll. 3, 5 and 7; *Sat. ŚS.*, vol. V, p. 237, ll. 17 f. According to W.YV. only a hundred; *Kāt. ŚS.*, Weber, p. 971; according to the Scholiast, one hundred and one.

87 *Kāt. ŚS.*, XX, 6, 12; *Āp. ŚS.*, XX, 17, 12.

88 *Baudh. ŚS.*, XV, 29.

89 Scholiast on *Kāt. ŚS.*, XX, 6, 14, Weber, p. 973, ll. 1-2.

90 *ŚS.*, vol. V, p. 242, ll. 6 f.

91 *Tait. Saṃh.*, VII, 4, 12, 1; *Tait. Brā.*, 3, 9, 6, 1; *Āp. ŚS.*, XX, 17, 13; *Kāt. ŚS.*, XX, 6, 14, Weber, p. 973, l. 1.

their garments; for the first three times they tie in a knot the right locks of hair and let loose the left ones and walk from right to left, smiting their right thighs; then they follow the exactly reverse course in all matters.[92] The chief queen, now, shows anxiety to approach the slain horse, who represents Prajāpati, in order to have seed from him. Then the chief queen lies down by the side of the horse. She, along with the utterance of mantras, makes various attempts while the Adhvaryu cloaks them together with garments. While she does the obscene act, she feels reluctant and censures the horse.[93] Three times the chief queen censures, three times the others persuade her. All sorts of indecent acts and talks are the concomitant factors of fertility spells;[94] here, too, for the sake of fertility, indecent colloquy between the priests, queen and maidens, etc. begin. According to several schools only the maidens reply.[95] According to *Śat. Br.*,[96] the Brahman, the most important priest of all, addresses the queen consort, while the Udgātṛ addresses

92 *Āp. ŚS.*, *op. cit.*, Sūtras 13-16.

93 *Kāt. ŚS.*, XX, 6, 16-17, p. 973, ll. 6-10; *Āp. ŚS.*, XX, 18, 4, vol. III, p. 163, ll. 77 f.; *Vait. S.*, XXXVI, 30, p. 52.

94 Cf. the Dialogue between the Brahmacārin and the Hetaera in the Mahāvrata.

95 *Kāt. ŚS.*, XX, 6, 20; *Āp. ŚS.*, XX 18, 6; *Āśv. ŚS.*, X, 8, 13; *Vait. S.*, XXXVI, 32.

96 XIII, 2, 9, 1-8. It will be seen in this connection that from the very beginning the chief queen is, from the ritualistic point of view, dedicated to the Brahman. Most probably there is no other reason here than this that the chief queen holding the highest position can be dedicated to Brahman only who is the most important of all priests; *Āp. ŚS.*, XX, 10, 2, vol. III, p. 153.

the Vāvātā and the Chamberlain, the fourth wife. The different schools vary very much, but there is no doubt that all of these insertions and omissions are meant for the fertility of the chief queen. All other queens as well as their maidens join herein only as help-mates in the Fertility Rite which is the chief one in the Horse-sacrifice. At the end of the obscene colloquy the qeen consort is raised up by her own maidens.[97] Now, the first three queens mark out with metal needles the lines for the dissection of the victim. Here, too, the chief queen has all the preferences. She marks the lines in the fore-part, down to the breast, while the Vāvātā does up to the navel and the Parivṛkti the rest. She, again, makes the knife-paths (Asipathas) with golden needles, while the second wife with silver ones and the Parivṛkti with iron or lead ones.[98] The scholiast on Satyāṣāḍha[99] says in this connection that the chief queen, Vāvātā and the Parivṛkti, holding as they do the supreme, intermediate and worst position respectively, should, accordingly, mark out the knife-path in varying parts of varied importance—the chief queen in the fore-part, i.e. the most

97 *Kāt. SS.*, XX, 6, 21, Weber, p. 973.

98 *Āp. SS.*, XX, 18, 7, vol. II, p. 163, ll. 2 f.; *Baudh. SS.*, XV, 30, vol. II, p. 235, ll. 9 f.; *Kāt. SS.*, XX, 7, 1, Weber, u. 973, ll. 18 f.; cf. *Kāth. Saṃ.*, X, 5; *Mait. Sam.* III, 12, 21; *Vāj. Saṃ.*, XXII, 33-38.

99 *SS.*, vol. V, p. 244, ll. 3-5:

राज्ञः पत्न्यस्त्रिविधा उत्तमा मध्यमाधमा चेति ताश्च महिषी वावाता परिवृक्तीत्येतन्नामधेयाः। ताश्च मृतस्याश्वस्यासिना छेदनाय तत्तत्स्थानेषु रेखाः सूचीभिः कुर्युः।

6

important part, the Vāvātā in the middle part and the Parivṛkti in the hind-part. She is the *uttamā patnī* and accordingly she has her own exclusive rights and in the remaining, too, she leads everywhere.

In the Rājasūya the chief queen is the permanent Ratnin in as much as authorities differ as to the reckoning of the Vāvātā and Parivṛkti as Ratnins, Jewels of the king.[100] The Śat. Br. reckons neither the Vāvātā nor Parivṛkti as Ratnin.[101] The king offers a pap for Nirṛti in the house of the Parivṛkti, not because she is a Ratnin, but because he likes to get rid of Nirṛti, calamity, while he is consecrated. As the Parivṛkti has no son, she is seized with Nirṛti; in order to propitiate Nirṛti, the king prepares a pap of black rice broken by nails with which to offer. According to Kātyāyana, [102] she is to betake herself to a Brāhmaṇa's house where the king has no power. The offering to Nirṛti, the use of black rice broken by nails and taking shelter in a Brāhmaṇa's house at once direct to the degraded position of the Parivṛkti: and it is only natural that a good many authorities, led by *Śat. Br.*, do not recognise her as a jewel. Several authorities of the Taittirīya school recognise the Vāvātā as a Ratnin and recommend the offering of a pap

100 The Rājasūya practically ends with the Sunāsīrīya offering; on the fourth to the fifteenth day after the Sunāsīrīya, offerings called Ratninām Havīṃṣī are offered in the house of the Jewels of the King, his wives and high officers. For the order of Ratnins, cf. *Śat.. Brā.*, V, 3, 1; *Tait. Brā.*, I, 7, 3; *Baudh. ŚS.*, XII, 5, 6; *Āp. ŚS.*, XVIII, 10, 12—II, 23; *Kāt. ŚS.*, XV. 3, 1-46; *Kāt. Saṃ.*, XV. 4, 5; *Mait. Saṃ.*, II, 6, 5, 6; etc.

101 For its eleven Ratnins, cf *op. cit.*, Sūtras 1-12.

102 XV, 3, 36, p. 974, Weber's Ed.

to Bhaga in her house,[103] but this recommendation in her favour loses importance as no other Vedic school gives her the position of a Ratnin. According to all the authorities a pap to Aditi or Āditya is to be offered in the house of the chief queen. She offers a cow as the sacrificial fee of this rite.

It is the chief queen who is to sit touching the king in the offering of scrapings of the consecrated waters which is offered at the house of a favourite son.[104] While mounting the chariot for a symbolic conquest of the quarters (dig-vijaya) the king touches the chief qeen and the horses with the tip of the bow so that by the quickening of the Maruts they might bring him victory and that he might be united with power.[105] This bow he hands over to the chief queen for safe preservation so that their (eldest?) son might be victorious by means of this (symbolic) bolt (vajra).[106]

While adoring the king, the Brahman hands over the sword to the king, which he again lets pass amongst the Ratnins from hand to hand. They touch the sword to assure the king of their faithfulness. The chief queen is the only wife who, in common consent of all the authorities, is entitled to touch the sword which is the symbol of unity

103 E.g. *Āp. ŚS.*, XVIII, 10, 14, vol. III, p. 88, I. 1.

104 *Baudha. ŚS.*, XII, 11; vol. II, p. 102, I 4; *Tait. Saṃ.*, I. 8, 14, 1. etc.

105 *Āp. ŚS.*, XVIII, 17, 10, vol. III, p. 97; cf. *Vāj, Saṃ.*, X, 21.

106 *Āp. ŚS.*, *op. cit.*, Sūtra II; *Sat. ŚS.*, XIII, 6, 10, vol. V, p. 179.

among the jewels of the king as well as of loyalty of them all to him.[107]

In the Human sacrifice,[108] too, the chief queen lies down by the side of the victim[109] as she does in the Aśvamedha. They are cloaked together under garments and the sacrificer exhorts her to do the obscene act. A similar colloquy as in the Aśvamedha follows. When it is finished, the Hotṛ and others[110] (most probably, the Udgātṛ, Adhvaryu and Brahman,[111]) raise her up. According to the Vaitāna only the Brahman is to do so. Now, the Hotṛ consecrates her with prayers in which he invokes the spirit of the parted sires (of the sacrificer);[112] the Udgātṛ consecrates her with the formulas in which he prays that the manes may live in happiness and sojourn during the sacrifice to the sacrificial place;[113] and the Adhvaryu with the prayer that she may live long and secure.[114] The Brahman makes her utter the Mantra in which she prays for the long life of herself as well as for her husband.[115]

107 *Āp. ŚS.*, XVIII, 18, 9 and 14, vol. III, p. 99; *Sat. ŚS.*, vol. V, p. 181, ll. 27 f.—p. 182, l. 2.

108 This sacrifice is prescribed in two texts only, viz. the *Śāṅ. ŚS.*, XVI, 10 f., and *Vait. S.*, XXVII, 10 f. In the Puruṣamedha dealt with by the *Śat. Brā.*, (XIII, 6) only symbolical human victims are offered.

109 *Śāṅ. ŚS.*, XVI, 13, 7; *Vait. S.*, XXXVIII, 3; cf; cf. *Kāṇ. ŚS.*, 80, 15.

110 Scholiast on *Śāṅ. ŚS.*, XVI, 13, 13, vol. III, p. 375, l. 4.

111 Compare the following Sūtra and the Scholiast theron.

112 The Mantras: *RV.*, X, 57, 3-5.

113 The Mantras: *RV.*, X, 58, 1-3. 114 Mantras: X, 60, 8-10.

115 Mantras: *RV.*, X, 59, 5-7; cf. Scholiast on *Śāṅ. ŚS.*, XVI, 13, 15, vol. III, p. 375 and also, the foot-note.

In the Rāḍ-yajña[116] which has been mentioned in the *Pañc. Brā.* alone and is intended to restore a deposed king to his kingdom, the chief queen is one of the eight vīras who surround and sprinkle the celebrant.

Now, we set out the duties of the chief wife in establishing and keeping up of the sacred domestic fire. If the newly-married couple desire to establish and keep up fire from their marriage time,[117] they carry the Marriage Fire to their new house—or if they like to live under the same roof as the father, to that house, and establish it there. They constantly keep it up by offering morning and evening oblations. According to certain authorities,[118] it is only she, and not the husband, who should offer these oblations, because she is the House and this Fire is Domestic. Either of them seems, however, to be equally entitled to offer it;[119] it is only natural that in case of the absence or sickness of either, the other will offer. The presence of both, or at

116 XIX, 7, 1-4.

117 This fire could also be established at the time of the division of the property of the family, return of a student from his studentship, and on the death of the head of the family.

118 *Khā. GS.*, I, 5, 17-18, p. 40; *Gobh. GS.*, I, 3, 13.

119 *Pār. GS.*, p. 113, Bom. Ed., "Tyāgaṃ tu sarvatLā kuryāt tatrāpy anyataras tayoh, etc."

पत्नी चेत् कर्मकामा भवति, तदा पुमांसौ मित्रावरुणौ पुमांसावश्विनावुभा।
पुमान् इन्द्रश्च सूर्यश्च पुमान् स वर्त्ततां मयि पुनः स्वाहेति...जुहोति।

Karma-pradīpikā by Kāmadeva F. 12b.

यजमानः प्रधानः स्यात् पत्नी पुत्रश्च कन्यका।
ऋत्विक् शिष्यो गुरुर्भ्राता भागिनेयः सुतापतिः॥

op. cit. F. 12 b

least, either of them is necessary.[120] If she cannot be bodily present, the Adhvaryu acts as her substitute with her permission, which, of course, follows automatically in case of her pregnancy, madness,[121] etc.

If the fire goes out, she fasts;[122] according to Vaikhānasa,[123] performs a Kṛcchra. She also fasts if the time of kindling up the fire elapses.[124]

If the existence of the fire is interrupted for twelve days, it is to be re-established. The Vivāhājyāhuti, the Lājāhuti, the Gṛhapraveśanīyāhuti, have to be repeated herein; however, the wife herself and not her brother offers the Lājāhuti now. According to Vaikhānasa, however, the rite of establishing fire is to be observed again if the husband and the wife remain without fire three days, and in this case the wife is required to undergo the Prājāpatya or Pādakṛcchra penance while the husband fasts one day.[125]

Either the chief wife or the husband offers the Bali,[126] but Gobhila[127] makes a special rule that the wife should offer in the evening and the husband in the morning. Naturally the option ceases if the husband is absent.[128] According-

120 *Saṃskāraratnamālā*, vol. I, p. 613, ll. 1 ff.

121 *Pār. GS.*, *op. cit.*; *Saṃskāraratnamālā*, *op cit.*, ll. 9 f.

122 According to a good many authorities, only she should fast; according to some, the husband also may; Nārāyaṇa in *Saṃskāramayūkha*; *Āśv. GS.*, I, 9, 1, etc. Husband: *Āp. GS.* V., 17; *Hir. GS.*, I, 22, 5.

123 She does so also if it comes into contact with some other fire, too. 124 *Āśv. GS.*, I, 9, 3; cf. Nārāyaṇa and Gṛhakārikā.

125 *Vaikh. GS.*, VI, 15, p. 99, ll. 7-10.

126 *Vaikh. GS.*, III, 7, p. 41, ll. 14-15; cf. VI, 17, p. 101, ll. 3-4.

127 *Gobh. GS.*, I, 4, 17, p. 153; particularly Sūtra 19, p. 154.

128 *Śān. GS.*, II, 14.

ing to Bhāradvāja, it is only she who should offer the Vaiśvadeva, three times along with the utterance of the Yajus text and once silently.[129]

The cooking[130] and other preliminary things such as husking[131] are always done by her. Before beginning the cooking, she washes herself.[132] Having finished the cooking, she purifies herself by sipping water, etc., and in a sweet distinct voice reports to her husband that she has finished it.[133] The husband thanks her that it is welldone, and prays that the food which is Virāṭ may not fall short. Then she removes the cooking vessel to a secure place, and cleanses the upper part with water and the lower with cow-dung. She now takes four fuels in her hand, sprinkles and offers them along with the utterance of the prescribed formulas.[134] She makes offerings in praise of everything that helps her cooking, all the quarters and innumerable gods. During the Nṛ-yajña, either the husband pours water and she washes, or she pours water and he washes; they wash with mutual help simply the portion of the leg under the knee.[135] Daily she propitiates thus the Guests, the Gods, the Beings, Brahma, and the Manes.

129 *Bhār. GS.*, III, 12, p. 78, ll. 4 f. "Vaiśvadevaṃ nirvapet, etc." The husband is to offer only if she appoints him to offer the Bali, "Yukto vā svayaṃ nirvapet."

130 *Bhār. GS.*, *op. cit.*; commentator on *Gobh.*, "She is supreme in matters concerning food" and so on (cf. Manu IX, II). *Saṃskāraratnamālā*, p. 938.

131 *Bhār. GS.*, *op cit.*. 1. 6.

132 *Bhār. GS.*, *op. cit.*

133 *Gobh. GS.*, I, 3, 15, pp. 116-117; Khād. GS., I, 5, 17

134 *Bhār. GS.*, *op. cit.*, 1. 11. ff.

135 *Baudh. GS.*, I, 2, 22-23, p. 5.

According to Pāraskara, the husband and the wife may either take their meals together or the husband may take them earlier, but in any case they must partake of the remnant of the food after all the above-mentioned offerings.[136]

In the rites concerning the House, the chief wife enters first the newly-built house with a full jar on her head or lap[137]. It seems that only the chief wife as the mistress of the house should carry the jar. That she should enter first is indicative of her authority over the house; her decided authority over household affairs is also found in the statement that the wife is the house, occurring in various places[138]. Any way, it is certain that while entering the new house she heads the host of wives after whom come the husband and all others. It is on her lap that the husband should lie down and it is she whom the husband looks at again and again along with the prayer that they may together, in the house, overcome all hostile powers.[139] On this ceremonial day all the disputations are shunned by her as well as by others.[140]

136 *Pār. GS.*, II, 9, 14-15, p. 262 of Bom. Ed.; Karka, p. 263, ll. 3 f.; *Paddhati*, p. 266, I. 2; Gadādhara, p. 267, ll. 3 f According to Viśvanātha, the wife and the husband should take together if no guest happens to be present. For the procedure of offering the five Mahāyajñas, see Padhārthakama as given in *Pār. GS.*, pp. 267 f.

137 III, 12, 8.

138 न गृहं गृहमित्याहुर्गृहिणी गृहमुच्यते, commentary on *Gobh. GS.*, I, 3, 13 p. 95; *Drāh. GS.*, 1, 5, 17; *Śāṅ. GS.*, II, 16, 3.

139 *Hir. GS.*. I, 29, 2, p. 57, ll. 6-7.

140 *Op. cit.*

In a rite named Gṛhaśānti her apartments are swept clean by the husband with the leaves of Apāmāga or palāśa or udumbara or of some other tree or plant mentioned in the list.[141] While sweeping, he prays to Rudra that none of them in the house might be harmed, that the mother, particularly, could not be harmed, and that no injury might be inflicted on the seed, progeny, cows or horses.[142]

After the animal has been killed in a domestic sacrifice, the chief wife bathes the apertures of the animal with water along with the utterance of the mantras.[143] With the water-jar in her hands she worships the Sun. The procedure is exactly the same as in the Śrautra rites.[144] At the end of the sacrifice the wife adds a fuel to the fire.[145]

In the Śūlagava sacrifice, too, after the animal has been killed, she washes the apertures in the above-mentioned manner.[146] According to Bhāradvāja[147] and Hiraṇyakeśin,[148] she should offer rice to the consort of Śiva after the husband has offered to Śiva. According to Pāraskara,[149] she also offers the Patnī-saṃyāja offerings to Indrāṇī and Rudrāṇī, Śarvāṇī, Bhavānī and Agni Gṛhapati.

In one rite named Bauḍhya-vihāra mentioned only in

141 *Baudh. GS.*, I, 18, 2, p. 220, ll. 4-6.

142 For the Mantras, *RV.*, I, 114, 7-8.

143 Ādityadarśana on *Kāth. GS.*, I, 10, p. 223, l. 22; cf. *Brahmbala* on *op. cit.* 51, 13, p. 228, l. 3 f.

144 See Paśuyāga, *supra*.

145 Brahmabala on *Kāth. GS.*, 51, 13, p. 230, l. 12.

146 Ādityadarśana on *Kāth. GS.*, 52, 6, p. 232, ll. 19 f. cf. *Baudha. GS.*, II, 7, 10, p. 51, l. 17.

147 II, 9, p. 40, l. 13.

148 II, 8, 7, p. 70, l. 10. 149 III, 8, 10, p. 342. Bom. Ed.

the *Hir. GS.*,[150] and elaborated in the *Sams. RM.*,[151] the chief wife observes all the rites beginning from spreading the black deer-skin down to husking as have been mentioned in connection with the Sthālīpāka.

The chief wife performs the Caitra sacrifice on the full-moon-day in the month of Caitra.[152] She together with her husband begins the Śrāvaṇa sacrifice on the fullmoon day under Śraviṣṭhā.[153] The sacrifice goes on daily until Āgrahāyaṇī sacrifice when the beds are placed on the ground with the advent of drier weather. The sacrifice is directed against any danger from snakes.[154] Every day the sacrificer makes offerings to serpents which she puts away silently[155] On the fullmoon day of Bhādra, she observes the Prauṣṭhapada sacrifice.[156] On the fullmoon day of the Āśvina she offers the Āśvayuga sacrifice or the Pṛṣātaka ceremony,[157] in which her principal duty lies in preparing a mess of boiled rice-grains. On the fullmoon day of the Agrahāyaṇa[158] she observes the Āgrahāyaṇī

150 II, 9, p. 71. 151 Vol. II, p. 914 f.

152 *Śāṅ. GS.*, IV, 19.

153 *Gobh. GS.*, III, 7, 3; *Āśv. GS.*, II, 1, 15; *Sāṃ. GS.*, IV, 15; II, 14, 9; *Āp. PS.*, XVIII, 5 f.; *Hir. GS.*, II, 16; *Mān. GS.*, II, 16; *Bhār. GS.*, II, 1; etc.

154 The modern Manasā-pūjā of Bengal seems to be a prototype of this rite 155 According to Śāṅkhāyana, IV, 15, 14-20.

156 Recorded by Pāraskara alone, II, 15.

157 *Āśv. GS.*, II, 2, 1; *Śāṅ. GS.*, IV, 16; *Pār. GS.*, II, 16; *Gobh. GS.*, III, 8, 1-8; *Khād. GS.*, III, 3, 1. This rite seems to be the older form of the Āśvinīkumāra Vrata in which the mothers wait so expectantly for the return of the sons away from home.

158 Āśvalāyana prescribes the 14th day as an alternative.

sacrifice.[159] She cleanses the house thoroughly, which is followed by a smoking. At this time the danger from snakes being over, the beds of all the members of the house are lowered down. At the end of the sacrifice, all the members of the household sit on straws and unwashed garments. According to Gobhila,[160] she sits immediately next to the sacrificer with her children on her lap or by her side; according to Āpastamba[161] she sits to his nortn. After this rite she descends together with her husband and children along with the utterance of the words, "Life, fame, strength, enjoyment of food, offspring." Then she lies down, together with all others on her right side, with her head towards the east along with the prayer to the Earth for propitiating her.[162] She and all others rise up, praying for the exuberance of life, for blessed life. For four months and even more, she and all others sleep on the ground.[163]

In the ancestral rites the most important rite that the chief wife is to perform is the cooking of the Śrāddha-

159 *Gobh. GS.*, III, 9; *Āśv. GS.*, II, 3; *Śān. GS.*, IV, 17; *Pār. GS.*, III, 2; *Āp. GS.*, XIX, 3; *Bhār. GS.*, II, 2; *Mān. GS.*, II, 7, 1-5; *Hir. GS.*, II, 17. This is, as the name denotes, the festival of the beginning of the New year.

160 III, 9, 17; *Drāh. GS.*, III, 3, 22. See the commentary on *Gobh.* for the arrangement of all others.

161 XIX, 8.

162 Mantra, *Vāj. Saṃ.*, XXXV, 21.

163 *Pār. GS.*, III, 6, 6 f., p. 318, Bom. Ed.; cf. th various commentaries: Karka, p. 320, l. 4 f.; Harihara, p. 320, l. 32 f.; etc.

pāka,[164] food to be offered to the Manes with honour. As she is supreme in all matters concerning cooking and such other domestic affairs, it is she who is to do this.[165] Gobhila, as quoted in the *Śraddhakriyākaumudī*[166] says she should, at the end of the cooking, say "finished", after which the actual ceremony begins. Vyāsa,[167] as quoted in the *Śrāddhakāśikā*, says the wife should, after cooking, take a bath. It is she who is to serve food to the manes. Kṛkala's manes incurred sins because Sukalā was deprived of her right to offer the cakes; and Dharma calls both him as well as the manes thieves.[168] The manes as well as the sacrificer, instead of acquiring religious merit, incur sin if the (eldest) wife does not serve during the Śrāddha, the food herself.[169] At the end of the ceremony she partakes with her husband of the remnants of food.[170]

On the 2nd aṣṭakā day after the animal is killed, it is

164 *Śrāddha-kriyā-kaumudī*, p. 96; *Śrāddha-mañjari*, p. 6, ll. 23-24; according to the Mañjarikāa she is to cook if her husband is unable to do so; *Pār. GS.*, p. 464, l. 7.

165 *Śrāddha-kriyā-kaumudī*, *op. cit.*, 1.

166 *Op. cit.*,

167 *Pār. GS.*, p. 442, l. 4.

168 *Padma-purāṇa*, bhūmi-khaṇḍa, p. 222, ll. 1 f., particularly ślokas 20 ff.. अमी पितामहाश्चौरा यैश्च भुक्तं तया विना । etc.

169 *Padmapurāṇa*, *op. cit.*,

भार्या पचति चेदन्नं स्वहस्तेनामृतोपमम् ।
तदन्नमेव भुञ्जन्ति पितरो हृष्टमानसाः ।
तेनैव तृप्तिमायान्ति सन्तुष्टाश्च भवन्ति ते ॥

etc. Also *Pār. GS.*, p. 470, l. 37; 71, l. 1.

170 *Śrāddha-tattva*, H. Sastri's ed., p. 251

she who washes all the fourteen apertures of the cow's body.[171] On the Anvaṣṭakya day she[172] places a stone in the Kuśa grass and pounds on that stone a fragrant substance called Sthāgara,[173] grinds some collyrium[174] and anoints therewith three Darbha blades. These are placed underneath the seats of three Brāhmaṇas who are invited to the sacrifice.

In the Pitryajña she, accompanied by the sacrificer, pays reverence to the manes. She also prays to Agni Gārhapatya for releasing her from any sin she may have committed to atmosphere, earth, sky, mother or father.[175]

The true significance of the performance of rites lies in the eating of Iḍā. The eating of Iḍā leads to the end of the sacrifice, the sacrifice of life, the fulness of human life and ultimately to Prajāpati, Lord of Sacrifices, the Self of Sacrifices. The successful completion of domestic and social life of man, of the material and spiritual life, of his earthly and divine life, in a word, of his whole life—lies in this. The Christians observe this rite under the name of the Eucharistic sacrifice. In this sacrifice they offer bread and wine to Christ and by means of the utte-

171 *Drāh. GS.*, III, 4, 8; *Khā. GS.*, p. 109, l. 7-9; *Gobh. GS.*, III, 10, 27, p. 177 (2nd part). For the fourteen apertures, see *Gobh. GS.*, p. 177, l. 7.

172 Cf. Commentary, 'Ca-śabdāt prakṛtā patnī,' p. 207 of Gobh. *GS.*, vol. II, ll. 2-3.

173 But see *Gobh. GS.*, IV, 2, 29. Comm., vol. II, p. 206 "Sthagaraṃ candanādigandhadravyam."

174 According to the commentator this kind of collyrium is known as Sauvīrāñjana.

175 *Tait. Saṃh.*, I, 8, 5 (K).

rance of holy mantras these are transubstantiated into flesh and blood of Christ. The Christians form a Holy Communion with Christ by means of eating these flesh and blood of Christ.[176] This eating of the Iḍā in Vedic ritual is nothing but the observance of the Eucharistic sacrifice and forming a Holy Communion with Prajāpati, Lord of Sacrifices. In the Agnihotra the remnant of the milk offered is to be taken. In the New and Fullmoon sacrifices, etc., the remnant of the Puroḍāśa offering is to be eaten. In the animal sacrifice a portion of the meat offered is eaten. In the Soma sacrifice, the remnant of the Soma offered is to be drunk.[177] In the Baliharaṇa, the husband and wife take the remnant of the food remaining after the five daily sacrifices.[178] In all the Śrāddha offerings, the remnant of the food offered is to be eaten[179] In this eating of the Haviś-śeṣa, the Iḍā, only the chief wife is to participate, as this rite *devolves* on the wife and the sacrificer all that the Sacrifice may, and consequently, is a rite designed to help in the other world as well. In this rite all the priests and the sacrificer also participate and together with them, she forms a Holy Communion between Prajāpati, the Supreme Soul, and the establishers of the sacrificer.

176 Groten, *Christian Eucharist*, pp. 30 f. and 162 ff.

177 *Baudh. SS.*, VII, 15, p. 225; VIII, 4, p. 240; *Kāt. SS.*, Chow. Ed., p. 552 "Patnī ca anyat, etc."

178 *Pār. GS.*, II, 9, 14, p. 261, Bom. Ed., of the varicus commentaries.

179 *Śrāddha-tattva* of Raghunandana, Hṛṣīkeśa Sāstrin's ed., Calcutta, 1909-10.

The Position of Wives other than the first in the Vedic Ritual*

Though the wives other than the first have no right to participate in those rites which are meant for Supreme Bliss, they are, however, allowed to participate in those which are considered as Saṃskāras, and those which are meant only for earthly bliss (ārād upakāraka). The Patnī (chief wife) observes those rites as well as those which only she and none of the other wives, can perform. In the rites dealt with here the first wife has, unless otherwise mentioned, the first claim and precedence over other wives.

In the New and Full Moon sacrifices[1] all the wives of the sacrificer are either girded by the Agnīdhra priest, or they gird themselves.[2] They sit either to the north of the Gārhapatya[3] or to the south-west[4] with bent or raised knees. With the pres-

* Reprinted from the *Indian Historical Quarterly*, vol. XVII, 1941, pp. 180-195.

1 As a rule, the wives take a bath and adorn themselves for their participation in sacrifices. According to Bhāradvāja, as quoted by the *Commentary* on Āpastamba (II, 6, 12, p. 32) they should anoint themselves with cow-dung. Baudhāyana also recommends both adornment and anointment, and Paiṭhīnasi adds the smelling of scented flowers. Comm. on *Āp.ŚS.*, 1.6.12, p. 23, vol. I.

2 *Sat.ŚS.*, vol. I, p. 159, I, 14 f.

3 *Sat.ŚS.*, vol. I, p. 161, I. 5 f; *Āp.ŚS.*, vol. I, p. 96.

4 The *Sat.Brā.* strictly forbids the wives to sit to the west of the sacrifice, with their faces towards the east, for in that case Aditi,

cribed formula[5] a triple cord of Muñja known as yoktrapāśa is put round their waist, either outside or inside the garment.[6] The *Śat. Brā.*[7] warns that a knot must not be made, while the *Tait. Brā.*[8] insists upon making it. According to Kātyāyana and the Scholiast Karka[9] the Agnīdhra priest is to wind the cord round their waist from left to right and having fixed the southern end by twice twisting round the northern one, he draws the southern end to the encircling cord upwards so that it may hang down.

Then the wives worship Agni Gṛhapati and Devānāṃ patnīḥ with the formula, "Agne gṛhapate upa mā hvayasva iti" and

who always sits like that, might be displeased with them. By sitting somewhat to the south (cf. I, 3.1.17) of the Gārhapatya fire they propitiate Aditi.

5 *VājSaṃ.*, I, 30; *Tait.Saṃ.*, III, 5, 6a (cf. *Āp. ŚS.*, X, 9, 16 and *Baudh.ŚS.*, VI, 5).

6 *Āp.ŚS.*, अभ्यन्तरं वा, vol. I, p. 96, I, 6; *Sat ŚS.*, vol. I, p. 160, ll. 3 f.

For the symbolic meaning of the act, see *Tait.Brā.*, III, 3, 3, 2-3; they should be girded on the garment so that Varuṇa's noose could not injure them.

7 I, 3.1.16. For a knot is Varuṇa's attribute and Varuṇa might cause some injury to the wife.

8 III, 3, 3, 4. Thus symbolically all the blessings are secured for her. Āpastamba and others belonging to the *YV.* prescribe the knot to be made on the north side of the navel; *Āp.ŚS.*, vol. I, p. 96, II, 13 f.; *Sat.ŚS.*, vol. I, p. 160, ll. 9 f.; etc.

9 II, 7, I; Weber's ed. p. 221, ll. 1 f.

"Devānāṃ patnīr upa mā hvayadhvam iti" respectively.[10] Now, the Agnīdhra takes the pot containing the clarified butter from the fire, puts on the ground before the sacrificer's wives, and bids them look at it.[11] They do so first silently and then again with the mantra[12] "Pervader of Viṣṇu art thou, etc." according to *W.Yv.* ritual and with "Thou art the milk of great one", etc., according to *B.Yv.* ritual. Then they again sit to the north[13] or south-east[14] along with the utterance of the mantra "Indrāṇī iva avidhavā bhūyāsam" etc. Having taken seats, they mutter "Suprajas tvā vayaṃ", etc., "Mama putrāḥ śatruhanaḥ," etc. They sit there till the unloosing of the girdle.

At the end of the sacrifice the grass cords of the wives are to be united. As a preliminary to this rite the Hotṛ gives to the wives Kuśa grass along with the mantra "Vedo'si: Thou

10 *Āp.ŚS.*, 2, 5, 6-7; *Sat.ŚS.*, *op. cit.*, *ll.* 14 f. इदमारादुपकारकं किमपि प्रतिपत्न्यावर्तते, Mahādeva on *Satyāṣāḍha*, 1. 20-21; cf. Rudradatta on *Āp.* 2, 5, 10, संवहनादिः प्रतिपत्न्यावर्तते । संप्रैषान्तो विधिः पत्नी-संस्कारत्वात् प्रतिपत्न्यावर्तते.

11 *Baud.ŚS.*, pp. 18 l. 4.

12 *Vāj.Saṃh.*, I. 30; cf. *Tait. Saṃh.* I. 1.10. k "Thou art the milk of great one's", etc.; *Āp.ŚS.*, 2.6.2, vol. 2, p. 98; *Baud.ŚS.*, vol. I, p. 18, l. 4 f. For the rite to be observed by all the wives, cf. Rudradatta on *Āp.*, पत्न्यनेकत्वे चावृत्तिः बौधायनेनोक्ता, etc.

13 *Sat.ŚS.*, p. 14, 1-5.

14 *Āp.ŚS.*, 258

art Veda", etc.[15] If they are desirous of children, they touch their navels with the tips of the Kuśa grass.[16] The wives place the Kuśa grass on their laps with the mantra "Ghṛtavantaṃ kulāyinam," etc.[17] Then they themselves or the Hotṛ throw them away. According to some schools mentioned in *Sat.ŚS.*, it is done thrice.

Then the wives themselves unite the grass-cords, optionally using the Yajus text,[18] or the *ṚV* text[19] as the case may be.

15 According to the *Āśv.* school, the mantra is to be uttered by the wife after the Kuśa has been given to her; p. 32, l. 25. For an alternative mantra, see *Sat.ŚS.*, vol. I, p. 227, ll. 26-27. See particularly in this connection the *Vaijayantī* on *Satyāṣāḍha*, vol. I, p. 228, ll. 16f. तेन प्रतिपत्ति वेददानादीति गम्यते, etc."

16 According to *Āśv.*, *ŚS.*, Ānandāśrama ed., p. 33, ll. 3-5; Bib. Ind. ed., p. 55, l. ii. 2.

17 *Tait. Saṃh.*, I. 6.4.4; 7.4.6; *Mait. Saṃh.*, 1.5.3; *Kāṭh. Saṃh.*, and *Āp. ŚS.*, *Śāṅ. ŚS.*, 1.15.13. p. 226, ll. 10 f.; also *Āpastmba* III, 10, 3 (see Rudradatta: पत्नीसंस्कारश्चायं विन्दते प्रजामिति लिङ्गात् । तेन प्रतिपत्ति प्रास्यति ॥)

18 *Vāj.Saṃh.*, II, 21a; *Tait.Saṃh.*, III, 5.6 (to be used before 1.4.45 according to *Āp. ŚS.*, VIII, 8-14; cf. XIII, 20.15). The use of the Ātmanepadī verb *viṣyate* shows that wives themselves are to do so; see, however, Nārāyaṇa on *Āśvalāyana* (l. 11; 5, p. 33, l. 8;) who assigns this ceremony to the Hotṛ. For the use of the Parasmaipada or the Ātmanepada in this case, *Sat. ŚS.*, p. 228, l. 22 ff.

19 प्र त्वा मुञ्चामि वरुणस्य पाशात्, etc. *Śāṅ. ŚS.*, vol. I, p. 10, l. 21-22 (I, 15.9); *Āśv. ŚS.*, l. 11. 3, p. 33, l. 6, of Ānandāśrama ed.

The united cords[20] are placed on the hands of the wives and some Kuśa grasses are placed on them. A pitcher full of water is placed in front of the wives. Now water is poured on the grasses and the cord after which they place the grasses within the thigh.[21] They wash their mouths with the water from the pitcher[22] and pray for cattle, children, etc.[23] Then they worship Agni Gārhapatya which is the final rite.[24]

In the Varuṇapraghāsas the wives should be girded with grass-cords.[25] The *Vaitāna Sūtra*[26] says the wife should have a wash after the interrogation by Pratiprasthātṛ as to how many lovers she has. Though the Sūtras do not refer to any wash, the purificatory nature of the rite is in itself manifest

20 *Sat.ŚS.*, p. 229, l. 4 f.; *Baudh. ŚS.*, p. 31, l. 9 ff.; *Śāṅ.ŚS.*, vol. I, p. 10, l. 22; *Āśv. ŚS.*, p. 33, l. 10 f., etc. According to *Āśv.*, the cord is to be folded twice.

21 *Śāṅ.ŚS.*, p. 11, l. 1 ff.; also see immediately after the above references. See Varadattasuta Ānartiya on *Śāṅ. ŚS.*, I, 15, 14; vol. II, p. 11 "Anekā api kuryuḥ."

22 E.g., *Sat.ŚS.*, p. 229, l. 21. मुख-मार्जनं पत्नी-संस्कारत्वात् प्रतिपत्न्यावर्तते ॥ These rites are also accompanied with Mantras. Cf. Nārāyaṇa on *Āśv.* p. 34, l. 6 f. अत्र पत्नी-द्वित्वबहुत्वे सर्वासां वचनं कर्तव्यम्: also प्रतिपत्नि योक्त्रविमोचनमावर्तते, etc.

23 Cf. *Sat.ŚS.*, p. 229, ll. 26 28; *Āp.ŚS.*, Comm. on III, 10, 8.

24 *Baudh.ŚS.*, p. 32 अथ एनं ग्रहपतये, etc., *Sat.ŚS.*, p. 229, l. 29 f.; etc.

25 *Baudh. ŚS.*, vol. I, p. 135, l. 2; cf. *Āp. ŚS.*, VIII, 8, 14, *Kāt. ŚS.*, Chow. Ed. p. 334, l. 11.

26 VIII, 20, p. 12.

and therefore, all the wives should observe this. Moreover, the rite seems to have been originally intended for keeping a check over the wife and for keeping the blood pure; so all the wives should be subject to the interrogaion. They are to confess any illicit connections they have had, otherwise their kith and kin, near and dear ones, would die.[27] By declaring the names of their paramours or at least by giving out the number of the paramours by means of raising up as many stalks of grass,[28] they become themselves pure and cause their paramours to be seized by Varuṇa with his noose. If they have none, they straightly say so and the whole thing is then so clear.

After the husband and the chief wife have offered oblations with the Karambha-pātra, all the wives unite their grass-cords.[29] They all go now for the Avabhṛtha (final bath). They have baths, but do not put their heads under water; they simply pour water on their heads.[30] According to Kātyāyana

27 *Tait. Brā.*, I, 6, 5, 2 f.; *Śat. Brā.*, II, 5, 2; *Baudh. ŚS.*, V, 5-9; vol. I, p. 136, l. 5 f. *ĀpŚS.*, VIII. 6, 22. यज्जारं सन्तं न प्रब्रूयात् प्रियं ज्ञातिं रुन्ध्यात् । असौ मे जार इति निर्दिशेत् । निर्दिश्यैवैनं वरुण-पाशेन ग्राहयतीति विज्ञायते vol. II, p. 33. *Mān. ŚS.*, I, 7, 4; II, p. 55; l. 16 —p. 56, l. 1; *Kāt. ŚS.*, Chow. Ed., vol. I, p. 336, l. 8 f.; *Sat.ŚS.*, p. 465, l. 3-12.

28 *Kāt. ŚS.*, V. 5. 8-9; also, Chow. Ed., vol. I, p. 336, ll. 14-15.

29 *Āp. ŚS.*, VIII, 8, 14, इमं विष्यामीति पत्नी योक्त्रपाशं विमुञ्चते ।

30 *Āp. ŚS.*, VIII, 8, 15; Rudradatta, सलिलोत्क्षेपणेन सशिरस्कौ स्नात इत्यर्थः *Baudh.ŚS.* अनुपमज्जन्तौ ।

and the Scholiast Karka[31] the spouses should repair to some quiet part of flowing water and take a bath in the above manner. The chief wife and the sacrificer should wash the backs of each other and most probably, the other co-wives might help one another in washing their backs.

In the Sākamedha i.e. the third parvan of the Cāturmāsya sacrifices, when all the preliminary things necessary for the sacrifice have been done, the wives are brought forward and made to sit near the sacrificer.[32] According to certain schools, here, unlike in other sacrifices, there is no girding of wives (Patnīsannahana) or any other accessory rite. According to Satyāṣāḍha, the wife should look at the clarified ghee from her shed;[33] all the wives should do so as this is a part of the strīsaṃskāra. After the eating of the Iḍā, they should all anoint their eyes.[34] During the Tryambaka oblation, after the maiden has walked round the fire, the sacrificer pours into the hands of the wife the Māsara or rice-gruel, she in her turn pours this into the hands of the maiden along with the prayer that she (maiden) would achieve her object (Pati or Bhaga).[35]

31 स्नात इत्यर्थः. V, 5, 30-33.

32 *Mān.ŚS.*, I, 7, 5; II, p. 57.

33 *Sat. ŚS.*, vol. II, p. 479, l. 24; Rudradatta on *Āp. ŚS.*, VIII, 14, 21; vol. II, p. 65. But see *Baud. ŚS.*, p. 141 f. तूष्णीं पृषदाज्य-ग्रहणं सन्नह्य आज्येन च दध्ना च उदेहि इति ।

34 *Sat.ŚS.*, vol. II, p. 473, l. 11.

35 *Baudh. ŚS.*, p. 152, l. 12—p. 153, l. 1.

The object of this rite is only to obtain happiness in this world alone, and not in the other which is clear from the fact that only a single Vedic school (Baudhāyana) follows it. It is only reasonable that the rice-gruel should be handed over to the maiden, longing for husband or beauty, by her own mother and not by the chief wife. This offering of the rice-gruel means most probably a joint conferring of blessings upon the daughter by the parents and no doubt, her mother should offer her the material carrying her own blessings.

In the Paśuyāga, too, the wives are to be girded, says Baudhāyana.[36] After the animal is killed, they are raised up by Neṣṭṛ[37] or Pratiprasthātṛ[38] from their seats to the altar. They all look at and worship the Sun[39] with the prescribed mantra. Then they are led one by one to the east along with the prayer for offspring and increase of wealth.[40] All of them

36 Vol. I, p. 112.

37 According to the *W.YV.* Ritual.

38 According to the *YV. Ritual; Āp. ŚS.*, VIII, 18, I; *Mān.ŚS.*, I, 8, 4, 2.

39 *Baudh.ŚS.*, vol. I, p. 118, l. 8; *Mān.ŚS.*, I, 8, 4, 1; Rudradatta on *Āp. ŚS.*, VII, 18, 2 नमस्त आतानेति पत्न्यादित्यमुपतिष्ठते, अनेकाश्चेत् सर्वा युगपदुपतिष्ठन्ते, Mahādeva on *Sat.Ś.*, p. 424, l. 1 f., प्रतिपत्नि संस्कारत्वादावर्तते, etc.

40 अनर्वा प्रेहि, etc., *Baudh.ŚS.*, 118, l. 9, through the passage between Cātvāla and Utkara; Mahādeva on *Sat.ŚS.*, vol. II, p. 424; Rudradatta on *Āp ŚS.*, VII, 18, 3. vol. I, p. 436 बह्वीस्तु एकैकां नयति प्रेहीत्येकवचनात् ॥

touch the water of the Cātvāla with the object of purifying themselves.[41]

In the Agniṣṭoma the wives have their nails pared by a barber in such a way that they do not extend beyond the upper end of the finger tips; the paring should begin from the little finger of the left hand. They brush their teeth with bits of the udumbara twig, taking care that they may not bleed. They bathe in stagnant waters full of Raṅkha and Avaka plants on mossy bathing ghats. According to the Vājasaneya school they put a piece of gold in a pit and bathe therein. During their bath they invoke the waters for purifying them; while coming out, they mutter to themselves about the purity caused by the waters. Then they sip water. Unlike the priest, they are forbidden to have a hair-cut.[42]

During the consecration for a religious ceremony (Dīkṣā) they all wear on their heads nets made of thin silken thread or of wool collected from living rams or, at least, a net made of Kuśa grass;[43] these should hang on both sides of their head.[44] They are consecrated on their own seats with

41 आपो देवीः शुद्धायुवः Rudradatta on *Āp.ŚS.*, VII, 18, 4, स्पृशन्त्यपः सर्वाः पत्न्यः, similarly, Mahādeva on *Sat. ŚS.*, vol. II, 424, l. 10 f.

42 *Āp. ŚS.*, X, 5, 6—X, 6, 3 vol. II, p. 221, l. 1—p. 223, l. 10 (एवं पत्नी केशवर्जम्) ; *Sat. ŚS.*, vol. III, p. 584, l. 28 ff.

43 *Āp.ŚS.*, X, 9, 5, vol. II, p. 232, l. 4 f.; *Sat.ŚS..* vol. III, p. 592, l. 7 ff.

44 Mahādeva on *Sat. ŚS.*, op. cit., l. 27.

upper silken garments that are slightly washed, new, white, with skirts and used by nobody else. The Pratiprasthātṛ anoints and decorates them without mantras.[45] The sacrificer is made to wear a girdle; they tie plough-nooses.[46]

During the girding they observe the same rites as in the New and Full Moon sacrifices (Darśapūrṇamāsa).[47] Herein Āpastamba prescribes that the mantra "Āśānā saumanasam, etc.: Beseeching favour," etc.,[48] should be dropped and "Saṃ tvā nahyāmi, etc.: I bind thee, etc.,"[49] should be used while Baudhāyana recommends the use of both of them. The nets are now closely fitted in so that there may not be any chance of their loosening or falling down.[50] The Pratiprasthātṛ fastens pegs in the skirts of their clothes in order that they may scratch their skin, if required, with them.[51] They should not take meat and honey, nor do any impure act.[52]

45 *Kāt. ŚS.*, vol. I, p. 433, Sūtra 77.

46 *Āp.ŚS.*, X, 9, 16; vol. II, p. 233, l. 15 ff., अत्र दर्श-पूर्णमासवत् पत्नीं संनह्यति सं त्वा नह्यामीति विकारः । *Sat.ŚS.*, vol. III, p. 592, l. 22 f.

47 *Āp.ŚS.*, X, 9, 16, vol. II, p. 233, l. 15 f.; *Sat.ŚS.*, vol. III, p. 594, l. 14 f.; *Baudh.ŚS.*, vol. I, p. 160, ll. 18-19; *Kāt.ŚS.*, Chow. Ed., vol. I, p. 437, Sūtras 99-100.

48 *Tait.Saṃh.*, I. l. 10 (e-h). 49 *Tait.Saṃh.*, III, 5, 6, 1 (c).

50 Gopīnātha on *Sat.ŚS.*, vol. III, p. 595, l. 9 f.

51 *Baudh.ŚS.*, vol. I, p. 161, l. 8-9.

52 Rudradatta on *Āp.ŚS.*, X, 15, 13-14 vol. II, p. 248, ll. 17 ff. यावदुक्तं पत्न्या दीक्षित-व्यञ्जनानि (Sūtra 13); समानं ब्रह्मचर्यम् (Sūtra 14).

In the afternoon of the day of their consecration they all keep silent, breaking their vow when the stars appear.[53] They approach the Gārhapatya fire from behind the altar silently.[54] The milk for breaking their fast is boiled on the Southern fire while that of the sacrificer on the Gārhapatya; they drink it in their own seats in the mid-day as well as midnight.[55]

In the morning on the second Upasad (sacrificial festival preceding the Sutyā or pressing of the Soma; it is a part of the Jyotiṣṭoma and lasts several days) when the sacrificer gives dust of the cow's foot-print to the chief wife, all the wives look at it and pray that they may not be deprived of wealth.[56] Then either the Neṣṭṛ[57] or the sacrificer himself[58] makes the Somakrayaṇī cow look at them, whereupon they

53 *Āp.ŚS.*, X, 16, 1 f.; vol. II, p. 252 f.; *Kāt. ŚS* Chow. Ed., p. 439, Sūtra 107.

54 *Baudh.ŚS.*, vol. I, p. 163, l. 15-16.

55 *Āp.Ś.*, X, 17, 3 ff., vol. II, p. 253, l. 5 ff. (particularly Sūtras 6 and 13); *Baudh.ŚS.*, vol. I, p. 164, l. 4-6.

56 Gopinātha on *Sat.ŚS.*, vol. III, p. 629, l. 14-15, सर्वाभिरीन्त्रणं कार्यं संस्कार-कर्मत्वात्, cf. *Āp.ŚS.*, X, 23, 5.

57 According to the *W.YV. Ritual.*

58 According to the *B.YV.* Ritual.

pray for having children.[59] They in their turn look at the sacrificer and pray for having heroes.[60]

During the offering of the buck-goat to Agni and Soma on the last day of the Upasad session, the Neṣṭṛ leads them all towards the front of the sheds; near the sheds they utter a prayer for safe entrance into them with their desires fulfilled.[61] They all sit near about there and pray to Agni to draw his attention to them.[62] Now, the sons and grandsons together with their wives, unmarried daughters,[63] nephews and other relatives are invited to participate in the Family Union. The sacrificer touches Adhvaryu from behind, all the wives[64] similarly touch the sacrificer; the sons

59 *Vāj. Saṃh.*, IV, 23; *Śat.Brā.*, 3, 3, 1, 12; *Kāt.Ś.*, VII, 6, 26. *Tait. Saṃh.*, I, 2, 5, 2; *Kāth. Saṃh.*, II, 5; *Āp. ŚS.*, X, 23, 6: Rudradatta, vol. II, p. 272, ll. 3 अत्रानेकासामपि तन्त्रेण संस्थापनं विभुत्वात् । Similarly, Gopinātha on *Sat. ŚS.*, vol. III, p. 629, ll. 19-21; *Baudh.ŚS.*, vol. I, p. 170, l. 6-7.

60 *Tait. Saṃh.*, ,I, 2, 5, 2; *Baudh.ŚS. op. cit.*, l. 7; Rudradatta on *Āp. ŚS.*, X, 23, 7, सर्वाः पत्न्यः, etc.

61 *Tait. Saṃh.*, III, 5, 6, 13; *Āp. ŚS.*, XI, 16, 10; *Mān. ŚS.*, II, 2, 4, 9 अनुगामिन् instead of अनुकामिन् ; etc.

62 *Sat.ŚS.*, vol. III, p. 736, l. 10 ff.

63 But not the married daughters, as their Gotra has been changed (along with the Caturthikarma); Gopinātha on *Sat. ŚS.*, vol. III, p. 739; l. 6.

64 Gopinātha on *Sat. ŚS.*, vol. III, p. 739, l. 1. सर्वा अपि पत्न्यो यजमानमेवान्वारभन्ते सवर्णा असवर्णाश्च । They participate in this rite as

touch their mothers and the grand-sons touch their fathers; other relatives touch the grand-sons and so on.

In the night preceding the Sutyā or pressing day, all of them together with the sacrificer sit behind the altar or the Gārhapatya; the Adhvaryu places the Vasatīvarī water in front of them; after they have touched it, they are again circumambulated by the Adhvaryu.[65] This whole night they are all kept awake in the Prāgvaṃśaśālā* by the priests who tell them holy interesting tales.[66]

In course of the Prātaranuvāka (morning prayer) all of them should accompany the Maitrāvaruṇa, Neṣṭṛ, Agnīdhra and the bearers of the Ekadhana cups when they walk northwards out of the sacrificial ground.[67] As the object is to delude the Gandharvas with a woman so that the water,

amātyas (for the meaning of the word, cf. l. 5-7), not as Patnī which they are not; पत्युर्नो यज्ञ संयोग इति पाणिनि-प्रोक्तस्याभावेन, (l. 2-4), etc.

65 *Śat. Brā.*, III, 9, 2, 14 f.; *Āp. ŚS.*, XI, 21, i, vol. II, p. 346, l. i f.; *Kāt ŚS.*, Chow. Ed., p. 508, Sūtra 256-260; Gopīnātha on *Sat. ŚS.*, vol. III, p. 758, l. 25, पत्न्यनेकत्वे सव.:, etc.

* A room with some columns or beams towards the east where the family and friends of the sacrificer assemble.

66 *Āp. ŚS.*, XI, 21, 12, vol. II, p. 348; *Sat.ŚS.*, vol. III, p. 762, l. 1.

67 *Śat. Brā.*, III, 9, 3, 16 f. The Ekadhanas are water-vessels by means of which water is taken up during sacrificial observations.

sap of the sacrifice, may be carried to a safe place, all the wives should join in this rite.

In the early morning on the Sutyā (the extraction and solemn preparation of Soma) day all of them, each carrying one or two vessels, pass through the Tīrtha i.e. the path to the altar between the Cātvāla and the Utkara, carry water for washing their feet (pannejanī) and return by the same way as they go.[68] According to Āpastamba they should have their faces towards the west while filling the pitchers.[69] They enter the sheds by the east door, walk round the side-altars called Dhiṣṇīya and place the pannejanī pitchers to the west of the side-altar or Neṣṭṛ.[70] Then they come back and enter into the shed called Prāgvaṃśa.[71]

In the afternoon they are all given milk for breaking their fast.[72]

68 *Tait. Saṃh.*, 3, 5, 6, 2; *Kāt. ŚS.*, Chow. ed., p. 517, sūtra 44 "two vessels." Gopinātha on *Sat. ŚS.*, vol. III, p. 793, l. 15 f.; सर्वाभिरपि पत्नीभिः स्व-स्व-स्थाल्या ग्रहणं कर्तव्यम्, also l. 27 f.; similarly Rudradatta *on Āp. ŚS.* For passing through Tīrtha, Rudradatta on *Āp. ŚS.*, XII, 5, 4.

69 *ŚS., XII*, 5, 12, vol. II, p. 366; पत्नी पन्नेजनीर्गृह्णाति प्रत्यङ्-तिष्ठन्ती वसुभ्यो रुद्रेभ्य आदित्येभ्य इति ; पत्न्यनेकत्वे सर्वा गृह्णन्ति । यज्ञाय वः पन्नेजनीर्गृह्णामीति मन्त्रान्तः । तथैव पेठतुर्बौधायन-भारद्वाजौ ।

70 *Sat. ŚS.*, vol. III, p. 794, l. 3 f.; *Āp. ŚS.*, XIII, 5, 13 f.; vol. II, p. 367; *Baudh. ŚS.*, VII, 15, vol. I, p. 225.

71 *Op. cit.*, l. 21-22.

72 *Śat. Brā.*, III, 6, 3, 4.

During the evening pressing of the Soma juice all other wives touch the chief when the latter looks at the Pūtabhṛt vessel containing the Soma juice after it has been strained.

After the Pātnīvata cup has been offered, the Neṣṭṛ leads all the wives[73] through the sheds, which they enter by the west door. They all take their seats to the north of the Chanters.[74] Now, the Neṣṭṛ makes them exchange looks with the Udgātṛ along with a prayer to Agni for children.[75] Now, they should remove clothes from their right thighs; according to Satyāṣāḍha[76] the thigh joints also should be denuded; this view is not upheld by Āpastamba.[77] They should pour water along their thighs so that it may run down towards the interior of the thighs, but it must not touch their navels.[78] According to the Kāṭhaka School, as quoted by

73 Gopīnātha on *Sat.ŚS.*, vol. IV, p. 932, ll. 17-18, पत्नी-संस्कारत्वात् प्रतिपत्ति : if any of them is in course of monthly period, every rite in connection with the Pannejani drops.

74 *Kāt.ŚS.*, X, 7, 3, Webers Ed., p. 817; Chow. Ed., p. 563, Sūtra 141.

75 *Śat. Brā.*, IV, 4, 2, 17-18, *Sat. ŚS.*, *op. cit.*, I, 1f.; *Baudh. ŚS.*, VIII, 14, vol. I, p. 255; *Lāṭ. ŚS.*, II, 10, 15, p. 181, l. 12 f.; *Āp.ŚS.*, XIII, 5, 8; particularly commentaries on *Lāṭyāyana* and *Kātyāyana* (*op. cit.*,). The Mantra: *Tait. Saṃh.*, III, 5, 6(k); *Vāj.Saṃh.*, VIII, 10, (*Śat.Brs.*, *op. cit.*, 18).

76 *Śrauta-sūtra*, vol. IV, p. 932, l. 3 f.

77 Rudradatta on *Āp. ŚS.*, XIII, 15, 11 यथोरु-सन्धिर्नाविष्कृतः स्यात्तथोपाद्धरेद्वासः ; also Gopīnātha Bhaṭṭa on *Sat ŚS.*, *op. cit.*

78 *Sat. ŚS.*, *op. cit.*, l. 9 ff.

Yājñikadeva, commentator of the *Kāt. ŚS.*[79] they should bend their knees and wet the skirts of their garments with water from the vessels. Kātyāyana and his scholiast, Lātyāyana[80] and the Kāṭhaka[81] say that they should exchange looks with the Udgātṛ three times at the sound *Hiṃ*. Three times they should uncover and pour Pannejanī water on their right thighs so that after the third time there will be no water left. On the order of the Udgātṛ they should retire to their own place.[82]

According to the *Baudh.ŚS.* the pegs that were fastened to their skirts during the Dīkṣā should now be silently thrown to the Cātvāla when they all together with the sacrificer and the priests are about to go for the final bath called Avabhṛtha.[83]

During the Avabhṛtha they also participate with others in the concluding passage called Nidhana sung in chorus three times.[84] When the water comes to their sight, they pray to Varuṇa for overcoming the enmity and removing the sins they have committed.[85] After the bath they wear the

79 X. 7, 4, p. 818, Weber's ed.

80 P. 181, l. 14—p. 182, l. 8; so also Drāhyāyaṇa as quoted therein. Yājñikadeva on *Kāt. ŚS.*, *op. cit.*, छन्दोग-सूत्रम्, p. 818, l. 2-3, Weber's ed.

81 Karka on *Kāt. ŚS.*, *op. cit.*, एवमेव काठकेऽपि ।

82 *Kāt ŚS.*, X, 7. 5.. 83 VIII, 18, vol. I, p. 259, l. 9-10.

84 *Sat.ŚS.*, vol. IV, p. 941, l. 10 f.

85 Mahādeva on *Sat. ŚS.*, *op. cit.*, l. 29; *Tait. Saṃh.*, *Mait. Saṃh.*, 1, 3, 39; etc.

Paryāṇahanas, outer clothes tied round the Soma bundle.[86] While coming back to the sheds by the same way they went, they together with the sacrificer or the priests with Hotṛ at their head are led by the priest called Unnetṛ.[87]

During the Udanīyeṣṭi[88] the Patnīsannahana or the girding of wives and Yoktra-vimoka (the untying of the rope) take place in the same way as in other sacrifices.

In the Pravargya or Hot Milk Sacrifices, when the Mahāvīra pot is heated, they all cover their heads, according to the *Śatapatha*,[89] for fear of being deprived of eyesight, because the Mahāvīra is the symbol of Āditya,[90] and according to the *Mānavā-śrauta-sūtra*,[91] for having children. The Prāgvaṃśa is also screened[92] so that they cannot see from their seats the preparation of the Pravargya; according to Satyāṣāḍha,[93] the doors are shut; and according to Baudhāyana[94]

86 *Mān.ŚS.*, 1, 4, 45, 1; also quoted in *Kāt.ŚS.*, X, 9, 6; *Sat.ŚS.*, vol. IV, p. 1092, l. 24.

87 *Sat. ŚS.*, vol. IV, p. 964, l. 26-27.

88 *Sat.ŚS.*, vol. IV, p. 448, l. 17-18.

89 XIV, 1, 3, 16; Weber's Ed., p. 1029; S.B.E., vol. XLIV, p. 463.

90 For the connection of the Pravargya sacrifice with the Sun-worship, cf. *Śat. Brā.*, XIV, 1, 2, 15; 3, 16; 3, 1, 35.

91 IV, 1, 33; p. 154.

92 *Baudh. ŚS.*, vol. I, p. 265, l. 20; *Sat. ŚS.*, (n. 5) and Rudradatta, *Āp. ŚS.*, XV, 5, 2, vol. II, p. 643, l. 4-5.

93 *ŚS.*, vol. IX, p. 359, l. 11 f.

94 Vol. I, p. 270, l. 18.

hanging load-carriers (śikyā) are hung from above to serve as screens. According to Kātyāyana,[95] even though they may be very near, they should not look at the Pravargya; they should themselves cover their heads during the preparation. All the wives should observe this injunction, as otherwise it would be prejudicial to their own good; and as, according to the *Mānava-śrauta-sūtra,* this is really a strī-saṃskāra. After the Mahāvīra has been revered, their heads are uncovered. They keep on looking at the Mahāvīra pot and pray to Him for cattle and offspring and a safe happy life to themselves as well as to their husband.[96] According to the *Mānava-śrauta-sūtra,*[97] the sacrificer also looks at it along with them.

During the setting out of the Pravargya, all the priests and the sacrificer meet upon the altar in the shed and three offerings are made to the Āhavanīya. While coming out of the shed, the Adhvaryu remains[98] behind them all. According to Āpastamba,[99] they are to go back to their shed while several sacrificial staff, viz., pegs, strings, etc., are

95 *ŚS.*, XXVI, 2, 3, Weber, p. 1098; Chow. ed., vol. II, p. 1027, Sūtra 30; XXVI, 3, 2, Weber, p. 1100; Chow. ed., 1030, Sūtra 49.

96 *Baudh. ŚS.*, vol. I, p. 276, l. 18-19; *Sat. Ś.*, and Vāñchiśvarasudhi, vol. IX, p. 872, l. 9 and 11; *Āp. ŚS.*, vol. II, p. 656, l. 14-16; *Kāt. ŚS.*, XXVI, 4, 12, p. 1102, Weber's Ed. etc.

97 IV, 2, 37; p. 153.

98 *Kāt. ŚS.*, Chow. Ed., vol. II, p. 1039, Sūtra 119.

99 *Āp.ŚS.*, XV, 13, 4.

carried away by attendants. They are to come back to the sheds when the Prastotṛ begins to sing the Sāman. He sings it three times, in the finale of which the wives[100] also join.

In the Piṇḍa-pitṛ-yajña the husband gives all the wives portions from the middle cake for having children. They all pray to the ancestors for children adorned with lotus-garlands.[101]

Now, we deal with the wives in general in the Domestic Ritual. The first sthālīpāka is really a part of the marriage ceremony and as such each wife is entitled to perform this rite. Each one should cook at other times, too, in so far as the cooking happens to be a part of any of the strī-saṃskāras. The wife takes her meal in the day time together with her husband and avoids meat, etc. During the night she sleeps on the floor and refrains from any impure act. Next day she cleanses thrice the sacrificial place with a duster and thrice all around the fire with water.[102] The husband, after having the paddy washed, spreads the hide of a black deer, places mill-stones thereon and pours some paddy into them. She husks the paddy thrice and gets the rice perfectly in order. She

100 *Sat. ŚS.*, vol. IX, p. 888; *Āp. ŚS.*, XV, 13, 10; vol. II, p. 671; *Lāṭ. ŚS.*, 1, 6, 4-6, p. 54-55; so also Drāhyāyaṇa as quoted in *Lāṭyāyana;* etc.

101 *Sat. ŚS.*, vol. I, p. 255; *Āp. ŚS.*, 1, 10, 10-11, vol. I, p. 36-37, Rudradatta: अत्र पत्नीबहुत्वे विभज्य सर्वाभ्यः प्रयच्छति दान-मन्त्रश्चाऽऽवर्तते; *Āśv. ŚS.*, (*ĀŚ. S.*,) 2, 7, 13, p. 73, l. 10-14.

102 *Āśv. GK.*, 1, 2, 13-14, p. 265.

8

washes it thrice and cooks it. While cooking, she sprinkles clarified butter upon it by means of the purifying Kuśa grass.[103] The husband places this full cooking vessel on strewn grass. Then she sits to the left of her husband and to the west of the Gārhapatya fire, and offers to Agni and Agni Sviṣṭakṛt. After the offering the husband does all the cleansing work during this particular occasion, but during the Puṃsavana, etc., she is required to cleanse the sacrificial staff, etc.[104]

As Garbhādhāna[105] is a strī-saṃskāra, each wife observes this rite.

103 *Op. cit.*, 1, 2, 30 f., p. 266, for husking and cooking, cf. *Hir. GS.*, 1, 23, 2-4; for cooking, cf. *Vaik. GS.*, III, 5. p. 39, l. 13.

104 *Āśv. GS.*, *op. cit.*, v. 57 f., p. 268.

105 *RV.*, Schools: *Śāṅ. G Saṃgraha*, i. 19. (*I.S.*, pp. 35, 130; p. 9, Benares ed.). *Śāṅ. G. Saṃgraha*, p. 19. *Āsv. G. Pariśiṣṭa*, 125, p. 217. *Śaunaka-kārikā*, p. 23; Kumārila's *Kārikā*, 1, 4; p. 269. *Prayogaratna* of Nārāyāṇa Bhaṭṭa, 37 f. Āśvalāyana does not deal with the sacrifice, but refers to some Upaniṣad. Śaunaka in his *Kārikā* (p, 30 of the MS.) refers to one *Yajñopaniṣad*. It seems from his statement that the ritual as is described in his *Kārikā* differs from that of the *Yajñopaniṣad*.

In the *Vaikhānasa-gṛhya-sūtra* III, 10, the Garbhādhāna is mentioned as distinguished from Ṛtu-saṃgamana (III. 9), and the Puṃsavana, according to this school, is to be held in the 4th month. But according to all other authorities who deal with the rite, it is the rite observed for having the wife's pregnancy. The Mantras uttered in this rite cannot mean otherwise. The *Ṛtu-saṃgamana* does not find place in any other Gṛhya-sūtra except the

The wife, on the night chosen for the rite, takes a bath and adorns herself with ornaments, clean clothes and

Vaikhānasa. This rite has, however, been given importance in the Prayogas, Paddhatis and specially in the Compendia.

Authorities differ whether the Garbhādhāna should be observed in each case of the wife's pregnancy, or it should be observed once for all. Thus, Bhaṭṭa Nārāyaṇa says "This sacrament purifying the womb named Garbhādhāna is in way of purifying the object itself. So, as the object, the wife, is once purified, and pregnancy that occurs in it (her), is purified. So this rite should be observed once only." So also is the case with "Puṃsavana and Sīmantonnayana." But Karkopādhyāya holds the opposite view: "These three sacraments are to be repeated in every pregnancy, otherwise no saṃskāra of the following pregnancies is to be considered as observed." Again, Vijñāneśvara says, "Garbhādhāna should be observed in each case of the wife's pregnancy, but not Puṃsavana and Sīmantonnayana." Śūlapāṇi says, "Sīmantonnayana is not to be repeated, but Garbhādhāna and Puṃsavana are to be observed again and again." Tarkālaṅkāra in the Commentary on Gobhila thinks that Garbhādhāna and Puṃsavana need be repeated in each pregnancy, but not Sīmantakaraṇa.

The question remains to be solved, if the Garbhādhāna is to be repeated in each case of the wife's pregnancy, and if the Puṃsavana rite should also be observed in that Ṛtu when the Garbhādhāna is also going to be performed. The Rtusaṃgamana really serves the same purpose as the Garbhādhāna does. Moreover, from the treatment by several authorities of the Garbhādhāna, it seems that according to them the Garbhādhāna is but a ceremonial observance of the Ṛtu-saṃgamana for the pregnancy of the wife, failing which first the Nārāyaṇa Bali, and still failing, the Nāga Bali are to be observed. So there does not seem to be any necessity of the separate observance of the rite Ṛtu-saṃgamana in that monthly period of the wife when the Garbhādhāna is held.

wreaths.[106] The husband pounds the root of the Adhyāṇḍā[107] or the Phalinī[108] plant or of the Aśvagandhā[109] or the Dūrvā grass, [110] and drenches some portions of a piece of cloth with the juice of it. When the wife comes, specially decorated for the ceremony, the husband presses out the juice into the right[111] or both[112] the nostrils of the wife with the appropriate verses of the *Ṛgveda* (X. 85. 21-22).[113]

Nārāyaṇa Bhaṭṭa mentions that the husband should bathe the wife in the morning with the water from the pitchers adorned with five twigs with new leaves. After the bath the wife adorns herself with auspicious dress and ornaments. After the offerings of the Prājāpatya and the Ājya oblations, the head of the wife is touched. Agni and Āditya are worshipped and during the worshp of the latter the wife joins her husband.

Kālesi in his Paddhati mentions that the juice of Śukaśimbi pressed out by ladies with husband and children living is to

106 *Ā. G. Pariśiṣṭa, op. cit.,* Kumārila's *Kārikā, op. cit., Prayogaratna* of Nārāyaṇa Bhaṭṭa, p. 38(2).

107 *Ś. G. Sūtra, op. cit.,* p. 9, l. 1.

108 *Ś. G. Saṃgraha, op. cit.,* l. 19.

109 *Ā. G. Pariśiṣṭa,* Śaunaka, Kumārila and *Prayoga-ratna, op. cit.*

110 *Ā. G. P., op. cit.*

111 *Ś. G. S.; Ś. G. Saṃ.;* Kumārila and Śaunaka; *Prayogaratna* of Bhaṭṭa Nārāyaṇa, *op. cit.*

112 *Ā. G. Pariśiṣṭa, op. cit.*

113 According to Nārāyaṇa Bhaṭṭa, the wife had to sit on her left knee.

be sprinkled into the right nostril of the wife. The rite is to be observed only once. According to Vaikhānasa,[114] the husband should first of all, sprinkle the clarified butter upon the fire and then make the wife adorned with auspicious ornaments and clothes, sit down. After sactificing oblations to Dhātṛ, Varuṇa and Agni Sviṣṭakṛt, the husband gives the wife some barley-corns. Then she is made to partake of the three-fold food (a mixture of the equal portions of milk, sour curds and melted butter). After the wife's ācamana (sipping water), the husband strokes her body from the navel upwards for three times with the stalk of a kuśa grass with the prayer for having a child as desired.

According to Baudhāyana,[115] if the husband and the wife want a "Śrotriya" son,[116] they are to worship Arundhatī, take unsalted food, lie on the floor and observe chastity for three nights. They wear unwashed clothes and ornaments every morning and evening, hold bow and arrow and worship fire during this period. On the 4th day they are to offer an oblation of cooked rice. If they want to have an Anūcāna[117] son they observe the vow for 12 days; if a Ṛsikalpa[118] son, for

114 III, 10.

115 *Baudh. GS.*, 1, 7, l. 48; p. 24 f. *Baudh. G. Śeṣa-sūtra*, 2. 2. l. 7, p. 236 ff.

116 A *Śrotriya* is one who has read one Śākhā of the Veda; see *Baudh. GS.*, 1, 7, 3.

117 अङ्गाध्याय्यनूचानः; *Baudh.*, 1. 7. 4.

118 कल्पाध्यायी ऋषिकल्पः; *Baudh.*, 1. 7. 5.

one month; if a Bhrūṇa[119] for 4 months; if a Ṛṣi,[120] for six months; if a Deva,[121] for one year.

In the due period the wife takes her bath with a view to observing the rite. In the night the husband adorns her and utters the appropriate mantras. On the following day, the Nāpita-karma[122] is to be observed. The husband and the wife give the barber rice mixed with milk (rice pudding) and go towards the east or the north of the village. When they come across an Udumbara tree, they walk round it, sprinkle water on it and anoint it with scented things. Having covered it with flowers, they offer the Bali oblation. Then they go down into knee-deep water (in some pond), put fish in an unwashed cloth with the skirts stretched towards the bank and ask a Brahmacārin to tell what he sees. He replies that he sees sons and cattle. Then they offer these fish as Bali to herons. Now they throw off the flowers, etc., cast off the remnant of food, put off their clothes and hang them on the Udumbara twigs. They take a bath, wash each other's back and swim towards the deep of the water. Having anointed each other and worn red or unwashed clothes, they go home in a carriage or on foot, have a wash, sip water and begin to

119 सूत्र-प्रवचनाध्यायी भ्रूणः; *Baudh.*, I. 7. 6.

120 चतुर्वेदादृषिः; *Baudh.*, I. 7. 7.

121 अत ऊर्ध्वं देवः; *Baudh.*, I. 7. 8.

122 The barber comes, pares the nails, and gets some remuneration.

sleep without a word. Next morning they talk again during the Vaiśvadeva.

The *Baudh G. Pariśiṣṭa*[123] prescribes a different procedure. Here the husband, after entertaining Brāhmaṇas, worships the fire and offers oblations. Ājya oblations are offered to Sviṣṭakṛt. Then the husband and the wife partake of the rice which is offered to Savitṛ. Whatever they desire to obtain, they contemplate at that time. According to the *Paśupati-paddhati,* the husband should, after his morning duties, make his wife sit to his right, and touch her heart with his hand stretched over her right shoulder and murmur the appropriate mantras. If after the performance of the rite as described the object is not achieved, the husband, during the next time unearths the root of a white-flowered Kaṇṭikāri and keeps it in some secret place. On the due date the husband and the wife fast. After nightfall, the wife, having worn unwashed clothes and sipped water sits to the left of her husband with her face, towards the east. He pounds the above-mentioned root with sprinkled water and sprinkles it into the right nostril of the wife. According to the school of Hiraṇyakeśin,[124] the husband and the wife should, after their morning duties, sip

123 II, 2, pp. 236-37.

124 The *Gṛhya Sūtra* does not deal with the subject. But the *Paddhatis,* e.g., *Saṃskāra-paddhati* of Bhāskara Śāstrin, p. 40 f. and *Saṃskāratramālā* of Bhaṭṭa Gopīnātha Dikṣita, p. 649 ff. deal with the Ritual.

water. While the husband performs the preliminary rites the wife adorns herself with clothes,[125] ornaments and flower-wreaths, anoints and embalms herself and chews betel. She should become thinner by means of Three Nights' observance or inadequate meals.

According to Bhaṭṭa Gopīnātha, commentator of Hiraṇyakeśi GS., under certain circumstances, the Śānti rite should be performed before observing the Garbhādhāna rite.

If the object be not achieved after the Garbhādhāna rite has been duly performed, the rites known as Nārāyaṇa Bali and Nāga Bali should be performed.[126] The former is for averting the evil influence of the demons and the second for being relieved of the sin incurred by killing a serpent or serpents in the previous birth. On the day chosen for the performance of the Nāga Bali, both the husband and the wife, with the things necessary for the performance of the rite, go to a holy place, wear clean garments, make a serpent of the powder of rice, sesamum, etc., place it on a winnowing basket and utter the propitiatory mantras.

The *Saṃskāra-ratna-mālā* also prescribes the gift of a golden cow and the hearing of the *Hari-vaṃśa* for removing the barrenness of the wife.

125 According to Gopīnātha, she should wear unwashed clothes.

126 For the rite, see *Saṃskāra-paddhati*, p. 42 f., *Saṃskāra-ratna-mālā*, p. 696 f.

Bhavadeva in his *Paddhati* says that after nightfall an oblation is to be offered to Sūrya first of all, and then, the mantras as mentioned above are to be uttered. The husband stands behind the wife who sits with her face towards the East. While uttering the mantras, the husband should stretch his right hand from behind on the right shoulder of the wife. Then he touches the navel of the wife with a piece of gold and mutters: "Omn. Be the mother of excellent long-living children. May you, O all-blessed one, be the nourisher of the embryo without difficulty! O one dedicated to vows! give birth to a long-living child, prolonger of the race". Then a woman with husband and sons living should give the wife Pañcagavya sanctified with the above-mentioned mantras.

It does not seem necessary that the wives who have established śrauta fires need observe the domestic New and Full Moon sacrifices separately.[127] because they agree closely in the deity and other details with those of the śrauta; the only difference is that offerings of peps are substituted for cakes and no offerings to Indra or Mahendra are made. It is also distinctly clear that much importance cannot be attached to these rites as they have not been mentioned at all by a good many Gṛhya authorities like Bharadvāja, Laugākṣi (Kāṭhaka), Baudhāyana, Jaimini, and Sāṅkhāyana.

127 Cf. *Baudh. GS.*, IV, 9, 1. p. 33h.

Māṇ. GS.[128] and *Āśv. GS.*[129] simply mention them in names.

On each New and Full Moon night they perform these sacrifices together with their husband. They are required so bathe and eat the fast-day food in the afternoon.[130] They prepare a Sthālī-pāka from which the husband offers oblations to the various deities. Then they should, according to Pāraskara,[131] offer the Bali outside the house to the wife, the Man, Age, and the black-toothed white one, the Lord of bad women and those who, dwelling in the village or the forest, allure their offsprings. They then pray for welfare and offspring. They sleep that night on the ground; according to the Commentator on Gobhila,[132] they may sleep on the self-strewn grass (svastara), too. They together with the sacrificer are expected to, the Chief Wife must, pass that night with mutual entertainment recounting tales or other discourses. They commit nothing impure on that night. If the husband is on a journey, the chief wife acts as his substitute.[133]

128 II, 3, 3. 129 I. 10, 5.

130 *Drāh. GS., II.,* 1. 4; *Gobh. GS.,* 1, 5, 26, p. 219.

131 *Pār. GS.,* 1, 12, 4, p. 130, Bom., ed.; Karka, *op. cit.,* l. 23; Jayarāma, p. 131, l, 6f.; Harihara, *op. cit.,* l. 37f.; Gadādhara, p. 134, l. 10f.

132 *Gobh. GS.,* 1, 6, 5, p. 223, l. 5f.

133 *Gobh. GS.,* 1, 6, 9, p. 225.

In regard to the seasonal sacrifices, the *Mān* GS.[134] says, in the event of the absence of the chief wife and the sacrificer even a Śūdrā wife is entitled to offer the morning and evening oblations to Serpents in course of the daily observance of the Śrāvaṇa sacrifice up till the Āgrahāyaṇeṣṭi. So there is no doubt that all other wives are entitled to offer the same in the event of failure of the chief wife. As all the women of the household are allowed to participate in the rite of alighting from the bedstead,[135] there is no doubt that all the wives join in it; they should, with their children on their lap or by their side, sit in accordance with seniority of the time of their marriage one after another next to the chief wife.

Now, so far as the purificatory (Aurdhvadehika) rites are concerned, the same rites are performed for each of them without any distinction whatsoever. If the pregnant wife dies, she should be, first of all, sprinkled with water mixed with cow's urine. When the dead body has been removed to the crematorium, the husband cuts open the child from the left side of her womb; if the child is still alive, he gives it the breast of its mother along with the prayer that the breast may be an exhaustless spring of plea-

134 *Mān. GS.*, II, 16, p. 192; particularly, Aṣṭāvakra on the same. Cf. *Bhār. GS*, II, l. p. 32.

135 Harihara on *Pār. GS.*, III, 2, p. 321, 1. 5, अत्र स्त्रीणामपि मन्त्र-पाठः.

sure, wealth-giver, etc.,[136] and puts it in front of the dead mother. He then tries to revert the opened womb to its normal position, at least, to make it look as though no operation has been made; anoints it with curd mixed with sacrificial clarified butter; and bathes her with water mixed with mud, ashes, Kuśa and cow's urine. She is now wrapped up in new clothes and cremated.[137] Keśavasvāmin in his *Baudhāyana-paddhati*[138] says that if the husband sees the child still alive, he should offer a sacrifice there with the prayer expressive of his pleasure to get the child alive, bathe it and carry it home; then, fourteen offerings are made and then she is cremated in accordance with the usual rites. The *Karma-kāṇḍa-pradīpa*[139] also quotes the opinion that herein the wife should be laid with her head towards the south, the left side of her belly measuring four fingers from the navel should be cut open. If the child be dead, it

136 For the Mantra: *AV.*, 7, 10., i; *Vāj. Saṃh.*, 38, 5; *Maït. Saṃh..* IV, 9, 4. etc.

137 For these facts: Śaunaka as quoted in *Madana-ratna*, *Karma-kāṇḍa-pradipa*, f. 410a, l. 4f. Also cf. *Gṛhya-kārikā* (Reṇu) and Baudhāyana as quoted herein; Nārāyaṇa Bhaṭṭa's *Antyeṣṭikriyā*, f. 213a, l. 9f.

138 Folios 161-62. According to him if the child be living till then, another sacrifice should be offered on the 8th day in which cows, landed property, sesamum, gold, etc. should be given in gift.

139 *Op. cit.*, l, 7f.

should be washed and buried. The operated part should be sewn with a thread, and anointed with clarified butter. Then after due offerings and gifts, she should be cremated.

If the wife dies after child-birth, or during her courses, she should be bathed with water mixed with Pañcagavya, according to the *Karma-kāṇḍa-pradīpa*, hundred times,[140] covered with a new cloth and cremated in accordance with the usual rites.[141] According to *Vṛddhaśātātapa*,[142] no saṃskāras and such other rites should be performed for a menstruating woman; she should be bathed and cremated after three nights (most probably, after the passing away of the Impurity). Gadādhara in his *Kāla-sāra*,[143] thinks the cremation, either on the same day or after the passing away of the period of Impurity, is optional, i.e. it depends upon the intention of the chief mourner; preference, however, is given to cremation after the period of Impurity.[144] If she dies in a foreign country and as a consequence, the

140 Folio 409b, l. 1.; cf. Nārāyaṇa Bhaṭṭa, *op. cit.*, f. 212b., l. 12f.

141 *Karma-kāṇḍa-pradīpa*, f. 409a, l. 14; 409b, l. 1. According to the *Baudhāyana-paddhati* (f. 162) the water should be mixed with cow's urine.

142 As quoted in *Karma-kāṇḍa-pradipa*, f. 409. l. 4-5.

143 P. 123.

144 The *Madana-ratna* thinks cremation within the period of Impurity should take place in emergency cases; *Karma. KP.*, f. 409b, l. 6f.

above-mentioned rites are not performed, her bones are to be collected and purified with Pañcagavya bathing and ceremonially burnt again.[145]

If the wife of a Sāmavedin dies, be she the eldest one or any other,—she should be cremated with her face downwards.[146] During the collection of her bones, the sprinkling and such other rites should be done with water from an earthen water-vessel.[147] According to the Āśvalāyana school, a vessel should be marked as feminine with the sex marks made prominent.[148]

On the śrāddha days the wives should not have their hair dishevelled, should not cry, laugh or talk for nothing.[149]

As the eating of the cake is not meant for supermundane bliss, all the wives are entitled to partake of the cake or cakes; if there are six, they partake of the middle two.[150] According to Chāgaleya, as quoted in the *Śrāddha-mañjarī*,

145 According to Devayājñika, as quoted in *Karma. KP.*, f. 409b. l. 2-3.

146 *Karma. KP.*, f. 399c, छन्दोगानां स्त्री-मरणे विशेषः etc.

147 *Jaim. GS.*, II, 5, p. 30, l. 20; p. 31, l. i.

148 *Āśv. GK.*, i, 5, 4, p. 320, Bom. ed.

149 *Śrāddha-mañjarī*, p. 1.

150 *Śrāddha-mañjarī*, p. 39. *Śrāddhatattva*, p. 200. *Śrāddha-sūtra-kaṇḍikā, Pār. GS.*, Bom. ed., p. 481, l. 34; 485, l. 4. *Manu.*, Nir. ed., p. 126, v. 262; according to *Kullūka*, however, only the eldest wife should eat it. *Khā. GS.*, III, 5, 30, p. 118 (Aṣṭika). *Mantra-Brāhmaṇa*, II, 3, 1 .

the cake should be divided into as many portions as there are wives and each wife should be given a portion. According to the *Prayoga-pārijāta*, if six cakes have been offered in the Śrāddha and the sacrificer has two offered, each wife should be given one cake. If there are a good many wives, a selection should be made in accordance with qualities, age and period. Or, each of them may be given one cake at the end of each Śrāddha. According to the Mayūkha, the eating of the middle cake is only optional, and not indispensable. A wife who is sick, afflicted (with some mishap) or otherwise incapable,[151] should not eat the cake. According to Āpastamba, an ill-disposed or evil-hearted wife should also be avoided.[152] If the wives are not desirous of having children, they may not eat the cake.[153]

As the first wife and the husband raise up the fires and are really the protectors of them, the husband is not entitled to give up the fires on the death of any other wife than that of the first. In case of the death of the latter, an Āhitāgni is to cremate her with fire kindled from a new fire-drill or produced from the either half of a jar heated on the śrauta

151 *Candrikā*, p. 402, *Śankhalikhita* quoted.

152 *Āp.*, as quoted in *Smṛti-candrikā*, p. 403.

153 Cf. the *Śrāddha-kāṇḍa* in *Smṛti-candrikā*, p. 402, where various authorities have been quoted with reference to this. Also see *Gobh.*, *G. Pariśiṣṭa*, p. 125, पुत्र-कामा । *Jaim. GS.*, II, 3, p. 29, l. 9-11 (in all the Śrāddhas).

fires.[154] The husband is to relinquish the fires as he offers these to her in her death. The second wife (and naturally the third wife and the following) must not be offered the sacred fires in death; the husband is not entitled to relinquish the Agnihotra out of fascination for her in which case he would be considered as the relinquisher of Brahman.[155]

Miserable indeed is the position of a Śūdrā wife from the religious point of view. From the beginning the Ārya-Śūdrā marriage seems to be a matter of accident[156] and sometimes, most probably, of expediency,[157] on the part of the husband and as such the Śūdrā wife seems to have

154 *Jaim. GS.*, II, 5, p. 30 of *Caland's* ed.; for Comm., *op. cit.*, p. 66.

155 *Kātyāyana, Chandoga-pariśiṣṭa*, Ch. XX, p. 334.

156 The custom of giving slaves as presents to princes (*RV.* VIII. 19, 36) and priests (as sacrificial fee), ritualistic recognition of Ārya Śūdrā Union (*Tait. Saṃh.*, VII, 4, 19, 2; *Vāj Saṃh.*, XXIII, 50, 31), employment of Śūdrās as Anucaris and Pariveṣṭrīs (*Śat. Brā.*, XI, 2, 7, 4; *Kauṣ. Pan.*, 11, i, slave-concubinage, (cf. *AV.*, 22, 6; XII, 3, 13; 4, 9) etc. helped many Śūdrās to rise to the favour of Aryan Masters, so mueh so that most probably—not infrequently, they married them. Several Sūtrakāras make provision for one Śūdrā wife of one belonging to the higher castes (e.g. *Par. GS.*, i, 4, 10). Cf. *Vaśiṣṭha*, 1, 25. and for his own view, the following Sūtras.

157 It seems the King married the Pālāgali Queen for political purposes.

deserved nothing more than a few privileges from an Aryan husband; at least she has no claims in religious matters.[158] It is definitely stated by Manu[159] that she can never be the first wife of an Aryan. Even though married, she simply serves to lead the family of the husband to degradation and the progeny to the status of Śūdras; a Brāhmaṇa is strictly forbidden either to cohabit with or have a child by her.[160] The sacrifices offered by her husband are not acceptable.[161] If he enters her bed immediately after taking a funeral feast, his forefathers will suffer from lying in her Impurities for a month.[162] The Pālāgalī cannot participate in any rite in the politico-religious ceremonies as she is a Śūdrā by birth.[163] A Śūdrā wife of one belonging to one of higher castes is not entitled to churn the fire.[164] The only instance where a Śūdrā wife is allowed to act as a substitute in a rite is the Śrāvaṇa sacrifice, where in the absence of the chief wife and the sacrificer and all other wives she may offer the daily oblation

158 *Manu.*, III, 18; *Viṣṇu* XXVI, 5. For the legal incapacity of her children: *Baudh. DhS.*, II, 2, 3, etc.

159 III, 14.

160 *Op. cit.*, 15-17; also 19. *Viṣṇu* XXVI, 6; *Vaś. DhS.*, I, 27.

161 *Vāś. DhS.*, XIV, 11.

162 *Gauṭ. DhS.*, XV, 22.

163 *Śat. Brā.*, XIII, 2, 6, 7; V, 3. 1, 11.

164 *Karma-pradipa*, I, 8, p. 115.

to snakes. But the rule is by no means universal as it is found only in the *Māṇ.* GS.[165] and in no other text.

In spite of all these religious incapabilities, the *Śūdrā* woman considers herself fortunate in having an Aryan husband; the *Tait. Saṃh.*[166] says in this case she does not care for wealth or prosperity.

It is sure that in religious matters, and therefore in secular matters too, a certain number of women were compelled to lose many rights. There is no doubt that polygamy to a certain extent leads to the deterioration in the position of women. This was, however, counterbalanced by polyandry which has been known in ancient, and in a lesser form in modern[167], India.

There are reasons to believe that polyandry existed in ancient India. The ancient Seers would never have mentioned of a common wife of the Maruts and of the Aśvins if polyandry were unknown or discarded in the society.[168] The *Atharvavedic* verses[169] saying that a woman even after having had ten former husbands, can still marry more, can-

165 II, 16, p. 192; particularly, the scholiast Aṣṭāvakra.

166 VII, 4, 19.

167 Westermarck, *Short History of Marriage*, chap. X; *History of Marriage*, pp. 252-55.

168 Rodasī and Sūryā. *AV.* 1, 167, 4-5; the express reading of the *RV.* with reference to Rodasi, is साधारणी पत्नी common Wife.

169 V, 17, 8-9.

not but refer to polyandry. The case of Draupadī in the *Mahābhārata* is well-known; and the great epic asserts this much, that having many husbands is a desirable qualification for women.[170] In support of Draupadī's polyandrous marriage it cites the case of Jaṭilā Gautamī, Vārkṣī, etc. Gautamī married seven Ṛṣis; Māriṣā married ten Havirdhānas[172] and her son Dakṣa is known as the son of ten fathers.[173] The former in their turn married Tārā in common.[174] Āpastamba[175] says a daughter is given to the family of her husband though it is, in his time, forbidden. He, most probably, refers to the *Tait. saṃh.*[176] which says that the daughter is given to the family. Bṛhaspati[177] also mentions that the delivery of a marriageable damsel to a family is found in other countries (than his own). The Purāṇas also know about it.[178]

As the polygamous husband observes religious rites with

170 *Mah. Bh.*, 1. 202, 8. ईप्सितश्च गुणः स्त्रीणामेकस्या बहुभर्तृता ।

171 *Op. cit.*, 1, 126, 7266; cf. *Viṣṇu-purāṇa*, 1, 15.

172 *Op. cit.*, 1, 33, 3130; *Hari-vaṃśa*, V, 66 f.

173 *Rāmāyaṇa*, VII, 42.

174 *Op. cit.*, IV, (Kiṣkindhyā. Tārā-vākyam) *Padma-purāṇa*, IV, 112; 143-146.

175 *Dh. S.*, II, 10, 27, 3.

176 VI. 1, 6, 5.

177 *Dh. S.*, XXVII, 20.

178 *Brahma*, 15, 48; 54; *Matsya*, 44, 66-70; *Brahmāṇḍa*, III, 71, etc. The *Kunāla Jātaka* (Jt. No. 536) mentions that Princess Kaṇhā had five husbands at a time, all of whom she selected in a svayṃvara assembly.

the eldest wife, the polyandrous wife observes them with the eldest husband. The same reasons we have seen in the case of a polygamous husband in connection with the first wife would apply here, too. Draupadī had once to gaze at hell because she was more fond of Arjuna than her eldest husband Yudhiṣṭhira. Polyandry as well as Polygamy deprived a certain number of women as well as men of various religious rights. These twin usages seem to have counterbalanced the effects of each other on the society, and consequently, on the position of women as men and, at least, no emphasis can be laid on Polygamy as leading to deterioration in the position of women without any counteraction.

Just as the wife is enjoined to please the husband, the husband is also enjoined to please the wife.[179] Where the wife and the husband are whole-heartedly pleased with each other, they acquire the three objects of life (Tri-varga). They must remain satisfied with mutual partnership in all matters; they must not even think of others; for the violation of these rules they incur the same sin and undergo the same punishment without any distinction whatsoever.[180] For grave offences[181] they separate from each other or they may marry again. She may remarry, if her first husband is impotent, outcaste or dead or for other (similarly grave)

179 *Manu*, III, 60-61.

180 Parāśara, 4, 12-13; similarly, Devala, Bṛhaspati, etc.

181 For those of the wife: *Yājñavalkya*, 3. 72-73.

reasons.[182] She or he is to remarry, however, on the fullest knowledge that her or his marriage for the second time cannot be considered as a sacred ceremony (saṃskāra). Even though she or he remarries another unmarried man or woman, still the marriage cannot be accredited as a saṃskāra as each saṃskāra is to be observed only once in life and her or his marriage ceremony has been completed for ever in the first marriage.

From time immemorial[183] the wife has doubly blest her husband, by procreation as well as by participation in sacrifices. In this connection her epithets "Jāyā" and "Patnī"[184] are, no doubt to some extent, significant. But this "Jāyātva" and "Patnītva" are by no means separable in a clear-cut way as her Jāyātva serves really for her Patnītva. She performs a religious duty by means of procreation. She as well as her husband have been born as owing debts to the gods, to the Ṛṣis, to the fathers and to man.[185] In

182 *Vaś. DhS.*, XVII, 20; *Manu* IX, 175-176; *Yājñ.*, i, 67; cf. also *Kāma-sūtra*, p. 248 (Nir. Ed.), *Sūtra* 31 (with Yaśodhara's Commentary); *Baudh. DhS.*, IV, I. 16; II, 2, 3, 27; *Viṣṇu* XV, 7; *Nārada* XII, 45ff.

183 For the Indo-Iranian period: W. Geiger, *Ostiranische Kultur im Altertum*, p. 244.

184 *Pāṇini*, IV, 1, 33; cf. *Sat. Brā.*, 1, 9, 2, 14. But Patañjali does not observe this distinction.

185 *Sat. Brā.*, 1, 7, 2, 1; also IX, 4, 1, 5; *Tait. Brā.*, VI, 3, 5; 10; III, 7, 9, 8; *AV.*, VI, 117, 3; *Tait. Āran.*, VII, 11, 5; *Tait.*

order to liberate themselves from the debt to fathers, they are to marry and have children;] the fathers in the other world depend for their continuance on the offerings of their children.[186] The ardent desire for having children for religious purposes has given women an extremely high position.[187] So it is only natural that she almost always prays to gods for children.[188] Owing to the urgent necessity of having children, productive unions are always to be effected in rituals so much so that even the vessels, spoons or other sacrificial implements are often imagined as males and females. Progeny is one of the primary objects of performing sacrifices. The wife as the bearer of this highest

Upaṇ., 1, 9; *Ait. Āraṇ.*, 1, 3, 5, 6; *Bṛh. Up.*, VI, 4; *Vaś. DhS.*, VIII, 11; *Baudh. DhS.*, II, 3, 2, 1, etc.

186 It will be seen in this connection that in the water-libations and Śrāddhas, water and cake are offered to the parents of both the mother as well as the father.

187 *RV.*, 1, 9, 20; III, 1, 25; X. 85, etc. *AV.*, III. 23, 2; V, 25, 11; VI, 11, 2, etc. *Tait. Saṃh.* VI, 3, 89, 5; *Tait. Brā.*, 1, 5, 6; *Ait. Brā.*, VII, 13; *Ait. Āraṇ.*, II, 3, 7, 3; 5, 1, 1-7; *Chānd, Upaṇ.*, V, 9, 8; *Bṛh. Upaṇ.*, VI, 2, 13; etc.; etc.

188 Compare the references mentioned as "mantras", prayers, etc., in previous pages. Cook informs us in his *Zeus*, vol. II. p. 1114, that even at the present day women slide downrock in front of the church in order to propitiate Saint Marina for having children; cf. Miss M. Hamilton's *Greek Saints and their Festivals*, Edinburgh and London, 1910, p. 58f., as quoted by Cook.

blessing on earth deserves respect from the husband as well as from the society. The husband is bound to respect her as in her, the Jāyā, he is born again, and as she, offered as great Brilliance to him by the gods and the seers, is his mother again.[189]

According to Cook, Greek women are excluded from the cult of Theos Megus, Zeus and Tachnepsis,[190] from Mithraic rites,[191] and the race of Drypole;[192] but there is not a single Vedic ritual from which they are excluded. In the Pravargya sacrifice the wife wraps up her head. This does not mean exclusion at all; on the other hand, it is a part of her ritualistic observances in the sacrifice, as, after this observance, she joins in other rites in the sacrifice. According to a few authorities[193] the wife should be debarred from the Sapiṇḍana if she has neither husband nor sons. Mārkaṇḍeya[194] thinks even though her husband may be living, unless she has any issue she is not entitled to have the Sapiṇḍana, Hemādri[195] thinks the mention of the son is significant of the husband and so there is no contradiction in statements of these authorities. But there is no doubt

189 *Ait. Brā.*, VII, 13. 190 *Zeus*, vol. II, 985.

191 *Op. cit.*, p. 1053. 192 *Op. cit.*, P. 486.

193 *Paiṭhinasi* and *Vyāsa*, as quoted by Hemādri in *Caturvargacintāmaṇi*, p. 1654, l. 2-5, and 5-11.

194 सपिण्डीकरणं तासां पुत्राभावे न विद्यते ।

195 *Op. cit.*, l. 7-8.

that these authorities are opposed to equally outstanding authorities. The *Ṣaṭ-triṃśat-smṛti*[196] as interpreted by Kṛṣṇamiśra is in support of the Sapiṇḍīkaraṇa being held even though the wife may be a widow as well as sonless. The *Dharma-pradīpa*,[197] too, as quoted by the same authority holds the same view.

Even though the authority of the first school be followed, there is no reason to think that it would be prejudicial to the high position of the wife. Under similar circumstances the limitations are the same for the wife as for the husband. If the husband is a widower and sonless, the Sapiṇḍana may be performed for him by his brothers' sons; otherwise it is wholly omitted. It the same circumstances the Sapiṇḍana for the wife, too, may be performed by the sons of her co-wives, otherwise the omission is as inevitable as in the case of the husband. Moreover, the object of the Sapiṇḍana is to relieve the mane from the state of a mane; such a state of the wife in the above circumstances will cease because of the performance of other Śrāddhas.

The woman is always pure.[198] Soma gives them Purity, Gandharvas sweet voice, Fire All Purity—as gifts for their enjoyment with her. The woman can by no means be

196 *Pār. GS.*, Bom. ed., p. 504, l. 37; p. 505, l. 4.
197 *Op. cit.*, l. 6.
198 Yājñavalkya, I, 71.

contaminated.[199] Whatever be the sin of a wife in the meantime, it is sure to be drained out of her body and she becomes absolutely pure.[200] Her temporary Impurity is the cause of All Purity.[201] The Brāhmaṇa is pure only in the feet, but the woman is pure in all her limbs.[202] Her mouth is never impure.[203]

The stress laid by the authorities on the ritualistic impurity of women during their monthly course, pregnancy and childbirth is due to their physical incapacity or some other unavoidable cause or causes. The injunctions are all very reasonable pieces of advice and cannot at all hint at their inferiority in position.

During her period she is not in her normal state of health;[204] authorities, therefore, make compulsory rules

199 *Vaś. DhS.*, XXVIII, 5-6; *Bauh. DhS.*, II, 2, 4, 5.

200 *Vaś. DhS.*, XXVIII, 2-3. In mind also: *Manu* V, 108, *Viṣṇu*, XXII, 91; cf. *Mahābhārata*, 165, 32.

201 *Vaś.DhS.*, XXVIII, 4; III, 58; V, 4. *Yājñavalky*, 1, 72; *Baudh. DhS.*, II, 2, 4, 4.

202 *Vaś. DhS.*, XXVIII, 9. *Śat. Brā.*, V, 2, 1, 8 (some parts of her body to be covered with Kuśa grass) refers to the temporary Impurity and suggests an extra precaution,

203 *Yājñ.*, 1, 193; *Baudh. DhS.*, 1, 9, 2; *Viṣṇu*, XXII, 49.

204 Anton Nemilov, *Biological Tragedy of Women*, ch. VI, 105f.; particularly the section on "Menstruation and its significance," p. 115f. For the legendary cause of menstruation, *Tait. Saṃh.*, II, 5, 1; ch. *Bṛh. Up.*, 3, 4, 3; *Vaś. DhS.*, V, 5-9. Fear

which she should follow at that time[205] and declare that she must not be tempted to observe any rite as it is sure to make her undergo some painstaking observance at least. Even though she may not be bodily present therein, several rites, viz., the New and Full Moon Sacrifices, the Piṇḍa-pitṛ-yajña, the daily oblations, etc., are allowed to be performed. These are allowed, simply because they would otherwise cause some hindrance, necessitate some atonement owing to the lapse of the proper time. The performance of the optional sacrifices, the Paśuyāga, the Soma sacrifice, etc., is barred in her absence. Sacrifice continues, but in spite of her absence, she gets the benefit of its performance. Kātyāyana, however, mentions that if she becomes impure during the Soma Sacrifice, she should continue wearing her Dīkṣā-garments, stay in sand during the emission, and should, finally, take her baths before the Altar during the morning and evening with water mixed with cow's urine

for unclean women in Rituals: *Śat. Brā.*, III, 1, 2, 19. Impediment to Vedic Studies, *Śān. GS.*, II, 12, 10; VI, 1, 3; cf. *Āp, DhS.*, 1, 3, 9, 13. For the various taboos on women during menstruation and childbirth among various peoples: Frazer, *Taboo*, Part II, pp. 145-156.

205 *Baudh, GS.*, 1, 7, 22ff. For exhaustive treatment: *Saṃskāraratnamālā*, pp. 649-694 (various authorities have been quoted here). *Saṃskāra-paddhati.* p. 40: according to this Paddhati, during her first menstruation only, she may wear garlands of yellow and scented flowers and chew betels, not in others.

(on the fourth or fifth day:[206] as this a śrauta sacrifice she may have her bath on either). If she is observing the impurity for childbirth, she should take her (purificatory) bath after a period of ten nights and participate in sacrifices. Some think a pregnant woman should not be initiated to the Soma sacrifice. According to the Dharma-sūtras, she may participate in the Agnihotra even within the period of impurity for childbirth. According to Baudhāyana, she may participate in the New and Full Moon sacrifices, too.[207]

If the wife is herself to perform the Śrāddha for the dead husband, and in the meantime she cannot do so for some reason or other she does it later.[208] The wife has to cook the food to be served to the Manes. So, according to certain Authorities, if on the Śrāddha day she is impure, the Śrāddha should be performed with uncooked rice. If she has a co-wife, she might cook, but the Kalādarśa says it is improper (as cooking in the Śrāddhas is the absolute Right

206 *Saṃskāra-paddhati*, p. 40. l. 20-21.

207 For the above information: Commentary on *Āp.SS.*, IX, 2, 1, vol. II, p. 106; *Manu*, *Yājñavalkya*, *Jābāli*, *Bharadvāja*, and *Baudhāyana*, as quoted in the above (p. 107); *Sat. SS.*, XV, 1, 39-41, vol. VI, pp. 269-71. For the Garbhiniprāyaścitta: *Āp. SS.*, IX, 20, 7, vol. II, p. 200. For the Rajasvalā wife in the Soma Sacrifice. *Sat.SS.*, vol. IV, p. 993ff.

208 *Śrāddha-sūtra-kaṇḍikā*, *Pār. GS.*, p. 466, l. 17; *Śrāddha-mañjarī*, pp. 97 and 181.

of the Chief Wife) and the Śrāddha should be performed on the expiry of the period of her menstruation. It is, however, sanctioned that only the Annual Śrāddha should be performed with cooked rice (which, it seems, should be cooked by the sacrificer himself) even in this case.[209] The *Saṃskāramayūkha* quotes Vṛddhagārgya to show that the Vṛddhiśrāddha may be performed during her monthly illness.[210] The above rules hold good if the wife is observing Garbhāśauca (impurity for pregnancy).[211]

If the sacrifices are performed in her absence, the husband atones on the fourth night (after she has taken her purificatory bath). He tells her that half of the sacrificial merit could not be acquired on account of her absence; he is therefore atoning along with the utterance of the prescribed mantras and praying that the merit be now acquired after the observance of the atonement.[212]

The wife has been depicted throughout the Brāhmaṇic literature in the lovliest colour. Sachī boasts not a little to

209 For the varying opinions on the subject: *Śrāddha-mañjarī*, p. 181.

210 p. 16.

211 Ch. *Śrāddha-mañjarī*, p. 97, एवं गर्भिण्याम् अपि । As the eating of the middle cake is meant for pregnancy, it is only natural that during her pregnancy she is not given the same again.

212 *Āp.ŚS.* and *Sat.ŚS.* and scholiast thereon as mentioned above.

say that her husband must conform to her will and her frame is the most precious thing to her husband.[213] Her pride is quite justified as in prayers to gods the seers again and again refer to her as the ideal of love, sweet relationship, etc. Vāmadeva invokes Indra with the tenderness which a husband has for his wife.[214] Atri invokes and prays to the Āśvins with the faith a wife has in her husband.[215] Viśvāmitra prays to Pūṣan to accept his offerings, listen to his thought, and be to him what a husband is to his young wife.[216] Vāmadeva prays to Indra to love his voice as the husband loves the voice of his well-beloved wife.[217]

Vasu addresses Soma Pavamāna saying that Soma loves him just the same as a wife loves her husband.[218] When the husband goes out for fight, she orders that the generous Soma be prepared; when he has already gone, she prays to Indra for his protection.[219] The husband excites himself to all the mighty deeds with the sweet hope that she would proudly lean on his victorious arm after the victory.[220] With so much influence over her husband it is only natural that she, the most blessed gift from the gods Aryaman, Bhaga,

213 *RV*. X, 159, 2-3. 214 *RV*. IV, 20. 5.
215 *RV*. V, 78. 4. 216 *RV* III, 62. 8.
217 *RV*. IV, 32, 16 (3rd *Aṣṭaka*, 6th Adh., Sūkta II).
218 *RV*. IX, 82, 4. 219 *RV*. IV, 24, 8.
220 *RV*. X, 27, 12.

Savitṛ and Purandhi, would be the mistress of her household[221] having full sway over the father-in-law and others.[222] Careful and active,[223] benevolent,[224] untiring in endeavours to satisfy the husband[225] by any means whatsoever—the wife, best friend of her husband[226] in all her majestic glory, reserves the right of having her own favourite goddesses and gods to be worshipped towards the end of the sacrifice. She would not let the sacrifice be finished unless her Agni Gṛhapati has been satisfied with the oblation in the Patnī-saṃyāja. Of all gods her nearest connection with Agni is manifest. Agni enjoys her as her third God Husband.[227] He is her

221 *RV.* X, 85, 36.

222 *RV.* X, 15, 46; *AV.* XIV, 2, 18.

223 *RV.* I, 66; 79.

224 *RV.* V, 61; particularly, Ṛc. 9.

225 *RV.* IV, 3, 2; X, 71, 4. She has no grievance even against her guilty gambling husband. She suffers in silence, but has against him neither anger nor a hard word; her love for him and goodness towards his friends are constant. The guilty husband is sorely mortified—not so much for anything else, as for making her suffer. *RV.* X, 34.

226 She is so ever since she performs the Saptapadi (the rite of taking Seven steps) during the Wedding Ceremony. *Śāṅ. GS.*, I, 4, 5, seq.; *Gobh.* II, 2, 11; *Khā. GS.*, I, 5, 26; *Hiran. GS.*, I, 20, 9, seq.; *Āp, GS.*, 4, 16, etc.; etc. *Bṛh. Upaṇ.*, I, 4, 3; *Ait. Brā.*, VII, 13.

227 *RV.* X, 85, 40-41; *AV.* XIV, 2, 3-4.

Lover, her God[228] and is the Aryaman between her and her husband and makes them one-minded.[229] He brings about sexual union and causes pregnancy.[230] In rituals she always sits by the side of her Fire.[231] We have seen her in connection with Fire-worship before:[232] beginning from her marriage when she offers the oblations for the first time down to the end of her life she worships the Fire, but the worshipper is inseparable from the worshipped;[233] her Fire accompanies her in her death; if her husband dies before her, she gives Him (Fire) with him.[234] Her fire saves her from having a co-wife.[235] She herself feeds him with a log at the end of every sacrifice. So it is only natural that she would not allow the sacrifice to be finished without ceremoniously celebrating his worship. The priests, during the Patnī-saṃyāja, leave their respective places, come by her

228 *RV.* I, 66, 8.

229 *RV.* V, 3, 2.

230 *Śat. Brā.*, III, 4, 3, 4-5; *Śāṅ. GS.*, I, 17, 9.

231 E.g. Scholiast on *Āp. ŚS.*, VI, 5, 2; *Kāt. ŚS.*, Chow. ed. p. 274, Sūtra 193.

232 See *Indian Historical Quarterly*, March. 1940, The wife in the Vedic Ritual. For paticular stress laid on fire-worship by the wife, see *Śaṅkha.*, IV, 15; *Ūna. Saṃh.*, p. 409; *Kātyāyana*, XIX, 3; *op. cit.* p. 333.

233 *Gobh. GS.*, I, 3, 15: *Khā. GS.*, I, 5, 17; *Śāṅ. GS.*, II, 16, 3; *Gaut. DhS.*, V. 40; *RV.* III, 53, 3; *Śat. Brā.*, III, 3, I, 10f.

234 *Karma-kāṇḍa-pradipa*, f. 398a, l. 8ff.

235 *Āp. DhŚ.*, II, 5, 11, 13f.

side, and offer various oblations to Him. She thus firmly establishes her connection with her Agni.

She also sees that the wives of gods are worshipped before the sacrifice is finished. The wives of the gods worshipped before are invoked herein to have equal share of oblations with their husbands. The sacrifice cannot be ended without the satisfaction of the wives and their human counterpart. After the Patnī-saṃyāja she once again partakes of the Iḍā; the Samyu-vāc is recited and Saṃśrava-oblation is offered. She concludes the sacrifice by having uttered the greetings to the priests and bidding good-bye to them.

Thus we see that in Vedic ritual the wife holds as important a position as the husband. As equal halves they perform the sacrifices with equal results. If the husband has many wives, the chief wife is, really speaking, the patnī in the strict sense of the term; she has many rights, in fact, all the important rights in rituals in precedence over her co-wives. Other wives (excepting Śūdrās) also join in the sacrifices and perform certain rites; anyway, they are not non-entities in religious matters so far as their personal earthly benefit is concerned. But the Śūdrā wife of an Āryan has no right in rituals whatsoever. Polyandry and polygamy as existing side by side in the country in varying degrees have counterbalanced each other. Both of them are, however, abnormalities as monogamy is always the ideal of the society. The Vedic ritual imposes upon the widow as well as the widower equally formidable difficulties: the same are the problems for both; they are to decide which course would be the best for them. Even in the lifetime of both, they are allowed, in extreme cases, to remarry,—however, on the full knowledge that such marriages cannot be recognised as saṃskāras. The Vedic ritual nowhere gives any such evidence as to lead to the assumption that the wife is to be considered inferior in position to the husband: ritualistic injunctions on her in connection with her impurities are reasonable pieces of advice and cannot suggest any the least inferiority in her position. The ritual literature is full of praise for the wife, for her virtues, and it is no wonder that the concluding oblations are offered to satisfy her most revered and beloved God Agni and the Wives of the gods, and that she concludes the sacrifice with final greetings. Every Vedic sacrifice begins with the worship of the mother (Mātṛkā-pūjā), culminates in the worship of the wife (Patnī-saṃyāja) and successfully ends with the worship of the Daughter (Kumārī-pūjā) just in the same way as the sacrifice of man's life (Jīvanayajña) begins with the worship of the Mother, culminates in the worship of the Wife (Śakti-pūjā; Patnī-pūjā) and ends with the worship of the Daughter.[236]

236 Eor Patnī-pūjā, cf. *Manu* III, 55, p. 88, Nir. ed.

THE WIDOW

CHAPTER I

THE WIDOW IN THE VEDIC RITUAL
(NIYOGA)

CHAPTER II

WIDOW-MARRIAGE IN ANCIENT INDIA

CHAPTER III

WIDOW-BURNING IN ANCIENT INDIA

CHAPTER IV

THE WIDOW IN THE VEDIC RITUAL
(MISCELLANEOUS RITES.)

The Widow In The Vedic Ritual.*

CHAPTER I

In Vedic Ritual the position of a widow is no more miserable than that of a widower. In the absence of the equal half, the other half becomes useless—in religious matters as well as in worldly affairs—and what the surviving half can best do is to pass away the remaining part of his or her life in absolute self-abnegation, proving loyal to the deceased one and offering homage to him or her in thought as well as in action. If they cannot observe this ideal, they can do what they consider best; the way is no more blocked for one than for the other. On the other hand, the widow has some special privileges over the widower as will shown below.

NIYOGA

The propagation of children is enjoined as a religious necessity because they keep the ancestors living in the other world. On this score the widower sometimes marries again. The widow, too, can remarry if she likes; but if she prefers to keep up the memory of her husband and live with her husband's family and at the same time have children, she

* Modern Review, November, 1941, pp. 472-473.

may have them by having recourse to Niyoga, or levirate.[1] Niyoga is a social custom allowing widow or even women with husbands living to have children by persons other than their husbands. It has been known in India from Rig-Vedic times.[2] Whereas the commentators try to interpret Āpastamba[3] and Baudhāyana's[4] sūtras in support of Niyoga, there is no doubt that Manu[5] contradicts himself on the point as pointed out by Bṛhaspati.[6] Vaśiṣtha,[7] Gautama[8] and Nārada,[9] however, speak approvingly on the usage. Kauṭilya allows a queen to resort to Niyoga if an old king is badly in need of a competent and honest heir.[9] Yaśod-

1 It was known in various ancient civilizations; see Spencer, Sociology, 1, p. 661; Deuteronomy, 25,5-10, etc.; Plutarch's Lives, Lycurgus, p. 86.

2 Ṛg-veda, x. 40, 2; see also Nirukta, 3, 15 and Durgācārya on the same.

3 ii. 6, 13, 7.

4 ii. 2, 34-35. Haradatta, however, explains the Gāthā away by saying that it represents the sentiments of a neglectful husband.

5 ix. 68; 57-cp. v. 162; ix. 120f. In fact, he contradicts himself on this point as pointed out by Bṛhaspati.

6 E.g., Manu ix. 59-60.

7 xvii. 6-9, 63-64; cp. Manu ix. 50.

8 ii. 9. (xviii), 9-14. (No. 14). See Viṣṇu, xv. 3; see also Nanda Paṇḍita's comments on the same.

9 xii. 54f, see also xiii. 14.

hara also in his commentary on Vātsyāyana[10] mentions that a brother-in-law often becomes the lover of the eldest sister-in-law; this also seems to refer to Niyoga.

The Niyoga is nothing but making virtue of a necessity and after conception, she must not meet again the person appointed for Niyoga.[11] She can appoint for Niyoga her husband's younger brother, some kinsman or near relative of his or even an outsider during the life-time of her husband with his consent if he is incapable of procreating or after his death, if she is childless.[12] She may also do the same if the husband be away from home for some years, and for some reason or other, she does not like to leave her husband's family and remarry. As is only natural in ancient societies, the younger brother of the husband is preferred for the purpose as the issue, in that case, carries the maximum quantity of blood of the family of the husband possible under the circumstances.

10 Vātsyāyana, chap. 23. p. 262, 1, 8, "Jyeṣṭhabhāryā bahu-devarakā" commentary, *op. cit.*, p. 263, 1, 7-8 Nirṇaya-sāgara ed. 1891).

11 Nārada-dharma-sūtra, ii. 1. 20; ii. 2.

12 According to Gautama (xxviii. 45), issues raised are to be treated as sons of a śūdra wife by a Brāhmaṇa, cp. Viṣṇu-smṛti, xv. 37.

For a list of persons to be preferred, see Vaśiṣtha-dharma-sūtra, xvii. 79. For instances of Niyoga, see Mahābhārata i. 103, 104.

A wife or a widow must not, however, be forced to have recourse to Niyoga[13] for inheritance or similar purposes.

Baudhāyana[14] and Vaśiṣṭha[15] say that a widow desiring Niyoga should avoid meat, honey etc. and sleep on the ground for a short period not exceeding one year. After six months of the death of her husband, she offers a funeral oblation to her husband and with the approval and aid of her brother or father, and relatives of her husband, and also in consultation with the Gurus of her family, she chooses the man to have an issue by her.[16] A characterless, mad, diseased or very aged widow is not entitled to Niyoga.[17] Sixteen years after maturity is the proper time for Niyoga.[18] A sickly person is to be avoided for the purpose.[19] She must be economically independent of the person whom she appoints for Niyoga and provide for the necessary expenses for food, unguents, etc. herself i.e. from the estate of her husband.[20] An issue by Niyoga i.e. a kṣetraja[21] son is second in position only to the real son,

13 Vaśiṣṭha-dharma-sūtra, xvii. 65 रिक्थलोभान्नास्ति नियोगः ।

14 ii. 4, 7-9. 15 xvii. 55-56.

16 Vaśiṣṭha-dharma-sūtra, xvii. 56.

17 *op. cit.*, xvii. 57-58; Nārada, xii. 83-14.

18 *op. cit.*, 59. 19 *op. cit.*, xvii. 60.

20 *op. cit.*, xvii. 61.

21 For the definition of the ksetraja son, see Baudhāyana-dharma-sūtra, ii. 23, 17.

being decidedly better than an adopted son. In the list of inheritors, his position is second to that of the aurasa or real son begotten by the husband himself.[22] An adopted son or daughter coming as he or she does from outside cannot claim precedence over the Niyoga-son who has the blood of the family in him.

Thus we find that the Niyoga is sanctioned under the following circumstances:

1. When the wife (with her husband living) or widow is childless.
2. When the wife has children, but they are not honest and competent. This is a special concession granted only to a queen, with her husband incapable of any further procreation, for in this case a competent heir is absolutely necessary for the good of the whole country.
3. But when a wife or a widow has already a good and competent child or children, Niyoga is not allowed under any circumstances.

Further the Niyoga always needs the approval of her husband if living or of her father or brother and husband's families, and then alone the children begotten can be regarded as legitimate, enjoying all the social and legal privileges of

22 Viṣṇu, xv. 3; Manu. x 158-181; Yājñavalkya, ii. 127f. Nārada, xiii. 45.

those born in wedlock. Otherwise they are considered illegitimate. This strong emphasis on the approval of the husband, the heads of families and Gurus clearly shows that there is nothing underhand in this practice of the Niyoga, but it is a full-fledged social custom. approved, at least consented to, as necessary under certain circumstances. In course of time when Niyoga became unpopular in India the number of children to be raised by this device was lowered down to two, or even one.[23] But the Mahābhārata expressly states that the number should be three and no more,[24] though in still earlier times, it points out, a larger number of children could be thus raised. Thus Vyuṣitāśva's wife Bhadrā is said to have obtained seven sons.[25] Bālirāja had eleven sons; Kakṣivat and others had one maid[26] and five

23 Manu, ix, 61: Baudhāyana-dharma-sūtra, xviii. 8—not more than two sons. Haradatta, however, explains the word as "not more than one son". Saudāsa appointed Vaśiṣṭha to have one son (Aśmaka) by his wife Madayantī.

24 Kuntī says to Pāṇḍu, i. 123, 76-77. p. 218, Citraśālā Press ed.

नातश्चतुर्थं प्रसवमापत्स्वपि वदन्त्युत ।
अतः परं स्वैरिणी स्याद्बन्धकी पञ्चमे भवेत् ॥

Kunti's sister Śrutasenā had also three sons by means of Niyoga. Saradandayini also did the same, one of them being Durjaya; i. 120, 38-40, p. 212 Citrasala Press ed.

25 Mahābhārata, i. 121, vv. 19ff, Citrasala Press, p. 213.

sons by his queen Sudeṣṇā[27]. The Mahābhārata also makes the significant remark that further similar instances were not lacking.[28] Thus we see that whereas the widowers have three alternatives to choose from, viz., 1. the ideal one i.e. cherishing the memory of the departed wife, leading a celibate life; 2 remarrying for the sake of children i.e., for the sake of propitiating the forefathers; and 3. remarrying in spite of having children by the first wife, the widow is entitled to all these; in addition, she has another privilege, viz., having recourse to Niyoga. This is specially allowed in the case of the widow because her circumstances are different from those of the widower; she may desire to stay in her husband's family. If she, however, remarries outside her family, she has to leave her former husband's house. So a middle course was devised specially for her, viz. staying in her husband's family and having children by Niyoga. This proves that women were shown every possible consideration in Ancient India though it cannot be denied that this attitude unfortunately changed for the worse in later ages.

26 1,104, 42ff.

27 *op. cit.*, v. 53, p. 193, Citrasala ed.

28 *op. cit.*, v. 56.

CHAPTER II

Widow-marriage in ancient India.*

If the widow considers life-long celibacy or the Niyoga[1] unsuitable and she must have a second husband, she is entitled to remarry. The following evidences may be adduced in support of the above contention: The Ṛg-vedic verse X.18.8[2], "Rise, O' woman, come towards the world of the living; thou liest by the side of this one whose life is gone. Be the full-fledged wife of (this) your husband who (now) grasps your hand and wooes you" refers to widow-marriage. Hillebrandt's theory[3] that this verse does not apply to the funeral ceremony at all is not tenable. He thinks the verse was used for summoning the queen to remove herself from the side of the dead and for no other

* Modern Review, January, 1942, pp. 68-71.

1 See The Modern Review, November, 1941, The Widow in the Vedic Ritual (Niyoga).

2 उदीर्ष्व नार्यभि जीवलोकं गतासुमेतमुपशेष एहि ।
हस्तग्राभस्य दिधिषोस्तवेदं पत्युर्जनित्वमभि संबभूथ ॥

The only other place except RV. X. 18. 8 = AV. XVIII, 3, 2 = Tait. Āraṇyaka, VI, 1, 3, where the word Didhiṣu occurs is RV. VI, 55, 5. There also the word means wooer. See Pischel, Vedische Studien, 1. 21; Macdonell, Vedic Mythology, p. 35 and Geldner, RV. Commentur, p. 154.

3 Zeitschrift der Morgenlandischen Gesellschaft, 40,708; Cf. Ritualliteratur, p. 153.

purpose at all.[4] He formulates his theory on the evidence of the Śāṅkhāyana-śrauta-sūtra[5] according to which this verse is the first of the Utthāpinī verses that are employed for raising the queen. But he ignores totally the fact that the verse appears even in the Atharva-veda[6] and the Taittirīya Araṇyaka,[7] not to speak of the Gṛhya-sūtras[8] of the same standing as that of Śāṅkhāyana, as one of the mantras used during the funeral ceremony. There is no reason why the verse referring to the married woman, who is addressed as the wife of the person grasping her hand with a view to marrying her should be employed only during the Puruṣa-medha and not during the funeral ceremony. Again, the remaining Utthāpinī verses mentioned in the Śāṅkhāyana-śrauta-sūtra (16.13.13) do not seem to have any specific connection with the Puruṣa-medha sacrifice. The well-known Ṛg-vedic verses X. 85. 21-22, which refer to Gandharva Viśvāvasu, appears throughout the Vedic literature, as marriage mantras. RV.X.53.8. has been included in the list of the Utthāpinī verses simply because it begins as Ut tiṣṭhata. It seems that the four Utthāpinī verses have been so called in the Śāṅkhāyana-śrauta-sūtra,

4 Cf. Lanman, Sanskrit reader, Boston, 1888, p. 385; Delbrück, Die indische Verwandschaftsnamen, p. 175; Jolly: Recht und Sitte, p. 78.

5 16, 13, 13.

6 18, 3, 2.

7 6, 1, 3.

8 Asvalāyana, 4, 2, 18; Vaitāna, 3.8.3; Kauśika, 80, 45.

simply because all the four verses begin with Ut or Uta. Hillebrandt emphasises that A.V.XVIII, 3.1-4. can only be taken in connection with the Puruṣa-medha sacrifice. But Śāṅkhāyana himself on whose authority he has to base his arguments, takes only the second verse in connection with it. In explaining these verses he thinks Jīva-loka, in the first verse means Pati-loka, Gopati pati and so on. These are certainly forced interpretations. There is no doubt that the verse is used in connection with the funeral ceremony; but the real difficulty lies in deciding about the true interpretation of the verse. Sāyaṇa himself gives different interpretations in different places. In interpreting the verse (RV.X.18.8.) which occurs in the Atharva-veda (XVIII.3.2.) as well, Sāyaṇa interprets its second line with reference to the first husband while he explains the same verse in the Taittirīya Āraṇyaka (VI.1) with reference to the second husband. Sāyaṇa interprets "Abhi saṃ babhūtha" as "Ābhimukhyena samyak prāpnuhi", taking Bhū in the sense of "getting"[9] with the aid of Pāṇini's rule Chandasi Luṅlaṅliṭaḥ.[10] Modern authorities have likewise differed in opinion. Among those who think the

9 See Bāla-manoramā, Uttarārdha, p. 300; Dhātu-pradipa of Maitreya Rakṣita, Rajshahi, 1919, p. 146. It is a *curādigaṇīya* root.

10 III. 4, 6,

verse refers to the first husband are Roth,[11] Maxmüller,[12] Weber,[13] Geldner[14] and Monier-Williams.[15] Whitney,[16] Caland,[17] Ludwig[18] and Macdonell[19] interpret the verse as referring to the second husband. According to these latter authorities, therefore, the verse sanctions widow-marriage. Some of the medieval authorities[20] have, no doubt, employed the verse as the prescribed mantra for the

11 Zeitschrift der Morgenlandischen Gesellschaft, VIII, Die Todtembestattung indischen Altertum.

12 *Op. cit.*, Bd. 9. 1895, p. vi.

13 Sitzungsbar der Berliner Akademie, 1896, p. 255.

14 In A. Bertholet's Religious Geschicht und Lesebuch, Tubingen, 1908, p. 136.

15 Brahmanism and Hinduism, 4th edition, London, 1891, p. 280.

16 Harvard Oriental Series, Vol. 8, p. 849. His opinion that the widow is to be remarried immediately after the misfortune befalls her is untenable.

17 Die altindische Todten und Bestattungs-gebräuche, p. 44.

18 Der Rig-veda, Bd. V, p. 525.

19 History of Sanskrit Literature, p. 126.

20 Kṛṣṇa Dīkṣita, Aurdhvadehika-prayoga, India Office MS, No. 1270a, F. 96b.

उदोर्ष्व इति द्वाभ्यां मन्त्राभ्याम्...उत्थापयेत ॥

Bhaṭṭa Harihara's Antyeṣṭi-paddhati, India Office Library MS. No. 674, F. 11b.

उदीर्ष्व देवरः शिष्या वा…करे धृत्वा उत्थापयेत् ॥

widow-burning in which case it can by no means refer to the second husband, but a reasonable doubt gains ground in view of the fact that none of the ancient authorities employ it for the same purpose. According to the former "Ud īrṣva" refers to the raising up of the wife on the funeral pyre and the "Jīva-loka" then, according to them, must mean some part in heaven. But this idea is a later development and represents a very small section of the Smārtas who sanctioned widow-burning. All the ancient authorities unanimously prescribed the verse as a mantra for removing the wife from the funeral pyre wherein she lies by the side of her dead husband, strictly in accordance with the direction found in the first line of the same. Āśvalāyana employs it as a mantra with which the younger brother of the deceased husband (or some such person), a disciple or an old servant should raise the widow from the funeral pyre.[21] Nārāyaṇa[22] and Haradatta[23] commenting

21 IV, 2, 15 (Trivandrum edition), Trivandrum Sanskrit series, No. 78, 1923,

तामुत्थापयेद् देवरः पतिथीयोऽन्तेवासी जरद्दासो वा नार्यभि जीवलोकमिति

The old servant or the discipie is not entitled to utter some mantraś or do all the rites; see commentaries on iv, 2, 17-18.

22 Āśvalāyana-gṛhya-sūtra, ed. by J. Mukundaji, second ed., Bombay, 1909.

23 Trivandrum edition, p. 178. Haradatta, however, refers to the opinion of a school according to which the brother-in-law

upon the sūtra of Āśvalāyana say that the younger brother of her husband only is entitled to be her second husband. According to Baudhāyana,[24] Āpastamba[25] and Hiraṇyakeśin[26] a Patistha (one who is entitled to marry her, i.e., the younger brother of her husband or Patihita or a kinsman of her husband) should utter this mantra while raising up the widow by her left hand. This Patistha or Patihita is recommended to raise her up so that she may be his wife if she intends to remarry or be maintained by him if she decides to have recourse to Niyoga. Thus none but Āśvalāyana refers to an old servant or a disciple as a fit person for raising the widow up from the funeral pyre. This old servant or disciple is really a substitute for the Devara who may be absent for some reason or other. So the Devara or the husband's younger brother is the fittest person to remarry the widow.

This is further supported by the etymological meaning of the word "Devara" (Dvitīyaḥ varaḥ)[27] (husband's youn-

who is like a husband (पतिथीयः पतिस्थानीयः) should only maintain her and do similar duties.

24 Pitṛmedha-sūtra, VIII, 2; Mysore University ed., p. 386.

25 ZDMG., X, No. 3, p. 38.

26 *Op. cit.*

27 Yāska gives this interpretation; see also Govindasvāmin on the Baudhāyana-dharma-sūtra, 2, 2, 9; cf. also RV, X, 40, 2b—a widow draws her husband's brother in bed.

ger brother) and certainly he was the most eligible second husband of his elder brother's widow. Kauṭilya points out that she may, no doubt, remarry but if she does not marry the person selected by her father-in-law, she will forfeit the right of possessing any longer the dowry received during her former marriage or other gifts from the father-in-law or husband.[28] The Mahābhārata also expressly states that [29] a woman marries her brother-in-law after the death of her husband. In later times Samudragupta's son Candragupta II is said to have married his elder brother Rāmagupta's widow Dhruvadevī.[29a] Thus it is evident that this custom of remarrying the husband's younger brother continued for a long time even after the Vedic period.

Though remarriage with the husband's younger brother was preferred, it was by no means compulsory. The passages referring to widow-marriage in the Atharva-veda, etc., do not refer to it at all; as a matter of fact, it not only does not question the validity of the eleventh

28 Artha-śāstra, III, 2.

29 12, 19: नारी तु पत्यभावे वै देवरं वृणुते पतिम् । See also शान्तिपर्व, 72, 12; अनुशासनपर्व, 8, 22.

29a Malaviya Commemoration Volume, Early Gupta History, p. 203.

marriage—of a woman,[30] but also assures in indubious language that by performing the Aja pañcodana rite (offering a goat with five rice-dishes), a remarried woman and her second husband may ensure for themselves a lifelong union.[31] In the following stanza, the husband of the remarried wife is assured that he will be able to live with his wife in the same world even after death and the next stanza assures both the husband and the remarried wife that they may go even to the highest heaven.[32] The Aitareya Brāhmaṇa (III. 22) stating that one wife cannot have many husbands together, indicates that she connot have more than one husband at the same time, implying thereby that she can remarry when her husband is dead.[33] This also has no direct

30 V. 17, 8f; if a woman marries a Brāhmaṇa for her eleventh husband etc.

31 AV, ix, 3. 27.

या पूर्वं पतिं वित्त्वाऽथान्यं विन्दते परम् ।
पञ्चौदनं च तावजं ददातो न वि योषतः ॥

32 AV. ix. 3. 28-29.

समानलोको भवति पनर्भुवा पुरः पतिः ।
योऽजं पञ्चौदनं दक्षिणाज्योतिषं ददाति ॥
अनुपूर्ववत्सां धेनुमनड्वाहमुपवर्हणम् ।
वासो हिरण्यं दत्त्वा ते यन्ति दिवमुत्तमाम् ॥

33 तस्मात् नैकस्यै बहवः सहपतयः ।
See also Mitra Miśra in his Vīra-mitrodaya, Adhivedana-prakaraṇa

reference to the husband's younger brother. The words Didhiṣu, Didhiṣupati,[34] Parapūrvā, Paunarbhava, etc. do not necessarily refer to the younger brother of the dead husband, though they undoubtedly show the prevalence of widow-marriage in ancient India. There are many instances in the Mahābhārata where widows are found married[35] or widows are sought for as wives.[36] Baudhā-

—सहशब्दसामर्थ्यात् क्रमेण पत्यन्तरीभवतीति गम्यते ; Nilakaṇṭha in his Bhāratabhāva-dīpa on Mahābhārata (i, 195. 29) remarks:—सह इति युगपद् बहुपतित्वनिषेधो विहितो न तु समयभेदेन। Cf. Tait. Samh. VI. 6, 4, 3. यदेकस्मिन् यूपे द्वे रशने परिव्ययति...द्वे पती विन्देत ; here too a woman is forbidden to have more than one husband at the same time.

34 Kāṭhaka-saṃhitā, XXXI, 7; Kapiṣṭhala-saṃhitā XLVII, 7; also found in Dharma-sūtras. See also Manu III, 173. Manu seems to apply the term to the brother-in-law who is married to his sister-in-law after his brother's death for the purpose of begetting a child, if he displays conjugal affection to her (Cf. Leist, Alt-avisches Jus Gentium, 106).

35 E.g., Arjuna had a son by the widowed daughter of Airāvata, the Nāga king.

36 Ugrāyudha seeks for the hands of Satyavatī, widow of Śāntanu (Hari-vaṃśa XX) etc.

yana,[37] Vaśiṣṭha,[38] Parāśara,[39] Manu,[40] etc., also recognize widow-marriage not necessarily with the brother-in-law but with outsiders as well.

The Buddhist literature, too, furnishes a large number of instances of widow-marriages.[41]

Even in subsequent periods many widows are found married and their issues become powerful kings too; e.g., Kings Candrāpīda, Tārāpīḍa who successively ruled Kashmir in the 8th century A. D. [42] and King Vīradhavala of Dholka.[43] Even Vastupāla of outstanding fame, and exponent of the Jaina religion in later ages, was the son of a twice-married woman by her second husband.[44]

37 Dharma-sūtra, IV, 1, 16.

38 XVII. 39-20; 72-74.

39 IV, 30;

नष्टे मृते प्रव्रजिते क्लीबे च पतिते पतौ ।
पञ्चस्वापत्सु नारीणां पतिरन्यो विधीयते ॥

Also found in Garuḍa-purāṇa, 107, 28 and Agni-purāṇa, 154. 5 and Narada-smṛti.

40 IX, 175.

41 E.g., Asatarupa Jataka; King of Kośala makes the widowed Queen of Kāśi his chief Queen.

42 Rāja-taraṅgiṇī, IV, 35-42. They were the sons of King Durlabhaka by the wife of a rich merchant subsequently married by him.

43 See Merutuṅga's Prabandha-cintāmaṇi.

44 *Op. cit.*

Hammīra of Chitor married the widowed daughter of Maldeo; their son Kṣetrasiṃha experienced no difficulties in becoming the ruler of Udaipur.[45]

The great philanthropist Paṇḍita Īśvaracandra Vidyāsāgara, while attempting to legalise widow-marriage in Hindu Society in 1856 based his evidence upon a few Smṛti works and the Mahābhārata, but the evidences adduced above clearly show that the widow-marriage is supported not only by the Smṛtis but also by the Vedic literature. A widow is allowed to marry as many times as she likes, either the younger brother of her husband or somebody else.

Regarding the legal position of the son of a widow, Gautama[46] allows one-fourth share of his father's property to the son of a widow by her second husband. Vaśiṣṭha[47] and Viṣṇu[48] declare the son of a married widow fourth in the list of inheritors in oder of preference and better than an adopted son. Manu[49] says that a Paunarbhava, son of a remarried widow, is to be regarded as a Brahman living by trade. This discrimination between the sons of the first husband and those of the subsequent

45 Tod's Annals and Antiquities of Rajsthan. For the family tree of Hammīra see Sanskrit Poetsses by Dr. J. B. Chaudhuri, Appendix.

46 Smṛti, XXIX, 8.

47 Dharma-śāstra, XVII, 18.

48 Smṛti, XV, 7.

49 III, 181.

ones seems to be a later development. However, the Vedic literature is silent about it.[50]

Thus we have shown above that widow-marriage was neither prohibited nor highly recommended in Ancient India.[51] The ideal was a life of celibacy after the demise of the partner in life, failing which a widow might either take recourse to Niyoga or remarriage.

50 From the Mahābhārata it appears that widow-marriage began to fall into disrepute in its time though it was even then, probably, widely in vogue. In the Ādi-Parvan (104), Dīrghátamas is said to have decreed that a woman must not marry a second time.

51 Cf. Vātsyāyana's Kāma-sūtra, 1.5.3.

CHAPTER III

Widow-burning in Ancient India

When in course of time the Indian society did not approve the rites of Niyoga and Widow-marriage,* widows became victims of a cruel intrigue against them, viz., the Suttee or widow-burning. The right of Sahamaraṇa or dying with the husband on the same funeral pyre is certainly not Vedic.[1]

Colebroke in 1795 stated that the Ṛg-vedic verse, X. 18. 7 is "the only Vedic authority for the rite of Satī".[2] But this view is not tenable for two reasons. Firstly, the reading that he accepts cannot be traced. He somewhat followed Raghunandana's reading as is found in the Serampore edition of his works. Then Raghunandana enjoined widow-burning (Sahamaraṇa or Anumaraṇa)

* For these, see Modern Review, November, 1941, pp. 472-473 and January, 1942 pp. 68-71.

1 Some later Smṛtikāras recognise also the Anumaraṇa, i e. the death of a widow after some time as prescribed, though not on the same pyre, in the fire lighted up with the fire preserved from the funernal pyre of the husband. Pregnant widows in an impure state cannot immolate themselves.

2 Miscellaneous Essays. Modern, 1872, 1, 114ff.

on the basis of a wholly wrong Vedic text which runs as follows:—

इमा नारीरविधवाः सुपत्नीराञ्जनेन सर्पिषाऽभिसंविशन्तु ।

अनश्रवोऽनमीवाः सुरत्नाः प्रविशन्तु जनयो योनिमग्नेः ॥

Colebrooke probably got the reading from some Bengali paṇḍita of his own time who knew evidently Raghunandana's reading of the last few words as given here.[3] As the reading followed by Colebrooke cannot be traced anywhere, it is to be rejected altogether. The right reading is:—प्रविशन्तु जनयो योनिमग्नेः ॥[4]

The translations of the verse by Wilson[5] and Max Müller[6] is not satisfactory. The Verse should be translated as follows:—

"Let these women, not widowed, having good husbands, dress their eyes with butter serving as eye-salve; without tears, without disease, well-ornamented, let these wives enter the house first."

3 Caṇḍeśvara about 1400 A.D., quoted the verse as the authority for widow-burning. Caṇḍeśvara cites a corresponding verse from the Brahma-purāṇa as well. So about 1400 A.D. this verse of some Khila Sūkta not now-a-days known beginning as such appears to have passed as an authority for widow-burning.

4 Prof. Wilson's reading, *JRAS.*, vol. XVI, p. 205, सुरत्ना रोहन्तु जनयो योनिमग्रे । Dr. Max Müller accepts this regarding, only correcting Suratnā-rohantu as Suratnā ārohantu.

5 Asiatic Researches, IV, p. 213.

6 Max Müller (Essays, Leipzig, 1869, II, p. 31f) who once

In any case, it cannot have any reference to widow-burning whatsoever.

Secondly, Colebrooke takes it for granted that it is an appropriate mantra uttered during the funeral ceremony. But it is quite otherwise. The ancient authorities on Vedic rites such as Āśvalāyana,[7] the Bṛhad-devatā,[8] the Taittirīya Āraṇyaka,[9] Baudhāyana [10] and Bharadvāja,[11]

thought the verse to be "eine Anspruche an die ubrigen Frauen, die dem Leichenbegangnis beiwohnen und ol und Butter auf Holzstoss zu giessen haben" translated it as:

"Lasst diese Frauen, die keine Witwen sind, sonder gute Manner haben, sich mit ol und Butter nahern. Die welche Mutter sind lasst zuerst zum Altar hinauf schreiten ohne Tranen, ohne Kummer, sonder geschmuckt mit schonen Edelgestein" again translated it as follows in ZDMG., Band IX, p. XXV:—"Es treten ein die Frau'n mit ol und Butter, nicht Witwen sie, nein, stolzauf edle Manner. Die Mutter gehn zuerst hinauf zur statte, in schonen schmuck and ohne Leid und Tranen."

7 Gṛhya-sūtra, IV, 6, 8, The commentators Gārgya Nārāyaṇa and Hardatta Ācārya differ as to the manner of salving the eyes, However, the women are to salve their eyes with bundles of Kuśa stalks and then throw them to their back and then the chief mourners look at them with this verse.

8 VII. 12.

9 VI, 10, 2.

10 Pitṛ-medha-sūtra, ed. in ZDMG, X, No. 3, pp. 28, 1. 21, 11

11 Pitṛ-medha-sūtra ed. in ZDMG, *op. cit.*, pp. 44.1.22.

prescribed it as a mantra to be used during the Śānti -karman which is performed on the tenth day after death. When the relatives of the deceased assemble in the burning ground for the Śānti-karman i. e., the rite for the well-being of the living, a fire is lighted up and all sit down on a bullock-hide.

The chief mourner then offers four oblations to the fire with a spoon made of varuṇa wood. All the relatives then rise up and recite a mantra. The women are then requested to put on collyrium and the chief mourner looks at them while uttering this verse,

In the Atharva-veda too, the verse appears twice (XII.2.2. XVIII.3.57). AV. XII.2,3 appears among verses meant for Śānti, i. e. the appeasing of Agni Kravyāt and for the consecration of the new house-fire. According to the Kauśika-sūtra 72. 11, the verse is used for the preparation of the new domestic fire wherein the women are presented with grass-shoots dipped in butter. Thus it is the same rite as Śānti Karman. A.V. XVIII. 3. 57 is used in connection with ancestral rites. The Kauśika does not mention its specific ritualistic application. Following the other schools, the verse is to be taken as a mantra of the Śānti rite.[12]

12 It is interesting that the Paippalāda recension adds another corresponding verse for the use of men.

As the various Vedic schools mentioned above to which more may be added, all prescribe the verse as an appropriate mantra for the Śānti-karman which is performed ten days after the funeral ceremony, Colebrooke's contention that this verse applies to the funeral ceremony is thus utterly baseless,

Rājā Rādhākānta unhesitatingly declares that the Ṛg-vedic verse X. 18. 8 refers to the Suttee.[13] He says when a Satī lies on the pyre, she intimates her resolution to immolate herself. She is then requested with this verse to come back to the world of the living, but she shows her valour by refusing the requests of her kinsmen. Rādhākanta cites in his support the fact that even at the latest phase of the Satī, the widow is requested by her friends and relatives to live.[14] If even then she remains firm in her determination, she is burnt to death. But this view is not tenable.

The first half of the Ṛg-vedic verse, X.18.8 represents, probably, a relic of widow-burning that was known in the Indo-European period;[15] but nevertheless it shows that widow-

13 Journal of the Royal Asiatic Society, XVII, 1860, p. 215 f.

14 Compare the identical fact in the last act of the Mṛccha katika where the relatives of Cārudatta endeavour to dissuade his wife from her resolution to immolate herself.

15 Schrader, Pre-historic Antiquities, pp. 390-391; Reallexicon der Indogermanischen Altertumskunde, p. 958. For the custom

burning was at the period of the composition of this Ṛg-verse forbidden. A similar relic is also traced in the Atharva-veda (18.3.3)[16] which refers to some rescue of a young wife from self-immolation. In fact, this symbolical burning is self-evident from the ritualistic application of the verse itself. Thus, Baudhāyana says that the wife should lie down on the left side of the corpse. Āśvalāyana recommends that she should be placed near the head of the corpse on the north side. But it must be a matter of ritualistic observance pure and simple as irrespective of the RV.X.18.8 we see that in a subsequent mantra[17] the widow of a Brāhmaṇa is asked to carry in her hand a bit of gold, the widow of a Kṣatriya the bow and the wife of a Vaiśya the jewel which is offered along with the corpse of a Brāhmaṇa, Kṣatriya or Vaiśya respectiveley.[18]

of burning widows among the Northern Indo-Europeans, see V. Nehn's Kulturpflazen und Haustiers, 7th Auft, published by O. Schrader, p. 473 f; for other peoples see p. 533 ff. For the custom prevailing among the ancient Germans, see K. Mullenhoff, Deutsche Altertumskunde, Berlin, 1900, IV, p. 312 f. The custom of widow-burning is found also among the primitive peoples; cf. Ploss-Bartels, Das Weib in der Natur und Volkerkunde, 9, Aufl., II, p. 672 ff.

16 Harvard Oriental Series, Vol. 8, p. 849.

17 Taittirīya Āraṇyaka VI, 1.

18 The opinion of one of the scholiasts of Āśvalāyana (IV, 2, 17-18) slighly varies here.

The Atharva-veda[19] clearly shows that the wife comes back to a life of prosperity and bliss with children. The Rig-vidhāna says[20] a brother-in-law (Devara) should dissuade his sister-in-law from ascending the funeral pyre of the dead husband. The A-recension of the Bṛhad-devatā shows that this is the verse uttering which the younger brother of the husband dissuades the widow lying on the funeral pyre by the side of the deceased husband from burning herself to death.[21]

Thus it is clear that all the Sūtra Texts and other Vedic works prescribe that the wife should lie down by the side of her husband and she is to be raised up and is to return to the world of the living.[22] This verse can therefore by no means refer to Widow-burning.

Again, the silence of the entire Sūtra Literature, Buddhist Literature, Megasthenes, Kauṭilya and early

19 XVIII, 2, 1. 20 III, 8, 4.

21 VII, 13-15. The B-recension, however, seems to have been tampered with; or probably, it simply notices a later development; it says that the widow-burning is optional in the case of other castes than the Brāhmaṇa. The burning of Brāhmaṇa widows is, however, a heinous crime.

22 Only the later popular works such as the Paddhatis and Prayogas mention that "the raising up of the wife" (Utthāpana) is applicable to those cases only where the wives are not willing to immolate themselves.

Smārtas such as Manu and Yājnavalkya confirm that this abominable custom was not in vogue in India even in their times.

There is ample proof to show that even in later times when widow-burning became a religious practice in some parts of the country, well-known Smārtas as well as literary giants denounced it as strongly as possible. Thus, Medhātithi in his commentary on Manu vehemently protests against the custom and considers it wholly opposed to the Vedas.[23] Virāṭ as quoted by Aparārka on Yājñavalkya 1-87[24] also holds the same view emphasising that the Suttee is simply committing suicide for nothing; it means totally ignoring wifely duties for which a Suttee is liable to religious penalties. Bāṇabhaṭṭa opposed the custom tooth and nail.[25]

It is thus proved conclusively that widow-burning is not Vedic. It is not Tantrika either.

The Tantras hold a very important position from the point of religious practice in particular. They as a rule denounce the Suttee or Saha-maraṇa rite. Thus the Mahānirvāṇa-tantra[26] declares the Suttee a criminal; by following the husband on the funeral pyre, she herself paves her way to hell.

23 V. 157,
24 Ānandāśrama Sanskrit Series ed. Poona, 1903-1904. vol. I.
25 Kādambarī, pūrvārdha, Kale's edition, pp. 264-265.
26 X. 80.

Thus the rite of Saha-maraṇa is neither Vedic nor Tantric. It is at best Paurānic.

In the Mahābhārata, there is a single solid instance of widow-burning,[27] viz., that of Mādrī. But it is clear that her self-immolation was not at all prompted by religious considerations, for paving the way of the husband and his ancestors to heaven but on personal considerations pure and simple.[28] All the sages present tried to dissuade her from this ignoble act. Again in the original portion of the Rāmāyaṇa viz. Books II-IV, there is no reference to the Suttee rite. The instance of Vedavatī's mother in the Uttara-kāṇḍa (17.14) refers to a much later date. The burning of the widow as a religious rite did not develop certainly in the epic age about 5th century B.C.

Presumably this rite came in to existence about the beginning of the Christian era or soon after. In the fourth century A.D. in Kālidāsa's Kumāra-saṃbhava (Canto IV) Rati is depicted as ready to follow Madana on the funeral pyre. The incident in the last act of Śūdraka's Mṛcchakaṭika also represents this age. Subsequently a few centuries later this abominable custom is shown as receiving the support of some law-givers such as Aṅgiras,[29]

27 cf. also Mahābhārata, 1, 174, 44 f.; XI, 26, 28 ff; XVI, 7, 18, 24, 73 f.

28 MBH, 1, 138, 71-72.

29 Quoted by Aparārka on Yājñavallkya, 1, 87.

Vṛddhahārīta,[30] etc.[31] By the fourteenth century A. D. attempts seem to have been made even to adulterate the ancient texts such as the Mahābhārata and the Parāśara-smṛti. The verses "Avamatya tu yāḥ". and "Bhartranu-maraṇa-kāle" etc., attributed by Mādhava in his Parāśara-Mādhaviya on Parāśara-smṛti[32] are not traceable in the Mahābhārata. Verses IV, 31-32 of the Parāśara-smṛti which advocate widow-burning somewhat contradict the last but one verse (IV-29).

Raghunandana managed to find out even Vedic sanction for this custom as we have shown before. Instances of Suttee of this and subsequent times may by heaped up from various sources.[33]

It seems that for some reason or other widow-burning was resorted to by Kṣatriya-women, particularly for getting rid of the oppression of the invaders.

30 Verse 201.

31 Bṛhaspati, 24, 11; Vyāsa-smṛti, II. 52; Vijñāneśvara on Yājñavallkya, 1, 86.

32 IV, 32,

33 Caṇḍeśvara's Vivāda-ratnākara, Bibliotheca Indica, pp. 440-445; Daśakumāra-carita, IV.; Bāṇa's Harṣa-carita, at the death of Prabhākara Vardhana; and other references Kathā-sarit-sāgara, 9; Kalhaṇa's Rāja-taraṅgiṇi, many instances. For an account of the latest phase of the Suttee, the travelling accounts of Foreigners in India are instructive and interesting, though at times exaggerated.

It is significant in connection with the spread of this custom that some invaders such as the Hūṇas and the Scythians considered widow-burning as religious. Scythian rule in Northern India must have helped the spread of the Satī rite there. The example of the rulers in particular is bound to be followed at times by the people at large. The other reason seems to be that some widows, at the moment of their deepest grief, could not think they would be able to live without their husbands and had recourse to self-immolation. Their example, considered as noble, was also sometimes followed. By and by the Saha-maraṇa rite gained popularity and public approbation and subsequently, religious sanction in some parts of the country.

Thus neither the Vedas nor the Tantras sanction the Saha-maraṇa rite. The ceremonial procedure of the rite has, however, been detailed in the Purāṇas such as the Padma-purāṇa.[34] As such, the Saha-maraṇa may be called only Pauranic.

34 Pātāla-khaṇḍa, 102, 67 ff.

CHAPTER IV

The Widow In The Vedic Ritual.*

Miscellaneous rites

As the Sahamaraṇa rite is not at all Vedic, it cannot affect the position of the widow from the point of view of Vedic ritual. But it is of interest to note that even in later times widow-burning is sanctioned as an alternative course to be followed by those who are afraid of widowhood. Preference is always given to Brahmacarya[1]. Manu is absolutely silent about widow-burning and recommends Brahmacarya as the highest duty of widow[2]. Viṣṇu, mentioning the Brahmacarya before Anvārohaṇa, shows that he prefers the former to the later[3]. The Agni-purāṇa also upholds the same view[4]. Devaṇṇabhaṭṭa in the Vyavahāra-kāṇḍa of his Smṛti-candrikā specifically points out that a

* Prabuddha Bharata, Feb. 1942, pp. 79-81.

1 Cf. the Mantras she utters: वैधव्यभयपीडिता, etc.

2 V 157 H.

कामं तु क्षपयेद्देहं फलमूलजलैः शुभैः ।
न तु नामापि गृह्णीयात् पत्यौ प्रेते परस्य तु ॥ V. 150
मृते भर्तरि साध्वी स्त्री ब्रह्मचर्ये व्यवस्थिता ।
स्वर्गं गच्छत्यपुत्राऽपि यथा ते ब्रह्मचारिणः ॥ V. 160

3 XXV. 14.

4 221. 23.

life of celibacy is certainly preferable[5]. The religious injunction that Brahmin widows should not immolate themselves shows that widow-burning is not commendable except under special circumstances[6]. Leading a celibate life is thus the highest Dharma for the widower as well as the widow. Just as the wife is considered Vidhavā after her husband's death, the widower is also considered Vidhava[7] (really, without a wife) after the death of his wife if he has no sons of

5 तद्धर्मान्तरमपि ब्रह्मचर्यधर्माज्जघन्यं निकृष्टफलत्वात् ॥

6 The B-recension of the Bṛhad-devatā, ed. by Macdonell, VII. 15: वर्णानामितरेषां च स्त्रीधर्मोऽयं भवेन्न वा । Padma-purāṇa, Sṛṣṭi-khaṇḍa, XLIX. 72-73.

न म्रियेत समं भर्त्रा ब्राह्मणी ब्रह्मशासनात् ।
प्रव्रज्यागतिमाप्नोति मरणादात्मघातिनी ॥
नरोत्तम उवाच—सर्वासामेव जातीनां ब्राह्मणः श्रेष्ठ उच्यते ।
पुण्यं च द्विजमुख्येन अत्र किं वा विपर्ययः ॥ भगवान् उवाच—
ब्राह्मण्याः साहसं कर्म नैव कार्यं कदाचन ।
निःशेषेऽस्या वधं कृत्वा स नरो ब्रह्महा भवेत् ॥

Hārita, Gautama, Angiras, and Vyāsa recommended Sahamaraṇa for all widows except Brāhmaṇīs. In much later times, however, the rule became somewhat relaxed; see Aparārka on Yājñavalkya, I. 87; Mādhava on Parāśara, IV. 31; etc.

7 For the etymological interpretation of धव see Yāska, III. 15 —विधवनाद्वा । विधवनाद्वेति चर्मशिराः । अपि वा धव इति मनुष्यनाम तद्वियोगाद्विधवा । As धव means मनुष्य, both man and woman, the husband is विधव when he loses his wife.

excellent behaviour, versed in the Śruti, etc.[8] The lot of a widower is as unfortunate as that of widow; it is the losing of the equal half of life that renders either of them equally unfit for religious observances unless otherwise authorised. Just like a widow, a widower, too, is debarred from all religious affairs.[9] A widower is not entitled to be entertained in the Śrāddha ceremony, just as the widow is not entitled to cook food for ancestors during the Śrāddha.[10]

In the Vedic ritual the rights of the widower and the widow are perfectly counterbalanced. The surviving half performs the funeral and Śrāddha ceremonies for the departed half, provided the two have no children.[11] In case of

8 Smṛtīnāṃ Samuccayaḥ, Ānandaśarma Series, p. 93, verse 78—

यस्य पुत्राः सदाचाराः श्रुतिज्ञा धर्मसंमुखाः ।
पितृभक्तिरता दान्ता न वैधव्यं मृतस्त्रियि ॥

9 *Op. cit.*, verse. 77, अप्रजो मृतपत्नीकः सर्वकर्मसु गर्हितः । Widows are not allowed to participate in sacrificial matters, specially in wedding ceremonies (Sāṅkhāyana-gṛhya-sūtra, II. 5; I. 12. 1.) Old Brāhmin women, however, have some access as they are taken into consultation (*ibd.*, 1.14.8) in cases of doubt about rituals.

10 Pāraskara-gṛhya-sūtra, p. 437 of the Bombay edition, I.8.9; Ṛsyaśṛṅga and Jābāla quoted in the Śraddha-sūtra-kaṇḍikā, *op. cit.*, p. 442.

11 Śrāddha-sūtra-kaṇḍikā, Pāraskara-gṛhya-sūtra, Bombay edition, p. 462. I. 18. Smṛti-candrikā, Śrāddhha-kāṇḍa, p. 9 रेवं

their death without any issue, only the Ekoddiṣṭa Śrāddha is performed for either of them.[12] Even though they have children, either of them is to offer water-libation to the departed one.[13] Either survivor (he or she) performs the ancestral rites to appease the ancestors. The rights of the widow are by no means curtailed as she can offer Śrāddha to both sides, her husband's as will as her parents',[14] just as the widower does; the manes (Pitṛs) too, are six in number as usual in Śrāddhas unless the Śrāddha is an Ekoddiṣṭa one. She also perfoms four Pārvaṇa Śrāddhas in the sacred places or on the Mahālayā, etc.; and herein,

etc. Śrāddha-mayūkha, p. 20; also p. 24, अपुत्रा पुत्रवत् पत्नी पुत्रकार्यं समाचरेत् etc; Śrāddha-kriyā-kaumudī, p. 456, 1.7. f; also p. 459. 1.18 f. भार्या and particularly. l. 30 f, Śrāddha-viveka, ऊर्ध्वांस्तु, etc. भार्यापिण्डं पतिः कुर्याद्भर्त्रे भार्या तथैव च etc.; also p. 462, 1. 17 and p. 464. 1. 8. Śrāddha-mañjarī, Ānandāaśrama Sanskrit Series, vol. LIX Poona 1909, p. 110, पत्नीश्राद्धे तु etc. Karma-kāṇḍa-pradīpa, Bombay 1921, p. 425, सर्वबन्धुविहीनस्य, etc. etc.

12 Śrāddha-mayūkha, Collection of Hindu Law Books, vol. XVIII, p. 25, सपिण्डीकरणादूर्ध्वं, etc. Śrāddha-kriyā-kaumudī, p. 462, इति मार्कण्डेयपुराणे अपुत्रपुंवदपुत्रे स्त्रीणां, etc.

13 Śrāddha-kriyā-kaumudi, p. 456, I. 14. cf. Śrāddha-mañjarī, Poona 1909, p. 117, अपुत्रस्य विधवा पत्नी, etc.

14 Śrāddha-manjari, p. 115, स्वभर्तृप्रभृतित्रिभ्यः, etc. etc.

too, she worships the ancestors of both sides.[15] Just as in the case of the widower, all the male ancestors are worshipped along with their departed wives, if any of the ancestors has one half still surviving, she does not reckon the other half as a mane but worships the immediately preceding three as manes along with their deceased wives. The ritualistic procedure or Prayoga that she follows is exactly the same as that of the widower.[16] She is not debarred even from performing the Vṛddhi Śrāddha[17] which very few persons are entitled to perform. Thus while performing a Śrāddha, she uses an upper garment as the third sacred thread hanging over her right shoulder, and she herself perfoms all rites pertaining to the Sāṃvatsarika or other Śrāddhas.[18] In an Ekoddiṣṭa Śrāddha, she performs all the rites up to the Saṃkalpa and may then permit a

15 *Op. cit.*, p. 115, चत्वारि पार्वणानि, etc,

16 Cf. the 'Prayoga' as has been given in full in the Śrāddha-mañjari p. 115. f.

17 Srāddha-manjari, *op. cit.*, यदि विधवा, etc. Cf. वाजपेय-याजि-पद्धति as quoted therein.

18 For this and the following details, see *op. cit.*, p. 117;

स्वभर्तृप्रभृतित्रिभ्यः स्वपितृभ्यस्तथैव च ।

विधवा कारयेच्छ्राद्धं यथाकालमतन्द्रिता ॥

Smṛti-samuccaya; also quoted in the Śrāddha-manjari, p. 115.

priest to complete the rest on her behalf.[19] Of course she may herself perform the whole ceremony if she likes. If she permits a Brahmin to perform it, she alternately puts on the sacred thread on her left or right shoulder just as the priest does[20]. In the ritual literature nowhere is there any suggestion to debar her from performing any rite that a widower may perform.

During the lifetime of the husband, the wife is not required to fast nor is she entitled to observe any rite in her own exclusive right, just as the husband also cannot do so in his own. But after the death of either of them they perform several rites as mentioned above, apparently separately, but really the rites are performed for the acquirement of religious merit by them both, and neither of them is entitled in this lifetime or after the death of either to perform any rite for individual good. In her lifetime as well as after her death the wife is the only religious partner of the husband. The widower cannot disgrace his deceased wife in any way; on the other hand, her memory is to be cherished throughout the rest of his life in all religious matters.

The above principle is also upheld by the Purāṇas,

19 कंचिद् ब्राह्मणमृत्विक्त्वेन परिकल्प्य तं ब्रूयात् ममाज्ञया त्वमिद-मसुकश्राद्धाख्यं कर्म कुर्विति ।

20 Śrāddha mañjari, p. 113.

according to which, after the death of either the husband or the wife, he or she should, apart from observing the rites mentioned above, also observe the Trirātri-vrata, the vows for gifts, sacred bath, etc., the Ekādaśī-vrata, Dvādaśī-vrata as well as the Trayodaśī-vrata[21] for their common good.

Such stringent rules as are found in the Śuddhi-tattva of Raghunandana, Yama-saṃhitā (ii.53) etc. are only later growths, not at all warranted by the Vedic custom. These rigidities were not known in the Vedic days, when women were shown every possible consideration in social as well as religious matters. Regarding tonsure, it may be noted, that it must have evolved at a very late period. The Mahābhārata (XV.27.16), the Brahmavaivaratapurāṇa (83.101), etc. do not advise the widows to shave off their heads; in the former, widows are found arranging their hair, whereas in the latter they are simply advised not to dress it. The Śambhu-saṃhitā, Hayagrīva-saṃhita, and Manu-saṃhitā[22] (not the Mānavadharma-śāstra) are strongly opposed to the observance of this rite. Vedavyāsa (1.53), Mādhavācārya, Anantadeva, etc., who support this, are all later authors whose opinions do not count against the Vedic authority.

21 Skanda-pūrāṇa, Kāśī-khaṇḍa (Vaṅgavāsī ed.). p. 2072 ff.

22 Indian Antiquary, vol. III, pp. 136-137.

Thus it is shown that from the ritual point of view both the widower and the widow are, no doubt, under certain obligations, but none is more handicapped than the other from the social and religious points of view. Failing in cherishing the memory of the other half for the rest of life, either may remarry; but such marriage is of no religious importance whatsoever. The rites performed by or for them are just the same as in the Vedic ritualistic literature; there is no connivance at or partiality for either party.

CHAPTER V

The Mother

The Vedic Ritual shows that the Mother and the Father are one and the same in Life as well as after death, but so far as the children are concerned, they are to respect their Mother a thousand times more than they do their father.

If the Mother really becomes One with her husband by means of the Marriage and Cathurthīhoma Mantras,[1] how can it be proper that her Sapiṇḍīkaraṇa should be performed with the mention of her father's Gotra and not her husband's?

Āpastamba[2] says the young of the Cuckoos, depending upon others for livelihood, return to their parents after perfect development; so do women after their death. At the end of a year the son should perform the Sapiṇḍana for the mother with the Maternal grand father as the mane just as he should perform for the father with the paternal grand father, says Uśanas.[3] The Bhaviṣyapurāṇa[4] says the

1 Commentary on *Gobh. GS.*, p. 355, l. 10-14.

2 Hemādri, Pariśeṣakhaṇḍa, p. 1654.

3 This verse occurs in the Brahmāṇḍapurāṇa and has also been quoted by Kṛṣṇamiśra in the Śrāddhakāśikā, *Par. GS.*, Bom. ed. p. 499, l. 14 and also by Śūlapāṇi in the Śrāddhavivekasaṃgraha, p. 265. l. 12.

4 Hemādri, *op. cit.*

offerings should be given to the mother with the mention of her father's gotra, not her husband's; in birth as well as in danger women resort to their fathers.

The opinion of these Authorities is, however, clearly opposed to that of equally outstanding Authorities. According to Yama,[1] the Sapiṇḍana of the mother should be performed with the mention of her husband's Gotra and name. Hārīta[2] says the woman loses her father's Gotra in the seventh step during her marriage; (*so*) the offerings of cakes and water to her should be made with the mention of her Husband's gotra. Bṛhaspati, as quoted by Hemādri in the Śrāddhakalpa,[3] says the woman should be offered the cakes and water in her husband's Gotra.

The disputed nature of the question becomes still more manifest when the same Uśanas is found quoted by both the schools of thought. He is found on the side of the latter school when he says "Ekatvaṃ sā gatā bhartuḥ piṇḍe gotre ca sūtake. Tasmād Udakapiṇḍau tu bhartṛgotreṇa nirvapet; She has been One with her husband in Piṇḍa, Gotra, Sūtaka; therefore, the offering of cake and water should be made to her in the Gotra of her husband."

1 The comparisons that the Purāṇa gives in this connection are marvellous.

2 Hemādri, p. 1651.

3 P. 1651; also Śūlapāṇi in the Śrāddhaviveka, p. 256.

The Antyeṣṭyarka[1] says in connection with the Sapiṇḍanaprayoga "Mātuḥ sapiṇḍīkaraṇaṃ... *amukagotrābhiḥ* asmatpitāmahīprapitāmahīvṛddhaprapitāmahībhiḥ......sapiṇḍīkaraṇaṃ kariṣye". Here, "Amukagotrābhiḥ: with *all* of the Gotra N. N." shows that the Mothers all belong to the same Gotra. Unless they all belong to the Bhartṛgotra, it cannot be expected that all the three Mothers would have the same Gotra, because all of them are not likely to belong to the same Pitṛgotra; as coming from different families, it is only likely that their Pitṛgotra would vary. Therefore, the Mothers have their Bhartṛgotra after death.

Nārāyaṇa Bhaṭṭa in his Antyeṣṭikriyāpaddhati[2] says in regard to the Sapiṇḍīkaraṇa of the mother (the sacrificer is to make the Saṃkalpa like this): "I shall mix together the water of the vessel consecrated to the Preta of Gaṅgā of the Bhāradvājagotra with that of the Arghyapātras consecrated to Kṛṣṇadā, Veṇīdā and Narmadā[3] (all) of the Bhāradvājagotra, the mother, grand-mother and great-grand-mother of the husband of the Preta respectively, who represent Vasu,

1 F. 56, 1.9. F. 57, 1. 1f; also F. 58b, 1.2.f.

2 F. 197a, 1.4 f.

3 "Dā" is always to be added as a suffix to the name of females whenever they are used in Rituals; *Man. GS.*, p. 83, 1. 11-14.

etc."[1] Here, too, the Mother, who is a Preta now and all the three mothers-in-law are addressed as "of the Bhāradvāja Gotra." Because of the reasons mentioned above, the Gotra used here cannot but be the Gotra of their husbands. So they cannot but belong to their husband's Gotra.

The Maiden walking round the Fire in the Sākamedha Ritual expresses her ardent desire to be severed from her father's family and Gotra and be parmanent in the husband's Gotra.[2]

The Smṛti[3] says that by means of the Mantras uttered during the Caturthīhoma the wife unites with her husband-skin with skin, flesh with flesh, heart with heart, senses with senses: therefore, she belongs to his Gotra. Bṛhaspati[4] lays

1 The mother of the husband represents Vasu; his grand-mother the Rudra; his great-grand-mother the Āditya. Their husbands, too, represent the same deities. This also shows that the husband and the wife are One Soul and cannot have different Gotras after death.

2 See Mahidhara as quoted in part I, p. 10 of this Thesis.

3 *Gobh. GS.*, Bib. Ind., p. 355. 1. 10-11.

4 Hemādri, Śrāddhakalpa, p. 1651;

चतुर्थीहोममन्त्रैस्तु मांसमज्जास्थिभिः सह ।
एकत्वमागता भर्त्तुस्तस्मात्तद्गोत्रभागिनी ॥
पाणिग्रहणिका मन्त्राः पितृगोत्रापहारकाः ।
भर्त्तुर्गोत्रेण नारीणां देयं पिण्डोदकन्ततः ॥

Śūlapāṇi, *op. cit.*, p. 265.

particular stress on the Marriage Mantras in this connection. And in fact the Marriage and Caturthīkarma Mantras are decisive in this matter. "Your heart is my heart and my heart is your heart"-these sanctifying and soul-stirring Mantras would be meaningless if the Sapiṇḍīkaraṇa of the mother is performed with the mention of the father's Gotra.

So the use of the Mātāmahagotra during the Mātṛsapiṇḍana is rather an accident than a rule.

Baudhāyana and Yajñapārśva as quoted by Śūlapāṇi in his Śrāddhavivekasaṃgraha[1] recommend the use of the Mātāmahagotra if the Sapiṇḍīkaraṇa is performed by the son of a Putrikā. He should invoke with the first cake (Piṇḍa) his mother, with the second his mother's father, with the third his mother's father's father. A daughter is made Putrikā for the benefit of the father; she is given in marriage on the express condition that the children she will produce will perform as his own children all the religious rites.

Vyāsa[2] says, no doubt in this marriage, too, (i.e. of a Putrikā) the wife becomes One with her husband after her marriage, but as soon as she produces a child, she ceases to be One with him.

1 P. 265, 1. 15-16.

2 *Op. cit.*, Hemādri, p. 1656.

According to Vṛddhaśātātapa[1] the Sapindīkaraṇa of the mother married in accordance with one of the base forms of marriage (āsurādi)[2] should be offered in her father's gotra. The Śrāddhamayūkha[3] cites the Authority of the Mitākṣarā, etc. in support of this view. Hemādri in the Śrāddhakalpa[4] says that as in such a case the daughter is not offered to the bridegroom by the father of his own accord after the relinquishment of all his claims, she cannot be forcibly taken out of her father's family and Gotra. Śātātapa says, her Sapiṇḍana should be offered with her mother, grand-mother and great-grand-mother (on the father's side). The Madanapārijāta,[5] too upholds this view. Hemādri is of opinion that the Family Tradition should, however, be followed, and if it is in accordance with the Family Tradition, the mother's Sapiṇḍīkaraṇa should be offered along with the utterance of the Gotra of Maternal grand-father. It will be seen in this connection that these Authorities mention this rather as a concession than as a recommendation, and as such, it is only a Gauṇadharma.

The mother by all means retains her husband's Gotra and remains One with her husband after death, but deserves

1 As quoted by Śrāddhakāśikākāra, *Pār. GS.*, Bom. ed. p. 505, 1.14.

2 See Introd , J. B. Chaudhuri's Saṁbandha-viveka.

3 P. 86, 1.

4 P. 1655, 1.

5 P. 275, 1.15.

6 Śrāddhakalpa, p. 1656, 1.

preferential treatment from her children for the pain she undergoes during the pregnancy and in rearing them, and most probably, for the incomparable love and affection she has for her children which the father seems to develop in course of association with the children. The Love of the mother towards children is spontaneous and natural, and is not based on any earthly selfish end. The Mother is the embodiment of all Blessings from Heaven, all Hope, Ambition, and Devotion on Earth; she is the Sum Total of all Religious Merit for the child, as it were.

From the beginning of her conception, the mother undergoes a series of saṃskāras for various purposes, but always with one object in common—the welfare of the child. In the prebirth saṃskāras the father no doubt joins, but as these are Strī-saṁskāras, his participation signifies nothing more than helping the mother in the proper performance and observance of these rites. His service is dispensable in as much as in his absence the brother-in-law or some body else may join in the performance in his stead; but someone must help her as she, during her pregnancy, is ritualistically impure and cannot be supposed to offer the oblations, etc.[1]

1 *Saṃs. RM.*, p. 813, 1. 10f; *Drab GS.*, ii. 18; Kumārila, p. 291, 1. 12-13; for the injunctions the mother has to follow during her pregnancy, see *op. cit.*, p. 815, 1. 144ff.

In the fourth month[1] of her pregnancy[2] she has the rite for securing the safety of the embryo performed. Her limbs are besmeared with a salve of clarified butter along with the utterance of prayers[3] for having all sorts of maladies removed from every part of her body. According to Āśvalāyana as quoted in the Saṁ May.,[4] she remains lying in the shadow of the Fire-shed and a kind of herb named Ajitā is put into her nostrils. Śaunaka[5] mentions while she remains in the above-mentioned place, a girl (kanyā) should press some dūrvā-grass in the stones along with the sprinkling of water and get the juice out of it. The husband takes it, touches her, and murmurs the Prajāvat[6] and Jīvaputra[7] hymns. Having stood to the west of the wife he now pours into her right nostril the Dūrvā juice in such a way that it passes into her stomach. She then

1 Also not mentioned in the Āgniveśyasūtra, Trivandrum, 40.

2 According to the Vaijavāpagṛhya as quoted in the Saṃskāramayūkha, p. 20; and the SamMay., itself, this Anavalobhana may be performed together with the Puṃsavana or soon after it.

3 According to the Sank. School; *RV*., X, 863; cf. *Sams. RM.*, vol. II, p. 820, 1, If.

4 In the *GS*., he simply refers to some Upaniṣad. Śaunaka mentions this rite has been mentioned in Yajñopaniṣad, F. 23.

5 *MS*. Buhler, 4785 (I.O.L.), F. 24.

6 *Āśv. GS*., I, 13, 6; cf. *Āp. GS*., III, i, 13; *Hir. GS*., I, 25, 1.

7 *Āśv. GS*., I, 13, 6; cf. *Pār. GS*., I, 5, II; *Hir. GS*., I, 19, 7; *Āp. GS*., II, 5, 2.

sips water and keeps on touching the husband while he offers the oblation. Then the husband touches her heart with his (right) palm and prays for long life and welfare.[1] According to Śaunaka, this rite should be repeated in each pregnancy.

She takes particular care that the embryo may develop[2] and not fall. If there is any miscarriage,[3] the husband strokes her body from the navel upwards with wetted hand and prays for the long life of the mother as well as of the child.

In the third[4] or fourth[5] month of her pregnancy or even later[6] she observes the Puṃsavana rite.

1 Yat te susīme hṛdaye hitam, etc. This Mantra is also used during the Sīmantonnayana, cf. *Pār. GS.* I, II. 9.

2 *Saṃs. RM.*, p. 819, 1. 24ff.

3 *Op. cit.*, p. 820, 1. 7ff: *Hir. GS.*, 2.2.7, also quoted in *op. cit.*

4 *Gobh. GS.*, 2, 1.6; *Khād. GS.*, 2.2.17; *Pār. GS.*, 2nd or 3rd month; *Vār. GS.*, XVI, 5, p. 45 of Vīra's *ed.*; Kumārila: 4th month during the first pregnancy, 3rd month in others; *Jaim. GS.*, I, 5; 3rd month in the first pregnancy, 4th in others; *Bhār. GS.*, 1, 22 (p. 22) 3rd month or beginning of the 4th; *Saṃs. RM.*, vol. 2, p. 811 II, 3rd month; Vaijavāpagṛhya, as quoted in the Saṃskāramayūkha, p. 20: 2nd or 3rd: Jatukaranyā, *op. cit.*, 2nd or 3rd. Śaunaka, F. 23, 2nd or 3rd.

5 *Vaik. GS.*, III, II.

6 *Kāth. GS.*, 32, 2, p. 134: Devapāla, 8th moth; Brahm., 7th or 8th; Āditya, 8th month. *Āp. GS.*, XIV, 9; *Baudh. GS.*,

The earliest reference to the rite is found in AV. Here in III. 23[1] a charm has been prescribed wherein an arrow should be broken over the mother's head for procuring the child as desired. According to VI, II,[2] a rite for Puṃsavana, fire is generated between Śamī and Aśvattha and is variously applied to the pregnant woman. The AV. also prescribes a ritual[3] to be offered with an oblation in the lap of a woman desirous of offspring; in other places[4] a different ritual has been described.

According to the Vārāha school, she is wrapped up in an unwashed cloth, and the powder of the Nyagrodha shoot is poured into her right nostril. Then the husband touches her right abdomen with the prayer for the fulfiment of the object.

According to the Kāṭhaka school, Sthālīpāka oblations and Homas are offered thrice to Agni, Indra and Viṣṇu for having the child as desired.

I. 10, 1f (p. 29) when the pregnancy has become visible. cf. various authorities quoted in the Saṃskāramayūkha, and *Saṃs. RM., op. cit.* For the expiation to be made if the proper time expires, see *Drā. GS.*, II, 24; cf. Rudraskanda on *Drā. GS.*. II, 13.

1 Cf. Kaus. 35, 3.

2 Cf. Kaus., 35, 8.

3 VII, 17, cf. Kaus., 35, 16; VII, 19, cf. Kauś., 35, 17.

4 III, 23; VI, II, VII, 17; 19.

Vaikhānasa says she should sit, during the performance of the rite in the forenoon, to the west of the fire.[1] The husband gives her some barley-corns mixed with mustard-seed or their substitute, beans and grain-corns. Her belly is touched after which she partakes of the threefold food, a mixture of equal quantities of milk, sour curds and melted butter.

Bhāradvāja says a maiden should pound a Nyagrodha shoot in the mill-stones ; this pounded shoot should be poured into her right nostril when she, to the west of the fire, keeps her head up towards the east. She reciprocates her husband's wish for having the child.

According to Hiraṇyakeśin the husband should give her a barley-grain in her right hand and two mustard seeds, or two beans on both sides of the grain and pour a drop of curd on them which she eats. The following ritual is the same as in Vaikhānasa. The Baudhāyana school prescribes quite a different ritual.[2] The husband first offers oblations with cooked food and then oblation with clarified butter

1 The place she occupies and the position she takes have been variously mentioned. Place: *Āśv. GS.*, I, 13.5: in the shadow of a round apartment; *Gobh. GS.*, II, 6, 10; to the west of the fire; cf. *Āp. GS.*, 14, 11; *Drā. GS.*, II, 23. Position; *Hir. GS.*, II, 1, 2, 6: she keeps her head on the root of an udumbara tree; *Āp. GS.*, 14, 11: she lies on her back.

2 I, 10, If; p. 29.

with prayers for children.[1] Then he anoints her face four times with the remnant of clarified butter along with the utterance of the prescribed hymns.[2] According to the School of Āśvalāyana as described by Kumārila[3] and Śaunaka,[4] she should, after her bath and wearing two washed clothes, adorn herself with garlands, etc., and also observe the rite Kautukabandha.[5] The husband now begins to offer the oblation. After the Anuyāja, she sips water, sits with her face towards the east to the right side of the husband and keeps on touching him while he finishes oblation. Then she washes her (right) hand, stretches it and touches with it two beans and one barley mixed with curd. The husband asks her thrice what she is drinking, to which she replies thrice "Giving birth to the child (as desired)". She now drinks the curd together with grain-corns and the barley and sips water; she twice drinks the curd. She again carefully washes her mouth.[6]

According to Gobhila and Khādira she should sit, after her bath and dressing, on the Kuśa grass pointed northwards with her face to the East. The husband stands behind her and touches her uncovered navel with his hand

1 गर्भोस्योषधीनां, etc.

2 *Tait. Saṃh.*, III, 2. 3, 4.   3 Gṛhyakārikā, 1, 5, p. 269f.

4 MS. Bühler (I.O.L), 4785, F. 85.

5 This rite has been described in this Manuscript, F. 19f.

6 For the significance, See p. 231 of Gṛhyakārikā, 1. 4-5.

stretched over her shoulder.[1] The husband now puts into her nostril the Nyagrodha shoot which was purchased in due form and pounded beforehand by himself[2] or a young girl[3] or a student or a wife who is keeping a vow, or a Brahmabandhu.

According to Jaimini[4] she mutters, after she has been offered the beans and barley together with a drop of sour milk, the prayer for having the child, female or male as desired on this occasion, and also for bringing forth together with her husband long lived children (on later occasions). Then she fastens with two threads, one white and the other red, a Nyagrodha shoot having fruits and bears it on her neck.

According to the majority of authorities, she should perform this rite in each pregnancy.[5]

1 *Gobh. GS.*, II, 2, 6; *Khād. GS.*, II, 2, 19; cf. Mantra Brāhmaṇa, 1, 4, 8.

2 Cf. San., 1, 20, 3; *Hir. GS.*, II, 1, 2, 6.

3 *Khād. GS.*, II, 2, 22 mentions Brāhmaṇi instead of a Brahmabandhu; cf. Gobhila II, 6, 9. Cf. *Āp, GS.*, VI, 14, 11; "A girl" only.

4 I, 5.

5 Compare the Commentators on *Pār. GS.*, 1, 14; Saṃskāra-mayūkha, p. 20, etc.

In the 3rd or 4th month[1] or later[2] the Sīmantonnayana, the rite of parting the hair, is performed[3] for her.

In the morning she is bathed with water mixed with all the auspicious things (Māṅgalyaḥ) and dressed excellently.[4] According to Gobhila, she should, after her dressing, talk with a Brāhmaṇa. When the rite begins,

1 Āgniveśya-gṛhya-sūtra, Trivandrum, 1940, प्रथमगर्भायाश्चतुर्थे मासि, etc.

2 *Kāth. GS.*, p. 129, 3rd month; *Vār. GS.*, XVI, O, 5th, 6th or 7th; *Āśv. GS.*, *Hir. GS.*, *Bhār. GS.*, *Baudh. GS.*, and *Āp. GS.*, 4th month; *Gobh.*, *GS.*, 4th or 5th; *Drā. GS.*, (II. 24), 4th or 6th; *Pār. GS.*, 6th or 8th *Śān. GS.*, 7th; *Vaik. GS.*, 8th; *Jai. GS.*, 4th, 6th or 8th; *Mān. GS.*, 77, 1. 1. 6th or 8th; Kumārila (p. 271), 4th; Samskarāpaddhati, p. 53, any time beginning from the 4th month till the end of the pregnancy; Vaijavāpa, as quoted in *Sams. RM.*, p. 820, 4th, 5th or 6th; Yajn., 6th or 8th; Atri, 8th or 9th; Śaṅkha, when the foetus quivers till the birth of the child; Bṛhaspati, 4th, 6th or 8th (Solar month); for other Smṛti Authorities, see p. 821, *Sam. SRM.*, Prayogaratna, F. 68, 1. 7, 4th, 6th or 8th; Karmakāṇḍapradipa, F. 67a, 1. 4. 6th or 8th. This rite, according to several Authorities, need not be performed on each occasion of her pregnancy; Saṃskārapaddhati, p. 53, 1. 6-7. Pāraskara and his Commentators think it should be. For this difference in opinion, cf. Saṃskāramayūkha, p. 21.

3 Cf. Āditya's note on Laugākṣi's Text "Kārayate", *Kāth. GS.*, p. 129 f.

4 *Var. GS.*, p. 45, 1. 12; *Drā. GS.*, II, 25; she should be clothed by the husband. According to Vaikhānasa, she should be adorned and perfumed, p. 44, 1. 11.

she, according to several schools, sits to the west of the fire with her face to the East[1]; according to others,[2] behind the fire. According to ŚāṅGH.,[3] and JaimGS.,[4] she should keep on touching the husband while he offers the oblation along with the utterance of the Mahāvyāhṛtis.

According to the Kāṭhaka and the Varāha, the husband should first loosen all her hair and rub thereon his hands anointed with butter. Then she should part her hair with a porcupine quill having three white spots or a Sami-twig having leaves. According to Laugākṣi,[5] her hair should be dressed in two side-locks with a thread, partly blue and partly yellow. According to Brāhmaṇabala, the one on the right side should be dressed first. The Vārāha prescribes also the use of a woollen string for the purpose.

According to the Vaikhānasa school,[6] the porcupine quill with three white spots together with several objects[7] is to be placed on the parting line of the hair which is smoothed later on by the husband with the quill. Baudhāyana[8] says after her hair has been parted, some Barley-flowers should be fastened to it. Bharadvāja[9] also gives a similar ritual as Vaikhānasa, but adds that after

1 e. g. Āgniveśya-gṛhya-sūtra, p. 46.
2 *San. GS.*, ; *Var. GS.* : *Man. GS.*
3 I, 22, 3. 4 1, 7. 5 *Kāth. GS.*, p. 132, 1. 19.
6 III. 12. p. 44. 7 For these, see Text, *op. cit.*, 1. 10.
8 P. 30. 1. 7-8. 9 I, 21, p. 21.

the parting of her hair all the materials used for the Ritual should be placed in front of the fire, so also three rice mixed with sesamum and a water vessel. She is required to look at each of these and to answer, on the husband's question, what she sees, that she sees "Children and Cattle". One of these (three) rice should be used in feeding Brāhmaṇas, one for Brāhmaṇīs and the other she should eat together with sons or daughters as desired. Just like Baudhāyana, Āpastamba[1] also says that a few barley-shoots should be tied to her hair, but adds that she should keep silent till the stars appear and before she speaks it she should go along with her husband towards the East or North and murmur the Mahāvyāhṛtis.

According to Jaimini,[2] she should be made to sit on an excellent seat or on a mattress of Eraka grass and her hair should be parted from the beginning of the forehead to the top of the head. Her hair should be adorned with flowers. The husband asks, after having filled a vessel with water mixed with gold dust, what she sees therein, and she answers she sees Children, Cattle, good luck for herself and long life for her husband.

Like Jaimini, Āśvalāyana also recommends that her hair should be parted just from the front, but others think that the parting should begin from the middle. Some other

1 14, 7-8.

2 1, 7, p. 6-7.

material than the porcupine quill[1] might also be used,[2] but this material, according to Sānkhāyana,[3] should be left in her lap.

According to Pāraskara,[4] Sānkhāyana[5] and Gobhila,[6] the husband should tie an even number of Udumbara fruits on a string and fasten it to her neck with the prayer that she might be "Fruitful". He does so before the parting; so it seems that during the parting of the hair he touches the string on her neck with the left hand while he does the parting with the right.[7]

The Mān. GS.[8] mentions a rite to be observed in the 8th month of her pregnancy in which she should be bathed with water mixed with fruits. After she is dressed with unwashed cloth and adorned with scented flowers, the fruits should be kept hanging on her neck in the form of a necklace.

When the mother is about to be confined, ceremonies for easy delivery[9] are performed. According to the Vaikhānasa school the lying—in room is to be fumigated

1 त्रेण्या शलल्या त्रिभिर्दर्भपुञ्जीलैश्शलालुग्लुपसेनेति, ĀpGs. 6.14.3.

2 Viratara wood,—Udumbara branch or Sami branch; cf. *Pār. GS.*, 1, 15, 4; *Gobh. GS.*, 2, 7, 6; *Drāh. GS.*, II, 25; *Kāth. GS.*, and *Vār. GS.*, mentioned above.

3 1, 22, 9. 4 *GS.*, 1, 15, 6. 5 *GS.*, 1, 22, 10.

6 *GS.*, 2, 7, 4. 7 Cf. *San. GS.*, 1, 22, 8; *Hir. GS.*, 2, 1, 3.

8 1, 16, p. 79; Aṣṭāvakra, 1, cf. particularly, 1. 9.

9 Cf. Devapāla and Ādityadarśana on *Kāth. GS.*, p. 136, 3f.

before[1] she enters.[2] Sānkhāyana[3] says it should be salved against demons. According to several B. YV schools, a water vessel is placed near her feet and one Turyantī-plant near her head.[4] After her entrance into the room, Vaikhānasa says, three or four skilled women should rub her. According to the SatGS., ĀpGS., BharGS., and the PārGS., the husband should touch her on the head and sprinkle her. Hiraṇyakeśin says the husband should touch her belly and stroke her body from above downwards. According to the Kauśika Sūtra[5] four muñja stalks are to be placed on her head with the points towards the East and four reed-stems with points towards the West in case any evil omen be manifest, her right hair-lock may be washed. The husband should loosen her girdle after the womb has been dissolved, says Vaikhānasa. Laugākṣi[6] says when she is about to give birth, the husband should touch her head with his wetted hand and then proceed downwards to her heart along with the prayer for safe delivery. The

1 ĀpGs., 14.13—क्षिप्रं सुवनम् ।

2 *GS.*, III. 14. According to the Padmapurāṇa, as quoted in the Saṃskāramayūkha, the room should be well-built, auspicious, and either East-facing or North-facing.

3 *GS.*, 1, 20, The Padmapurāṇa; while entering she should be protected on all sides.

4 *Āp. GS.*, XIV. 14; *Sat: GS.*, II, 2, 8; *Bhār. GS.*, 1, 22, p. 22, 1. 14; *Vaikh. GS.*, III, 14, p. 45, 1. 14f.

5 33.

6 *Kāth. GS.*, p. 136, 1, 9f.

Saṁskāramayūkha[1] quotes the Padmapurāṇa to show that for easy delivery some powder of the Eraṇḍa root mixed with clarified butter should be rubbed on her back. If the child does not come out a Viśalya is squeazed out on her secret parts which are also fumigated,[2] also the root of yellow jasmine should be placed near her feet and in her hands.

For the safe coming out of the after-birth (Jarāyu), the husband offers his prayers; in case of delay the husband is enjoined to sprinkle water on her head.[4]

If the child dies during birth, certain special rites are observed for the good of her as well as her dead child.[5]

As soon as the child is born, a fire is lit up,[6] one of the reasons being, most probably, the smoking of the child. According to Gobhila,[7] she should not be touched by her husband until ten nights pass.

During the Jātakarman the father bathes the child in lukewarm water and places him on her lap along with

1 p. 22.

2 For the materials used, see *Vaik. GS.*, III, 14, p. 45, 1. 11.

3 *AV.*, 1, II, 4. This *AV.* hymn 1. 11, seems to be the earliest Ritual on successful child-birth.

4 *Āp. GS.*, XIV, 15.

5 *Kaus. S.*, 34; 3ff.

6 *San. GS.*, 1, 25, 4; *Pār. GS.*, 1. 16, 23; *Vaik. GS.*, 3, 15, 18; *Hir. GS.*, 2, 3, 4; *Āp. GS.*, 9, 3, 22; etc.

7 II, 7, 23.

prayers for the child's long life and immunity from diseases.[1] Then he expresses to her his wish that demons may not do any harm to the son and that she may become wealthy and live in prosperity.[2] According to Pāraskara,[3] Vaikhānasa,[4] Manu[5] and Laugākṣi,[6] before the breasts are first given to the child for sucking, they are to be washed by the father. Before washing the mother is promised Iḍā, daughter of Mitra and Varuṇa and a strong woman giving birth to a strong child; he prays also for more strong children. The right one is washed first and offered to the child along with the prayer for a long and joyful life for him. Similarly, the left one. The father then touches both the breasts with the wish that the child may not suffer or cry when parents touch him or speak to him.[7] She is commended to the protection of the Water by means of placing a water-jug near her head.[8]

1 *Vaik.GS.*, III, 15, *Hir.GS.*, II, 3, 10; *Baudh.GS.*, II, 1, 9, p. 33.

2 *Hir.GS.*, II, 4, 2; *Bhār.GS.*, 1, 25, p. 27, 1, 4.

3 *GS.*, 1, 16, 19.

4 *GS.*, III, 15.

5 *Man.GS.*, 1, 17, 7, p. 82, 1. 4-5.

6 *Kāth.GS.*, XXXIV, 5, p. 138; for Devapāla, see 1. 23-24; Ādityadarśana, p. 139, 1. 6f.

7 *Pār.GS.*, 1, 16, 20-21; *Āp.GS.* XV, 5; *Hir. GS.*, 2, 4, 3-5; *Vaik.GS*, 3, 15.

8 *Āp GS.*, XV, 6; *Pār.GS.*, 1, 16, 22; *Hir.GS.*, 11, 3.

The ceremonial observance[1] of her getting up from child-bed takes place on the 10th day[2] after child-birth[3] when the impurity due to child-birth ceases.[4] According to Sāṅkhāyana,[5] the parents should wash their heads, wear new clothes, and partake of the Sthālīpāka cooked on the Sutikāgni by the father.

On the 10th day or later[6] she participates[7] with her husband in giving a name to her child. The name of a girl should consist of an odd number of syllables, e.g. three (MānGS. 1.18.1.) The ending should be either Dā (MānGS., 1.18.1; Gobhila, 2,8.16) or Ā (JaimGS. 1.9)

According to the DrāhGS.,[8] the mother should, before commencement of the oblation, bathe the child, cover him with a clean garment and hand over the child with his head towards the north to the father who sits on her north on the

1 For these rites in the Āgniveśya *GS.*, see pp. 48-49.

2 Āgniveśya, 12th day.

3 *Ap.GS.*, XV, 8; *Pār.GS.*, 1, 17, 1; *San.GS.*, 1, 25, 1; *Jaim.GS.*, 8, 1; *Vaik.GS.*, III, 18; also 12th night.

4 *Gant.DhS.*, XIV, 16; *Manu* V, 62; *Vas.DhS.*, IV, 21.

5 1, 25.

6 Manu: 10th or 12th; Yāj.: 11th; Bhaviṣyapurāṇa: 10th, 12th or 18th; Gṛhyapariśiṣṭa, as quoted in Saṃskāramayūkha, 10th night, 100th night or a year; *Khād.GS.*, 11, 2, 31; the same as GP: same in Gobhila; *Vār.GS.*, III, 7, p. 7:, 10th night; *Man.GS.*, 1, 18, p. 83; 10th night.

7 e.g. Varāha: Pitāmātā ca.

8 11, 3, 6f

Kuśa grass. She then walks behind him and sits by his left side. The father gives various offerings and repeats[1] the secret (Guhya) as well as public (vyavahārika) name to the mother, and gives her the child back with his head towards the north.

According to Gadādhara on the VarGS.,[2] the mother or both the parents should sit behind the fire with the child on her lap. They participate in giving a name. The Sūtra[3] says the mother (as well as the father) should not eat meat for one year.

According to Āpastamba,[4] Hiraṇyakeśin,[5] and Bhāradvāja,[6] the mother and the father should pronounce the names together.

If the mother sees that for some reason or other her breasts have become insufficient for the child, she observes various rites as have been prescribed in the Saṁskāraratnamālā.[7] She also observes the rite of placing the child on the cradle (for the first time) on the 12th, 16th or 32nd day after its birth.[8]

1 Same in Gobhila *GS.*, 2, 8, 17.

2 III, 7, p. 7, 1, 10f, Vira's Ed.

3 *op. cit.*, 7; cf. *Man GS.*, 1, 18, 7, p. 84, Baroda Ed.

4 XV, 8.

5 II, 4, 11.

6 1, 26, p. 27, l. 13-14 "Pitā mātā iti...dve nāmnī" etc.

7 p. 869.

8 *Saṃs.RM.*, p. 870, 1, 24ff. Some authorities think the 13th day is better for the girl; p. 871, l. 6 and 8. Other women also join the performance of the rite, l. 10f.

The day of making the child[1] wear the first garment[2] is also a ceremonial occasion for her.[3] On the 10th, 12th or 16th day after its birth, she has the rite of the piercing of the child's ears[4] performed, the child remaining on her lap.[5] When the child is two and a half months old, it is given for the first time the betel.[6] The mother also gets similar rites performed for the child for its good and long life.[7]

According to the DrāhGs.,[8] the mother covers the child with a garment, and standing to the south, hands over the child to the father when the rite for its first going out is being performed on the 3rd day of the 3rd Bright Fortnight after its birth. With her face turned towards

1 Not mentioned in Āgniveśya.

2 The Āgniveśya describes an Āyuṣya rite, pp. 52-53.

3 *op. cit.*, p. 872, 1, 7ff.

4 *op. cit.*, p. 872, 1, 26f. Saṃskāramayūkha, p. 26. Cf. Gṛhyapariśiṣṭa, quoted in *Saṃ.RM.*, 874, 1, 29s, According to Viṣṇudharmottara, as quoted in *Saṃ.RM.*, p. 875, 1, 7-8 the child remains on the lap of the mother, The left ear of the daughter should be first pierced and then left; *op. cit.*, p. 876, 1, 15.

6 *Saṃs.RM.*, p. 876, 1, II. 6 *Saṃs.RM.*, p. 876.

7 *Saṃs.RM.*, p. 877.

8 II, 3, xf;cf. *Saṃs.RM.*, p. 886, 1, 16ff. *Baudh.GS.*, 4th month; Varāha; 10th day; Yama: 4th month; etc. For the Prayoga: *Saṃs.RM.*, p. 888, 1 6ff. This rite is also mentioned in Baudhāyana, Pāraskara, Gobhila, Khadira as well as Kauśika sūtras. Gobhila and Khadira: third day of the third bright half after the birth of the child. They really describe the rite Candradarśana under same Niṣkramana.

the west the mother sits by the side of the father. The mother is praised and the child is given back to her. She should circumambulate the child and bring it back home. For the special kind of food she would like to offer her child for the first time, she has to make a choice. She may choose the meat of a goat, partridge, Atibird, Bharadvāja or Kṛcaka with special objects in view. If child is desired to be all-round, various kinds of flesh should be mixed up and given. Āpastamba does not allow any alternative but suggests only partridge-meat*; Jaimini and Kāṭhaka no flesh but any sacrificial food.

According to Gobhila and Khadira, she should wash the head of the child in the morning. In the evening the father worships the moon and the mother, dressing the child, hands it over to the father with its face towards the north. She then goes behind the father, she being on his north. The father then recites the mantras (Mantra Brāhmaṇa 1.5. 10-12) in which the Moon is praised and gives the child back to the mother. with the prayer that it may never be separated from its mother.

She observes the rite of making the child[1] first sit on the ground in its 5th month; another rite when the teeth of the child appear.[2]

*Cf. *Āp.GS.*, 6.16.2, तैत्तिरेण मांसेनेत्येके ॥

1 *Saṃs.RM.*, p. 890, 1, 8f; p. 891, 1. "Kumārya apy evam".

2 *Vār.GS.*, p. 8, 1, 1.

She gives her child the first solid food[1] in the 5th month[2] or later.[3] She sits to the right of the father[4] with the child on her lap[5]. According to Sāṅkhāyana[6] and Kauṣītaki, she should take the remnant of the food after the child is fed. After the Annaprāśana she lets the child go and touch whatever he likes; the thing he touches shows what his profession is to be.[7]

When the child is one year old or more,[8] the rite of tonsure (Caula) is performed. She bathes the child and puts

1 Āgniveśya *GS.*, 2.2.4, p. 53.

2 Āgniveśya, षष्ठे मासि

3 *Man.GS.*, 1, 20, p. 87: 5th or 6th: *Vaik.GS.*, III, 22: 6th month; Cf. the various authorities quoted in *Saṃs.RM.*, p. 891f. The sixth month in the opinion of the majority of Sūtra Kāras. The Kāṭhaka after the appearance of the teeth.

4 *Saṃs RM.*, p. 894, 1, 13.

5 *Op. cit.*, 1, 25; Gadādhara on *Vār.GS.*, p. 8, Vira's Ed,, 1, 20.

6 1, 27, II.

7 Saṃskāramayūkha, p. 15; *Saṃs.RM.*, p. 895, 1, 5—6; Vad. on *Vār.GS.*, *op. cit.*, 1, 23-27.

8 The alternatives are: third year, first year; after the completion of 1st year. *Pār.GS.*, 2, 1, 1, one year; *Saṃ.GS.*, 1, 28, 1.: One year; *Vaik.GS.*, first or third; *Drāh.GS.*: 1, 28, third year; *Bhār.GS.*: 1. 28, first year; *Jaim.GS.*, 1, 11.; third year; Manu: first or third year; Yama: second or third year; *Āśv.Śmr.* : Third year; Nārada: third—eleventh year; *Sam.RM.*: third—eleventh; Saṃskayramūkha (p. 29) and *Sams.RM.*: (p. 897) quoted several authorities. *Baudh.GS.*, 2, 4, 1, 1st year or third year, *Man.GS.*,

on him or her an upper and under garment[1] and having the child on her lap, sits down to the west of the fire.[2] According to Gobhila,[3] she should sit on the Darbha grass pointed northwards with her face towards the east. But Rudraskanda on Drāhyāyana[4] says she should not sit on a seat made of Kuśa. She keeps on touchiug the father while he offers the Ājya oblations.[5]

According to Āśvalāyana,[6] each time the father cuts the hair he gives it together with Sami leaves to the mother; she puts it down on the bull-dung. According to Hiranyakesi[7] and Varāha[8], she sits to the north of the fire, holding a lump of bull-dung in her hands, therewith she receives the cut-off hair. It is then thrown into cow-dung so that it may not get into some wicked hands. According to Kauśika, the parents offer and receive the child three times between themselves.

1, 21, 1, 3rd year *Kāṭ.GS*,, 40, 1, third year *ĀŚVGS*. (1, 17, 1), *Vār.GS*., 4 and *Kāṭ.GS*., 40, 8; as is the custom of the family. *San,Gs* and *Kan,GS*., (1, 28): 5th year for Kṣatriya and seventh year for Vaiśya. The AV. (VI, 21, 136, 137) has spells to make hair grow.

1 Āgniveśya *GS*., pp. 53-54.

2 *Āśv.GS*., 1, 17, 2; *Pār.GS*., 2, 1, 5.

3 II, 9, 8. 4 III, I, 17. 5 *Pār. GS*., II, I, 6.

6 *GS*., I, 17, II. 7 *GS*., II, I, 6, 3-4.

8 *GS*., IV, 16, 13, p. 10, Prof. Vira's Ed., cf. Hiran.; cf. *Saṃs. RM*., p. 902, 1. 29f; *Vaik. GS*., II, 13.

The Kāṭhaka GS,, 40.2-5. makes it clear that the tuft of hair kept would show which family the child belongs to, thus a child of Vaśiṣṭha family is required to have the lock of hair on the right side of the head, those of Vaśiṣṭha and Atri families on both sides, those of Aṅgiras family five locks of hair and of the Bhṛgu family none at all.

According to VarāhaGS.[1] she should not long for any sour thing nor take any thing that excites; she should eat unsalted things silently.

If the mother is in the family way the Cuḍākaraṇa cannot be performed.[2]

The triple rites of the upanayana are: the vow of studentship, 2. learning Sāvitrī and putting a log of wood into the fire. The nāma-pṛccha or asking the name of the student is one of the supplementary rites. There are other minor rites which submerge in some one or other of the above three.

In connection with the upanayana* there is no reference to the father, but the girl or the boy approaches the mother

1 *Op. cit.*, p. 1.2, 1. 4-5.

2 Saṃskāramayūkha, p. 30; *Saṃs. RM.*, p. 900. 1. II. In case of the mother's pregnancy, there is a pratiprasava that the rite may be performed if the period of her pregnancy does not exceed five months; *Saṃs. RM. op. cit.*, 1. 14-15.

* Earliest trace of the upanayana: *ṚV*. III. 8.4.5.

for alms during the Bhikṣāṭana (roaming for alms.)* If she belongs to the Brāhmaṇa caste, she would be addressed as "Bhavati bhikṣāṃ dadātu" with "Bhavati" at the beginning; if to the Kṣatriya caste, with the same in the middle; if to the third caste, with it at the end. As soon as the son has begun Brahmacarya, he comes, first of all, to the mother for blessings. This shows that the mother is the best well-wisher of the daughter or son in life, particularly, in connection with the upanayana. This is quite in keeping with the fact that the student, after his Samāvartana, is instructed by the Guru to respect his mother most.[1] Āpastamba[2] says that after the return from the house of the Guru the student should give whatever he may obtain to his mother. On his reaching home the student should bow down, first, to his mother, and then to the father, as the mother is a thousand times more honourable than the father.[3]

The mother, so far as the Marriage is concerned, helps in every way possible the daughter as well as the son.[4] Her

* *Drāh. GS.*, II, 4, 29-30; Saṃskāramayūkha, p. 60; Viṣṇu, XXVII, 25; *Mān. GS.*, 1, 22, 20, p. 93, Bar. Ed.; *Vār. GS.*, V, 28, p. 18, Vira's Ed.; Manu II, 50; *Bhār. GS.* 1, 10.

1 *Tait.Āraṇ.*, 7, II, 12.

2 I, 2, 15.

3 Cf. Commentator on *Gobh.GS.*, II, 4, II, p. 353, 1, 16ff, "Pitres tu prathaman mātaraṃ eva", etc.

4 *RV.*, 1, 12, II; *AV.*, II, 36, etc.

choice in selecting a bridegroom is adhered to.[1] To incur the displeasure of a mother-in-law is considered most unfortunate by the son-in-law,[2] which shows that in matrimonial affairs the mother exercises much influence. During the wedding of the daughter the mother stands in front of the fire with some fried rice on a winnowing basket.[3] Her prayers to the Fire are essential for the good of the daughter.

Thus in all the saṃskāras performed at various stages of the children's life, the mother seems to lead in importance. She keeps on touching the father while he offers the oblations, and that means that she is at the same time offering the oblations. So long as she is living, none of the above rites can be performed without her participation and prayers to gods for the good of the children.[4] The principle of bowing down to the mother first on the student's return after Samāvartana is also uphold by the honour shown to the mother in Aurddhadehika rites,

So far as the śrāddhas are concerned, several special ceremonies are performed in honour of the mother.[5] The

1 *RV.*, V, 61, etc., with Bṛhaddevatā V, 49ff.

2 *RV.*, X, 34, 3.

3 *Drāh.GS.*, I, 18.

4 *Sams.RM.*, p. 900, 1. 3f; Saṃskāramayūkha, p. 30 "Caule ca vratabandhe ca", etc.

5 It will be seen in this connection that there is not a single rite performed for the father which is not performed for the mother just the same.

Candanadhenu śrāddha, the costliest and most ceremonial of all śrāddhas, is performed for the mother only.[1] The Anvaṣṭakās are also special rites performed for her in which she receives Piṇḍas along with her mothers-in-law (the grandmother and great-grand-mother of the sacrificer). The offering of the Piṇḍa in this Mātṛśrāddha is considered so important that Kamalākara, as quoted in the Śrāddhamañjarī says even a Garbhinīpati should offer the Piṇḍa in due time and even though the father of the sacrificer be living, it should be offered.[3] The Mañjarīkāra says in plain words that this rite is a very important one and should be performed even though several conditions may remain unfulfilled.[4]

According to Kātyāyana[5] the mother should not be offered a separate Piṇḍa except on the day of her death, as her satisfaction arises from the Piṇḍa awarded to the father. This prohibition or a separate offering to the mother applies to the followers of this particular school only, and even then it is designed to emphasise the fact that the parents are one and the same, and not that the mother is excluded from the right of having Piṇḍas. The statement that the

1 For the Prayoga of the Śrāddha, see Āryānuṣṭhāna, p. 360.

2 Śrāddhamañjarī, p. 130, "Navamyām mātuśrāddham", etc. It gives the Prayoga, too,

3 Maitrāyaniyapariśiṣṭa, as quoted in *op. cit.*

4 *op. cit.*, "Asya śrāddhasya atitaravasyam āva!:aspatvet", etc.

5 Chandogapariśiṣṭa, p. 329, v. 22, *Una.Samh.*

satisfaction of mothers arises from the Piṇḍas awarded to the fathers shows that they also share in the Piṇḍas just as the fathers do; and it shows that the Piṇḍas are offered conjointly for the mothers also.[1] Kātyāyana does not prohibit the performance for the mother,[2] which means that she is a regular mane as the father is. So what Kātyāyana means is that in the Śrāddhas the parents should be considered as one and the same Devatā, and no separate Devatātva should be attributed to the father. Again, this condition would apply only to the Pārvaṇa Śrāddhas as the same Kātyāyana remarks in another place[3] that no Vedic Ritual should be begun without worshipping the Manes and *even then* (Tatrāpi) the mothers should be worshipped first. In the Vṛddhiśrāddha,[4] the rite performed for the prosperity of the child, the mother must be worshipped first of all and then the father; so also in other sacrifices.[5]

Even when the rite Ābhyudayika is celebrated on three consecutive days, the mothers are to be worshipped on the first day.[6] Anyway, the very fact that the mother is enti-

1 See Hemādri, Pariśeṣa-khaṇḍa. 2 See the previous verse.

3 Saṃhitā, *Una.Samh*., p. 313, Sl. 17.

4 *Pār.GS*., Bom. Ed., p. 509, 1. 29; Saṃskāramayūkha, p. 6, see particularly Āśvalāyana quoted.

5 See Jābāli quoted by Gadādhara, *op. cit*; *Pār.GS*., p. 512, 1, 15.

6 Śrāddhakāśikā, *Pār-GS*., p. 512, 1. 15f; cf. in this connection

tled to the Sapiṇḍikaraṇa,[1] be it with the father[2] or the grand-mother,[3] at once shows the mother is a fullfledged Pitṛ and she has all the rights as other Pitṛs have.

The highest dignity of the mother's position is at once brought out by the fact that even her misconduct is not considered as a bar to the performance of the Aurddhvadehika rites for her—the sin being atonable by the son.[4] The father who is expelled from the caste for his crime is to be regarded as an outcaste by the son, too, but the mother[5] never is. Whatever be her crime the mother is the Mother for the son, and all the rites are performed for her.

That the mother is the highest Guru is also corroborated by the direct statements in the Mahābhārata[6] and the

the fact that in the Nāndiśrāddhas, too, the mothers are worshipped first of all, Upodghāta, p. 62, 1. 18.

1 Cf. *SānGS.*, IV.3; V. 9.

2 Yama as quoted in *Pār.GS.*, p. 499, 1. 12-13; cf. Śrāddhakriyākaumudī, p. 428, 1. 13-16; Bhaviṣyapurāṇa, as quoted in the Caturvargacintāmaṇi; Laghuhārita, as quoted in the Śrāddhakriyākaumudī, p. 426, 1. 17-21.

3 Vṛddhaśātātapa, *Smṛ.Sam.*, p. 234, 1. 6, verse 41; *Pār.GS.*, p. 499, 1. 9f.

4 *Hir.GS.*, II, 4, 10, 7; *San.GS.*, III, 14, 5.

5 *Vas.Dhs.*, XIII, 47; *Bau.DhS.*, XX, I; XXI, 15; *Āp.DhS.*, I, 10, 28, 9.

6 I, 196, 16; XII, 342, 18 and XIII, 105, 10.

Smṛti.[1] Manu[2] says definitely that she is a thousand times more honourable than the father.

The very fact that the mother should be worshipped at the beginning of any and every Vedic Sacrifice at once gives her the highest position as Guru.[3]

Thus it is seen in the pre-birth Saṃskāras, in the after-birth Saṃskāras, in the Aurdhvadehika rites, and in every other Vedic rite, that the position of the Mother is unique; she is the highest Guru and the rites performed by her and for her lead to the same conclusion.

CONCLUSION

Thus we have shown that in Rituals the Daughter holds no less important a position than the son; the Wife and the Husband hold an equally important position; and that the Mother holds a more honourable position than the father. On the whole, it can certainly be said that in no way does the Woman hold a less important position than the Man in the Vedic Ritual.

1 *Gaut.DhS.*, II, 51, Yājñavalkya, I, 35.

2 II, 145; cf. also 225-237; Iv, 160; Vaśiṣṭha, XIII, 48, quotes the same opinion.

उपाध्यायान् दशाचार्य आचार्याणां शतं पिता ।

सहस्रन्तु पितॄन्माता गौरवेणातिरिच्यते ॥—मनुसंहिता ।

3 *Pār.GS.*, Bom. Ed., p. 512, 1, 15.

Appendix I

The Sister

In this section on the Daughter, it is only meet to say something about the woman as Sister. It is true that we do not get copious informations about the Sister from Vedic Literature, particularly from the ritualistic point of view. Still, the little that we get is sufficient to throw a flood of light upon the position of the Sister in ancient India.

In the Vedic Ritual Literature, we do not get any rite of the type of Bhrāṭrdvitīyā as observed in Bengal to-day (popularly known as Bhāiphoṃṭā). Even then, sweet strong relationship between the brother and the sister is manifest from the Vedic Literature. The Vedic Literature records dissensions among sisters[1] and also among brothers[2] but there is no such record about any dissension between a brother and a sister.

The word Bhrātṛ is derived from Bhṛ, to maintain and, therefore, it means the maintainer of the sister. The etymological significance of this word is amply borne out by the Vedic Literature.[3] Both the Śruti and the Smṛti are unanimous that a brotherless sister must not be married.

1. AV. 2. 7. 6 2. 3. 70. 2; Sat Bra. 4. 1. 5. 3
3. AV. 1. 14. 2; VājSamh. 305

The Ṛgveda shows that a brotherless wife[1] was likely to return to her father's family[2]; moreover, a brotherless girl used to roam about in despair and was led astray.[3] The AV. explicitly states that a brotherless sister is shorn of all glory and has nothing to boast of; she is simply compelled to lead a wretched life.[4] Moreover, it warns everybody that a brotherless wife is bound to bring about disaster in the long run.[5] On account of the sin incurred by marrying a brotherless girl, the bridegroom had to pay the father-in-law a penalty of 100 cows and a chariot.[6] Vaśiṣṭha adduces Vedic evidence regarding the undesirability of marrying a brotherless girl as she is only likely to become a substitute for son in her father's family[7]. Yājñavalkya[8], Gautama[9], etc. are also of the same opinion.

The Atharva-veda represents the curse of the sister as a living being[10] and it was terribly dreaded by brothers[11].

1. अभ्रातेव पुंस एति प्रतीची, etc.

2. 1. 124. 7.

3. अभ्रातरो वे योषणो व्यन्त: । The reason of their being led astray is that brotherless girls were not married.

4. अभ्रातर इव जामयस्तिष्ठन्तु हतवर्चसः ।

5. 3. 8 अभ्रात्री, इत्यादि । There was every chance of their becoming Putrikās and staying with their parents.

6. ŚānGs. 1. 14. 16 "अधिरथं शत दुहितृमते"; Nārāyaṇa-bhāṣya, दुहितृमतेऽभ्रातृमतीपित्रे अधिको रथो यस्मिन् तद् गवां शत ं दद्याद् अभ्रातृमतीविवाहदोषनाशनार्थम् । Nirukta 3.5

7. 17. 16; cp. 3. 2, 8. 1. 52—53, भ्रातृमतीं etc.

9. 18. 20, Tait. 2. 5. 6. 3 10. 2. 10. 1 11. 9. 4. 15

In the Vedic Society, the Sister was considered indispensable and as a consequence, sisters were even adopted. Thus, Paṇis adopted Saramā as their sister.[1] In a list of close relations given in the Chāndogya Upaniṣad, the brother and the sister are placed together which shows that no other relationship can, according to the Upaniṣad, intervene between the two.[2] Bhaga means the combination of wealth, prowess, fame, fortune, knowledge and renunciation of the world; the sister is bhaginī, because she is possessed of these all for the brother.

In the Vedic Literature, there is an interesting discussion about the relative importance of the wife and the sister in the family. According to some seers, the sister was the more important of the two. They advocate that in the same sacrifice, the most important of all the Vedic sacrifices, after the utterance of the Mantra known as "Agni Gṛhapati", the Mantra called "Rākā" is to be uttered and not the one entitled "Devānāṃ patnīḥ."[3] Because "Rākā" represents the sister and as in the family, the sister was more important than the wife, in the sacrifice also the same must be the case and the sister must be shown more honour than the wife. And therefore, the Rākā mantra must be uttered first

1. 10. 188. 9

2. 7. 15. 2 स यदि पितरं वा मातरं वा स्वसारं वाचार्यं वा, etc.

3. तद्धाहू राकां पूर्वं शंसेज्जाम्यै वै पूर्वपेयमिति ।

and then the Mantra "Devānāṃ patnīḥ," and accordingly, the drinking of the Soma juice for the sister must precede that for the wife. The Aitareya Brāhmaṇa, however, passes a different opinion. Though the wife comes from outside still the sister is to be dependent upon her sister-in-law.[1] "Ātmā vai jāyate putraḥ"; and the wife is the progenitor of the self in the form of children. The husband prays that he himself may be her eleventh child.[2] The Aitareya Brāhmaṇa decides in favour of the relative importance of the wife, no doubt; still, it cannot be doubted that the opinion of the opponent school was a formidable one and had to be dwelt upon at length in the work itself. Again, the "Rākā" Mantra must have been given precedence in those parts of the country where matriarchy was the rule.

1. तस्मात् समानोदर्यां स्वसाऽन्योदर्याया जायाया अनुजीविनी भवति । Ait. Brā. 3. 37

2. तनयान् दश मे देहि मामेकादश कृधि ।

Appendix II

The Wife in Indian Literature

*The twin usages of polygamy[1] and polyandry have both been known in India from time immemorial in varying degrees. Brāhmaṇas have never advocated either of this—monogamy being always the ideal. The dogmatic explanations of the Taittirīya Saṃhitā,[2] Aitareya Brāhmaṇa[3] and Śatapatha Brāhmaṇa[4] about a man having more than one wife and a woman having only one husband draw our attention to what prevailed in some parts of the country and not what the Brāhmaṇas recommended. The unconditional union of heart and soul—serene, soleman and sublime—of the husband and wife,[5] the application of love-charms by the wife for having the husband as her own and other mutual solicitations for constancy in love[6] and the aspired

*This section was published in the Indian Historical Quarterly, Vol. XVI, 1940, pp. 70-8.

1. ṚV. X, 146; AV., III, 18 (a charm for having predominance over a rival co-wife); Ait. Br. VII, 13 (100 wives); Śat. Br. IV, 1. 5. 1 ff. and Jai. Br. III, 121 ff.; Sapatnī in St. Petersburg Dict.; Pār. GS.. I, 4, 6-10 and corresponding passages in other Gṛhya and Dharma Sūtras. 2. VI, 6, 4, 3. 3. III, 23; III, 47.

4. IX, 4, 1, 6. 5. प्राणैस्ते प्राणान् संदधाम्यस्थिभिरस्थीनि मांसैर्मांसानि त्वचा त्वचमिति (Mantra used in the Caturthikarma) Pār. GS. III, 6. 6. AV., II, 30, 2, 5; 36, 4; etc.

"Cākravākaṃ saṃvananam" mentioned by the Gṛhyasūtras in connection with the marriage,[1] Caturthīkarma[2] and the Garbhādhāna[3] cannot but lead to the conclusion that monogamy is the ideal of the society. The Vedic Literature depicts the wife in the loveliest colour[4] and this is possible in a society where monogamy is the rule. She is the absolute Master of the household; as a matter of fact, she is the house.[5]

The incorporation of many non-Aryan women in the Aryan fold in some form or other brought about a social revulsion. In later ages all the three higher castes were allowed to marry Śūdrās and the Aryans themselves could marry from castes lower to themselves, i.e. a Brāhmaṇa could marry a Kṣatriyā as well as a Vaiśyā in addition to a Brāhmaṇī and so on. The extensive performance of rituals in which a large number of women including the sacrificer's daughter, 'not to speak of Dāsīs, was given as

1. E. g. Baudh. GS., I, 4, 5, p. 13, II. 19-20 चक्रवाकं संवननं यन्नदीभ्य उदाहृतम् ॥ यद्दित्तौ देवगन्धर्वौ तेन संवनिनौ स्वः ॥

2. E. g. Hir.GS. 1, 246; p. 49, I, 11-12.

3. Hir.GS., I, 25, p. 57. 1. 17. Also see AV. XIV, 2, 64.

4. RV. X. 85. 46. सम्राज्ञी श्वशुरे भव सम्राज्ञी श्वश्र्वां भव। ननान्दरि सम्राज्ञी भव सम्राज्ञी अधिदेवृषु ॥ All the verses of X. 85 bear testimony to this.

5. RV. III. 53. 4, "जायेदस्तम्" etc. Sāyana: "अस्तम्। अस्यन्ते क्षिप्यन्ते पदार्था इत्यस्तं गृहम्। जायेत् जायैव गृहं भवति 'न गृहं गृहमित्याहुर्गृहिणी गृहमुच्यते" इति स्मृतेः।

sacrificial gift, encouraged polygamy which degraded Indian women to the lowest abyss.

The Supreme Soul created the first woman for love. As He found no delight without her, He divided Himself into two equal halves; as husband and wife they became one and complete again and again.[1] From the beginning the wife is thus the equal half of her husband. The husband hands over the dust of the foot-print of the cow to the wife for the increase of her wealth as she is the half of his self.[2] In the Vājapeya sacrifice he wants her to accompany him in mounting the post for Heaven for the same reason.[3] Yājña-valkya says, the wife and the husband are each like half a shell.[4] She completes him.[5] They are one body.[6] In the Vedas, the Smṛti and the popular usage she is declared to be the equal half of her husband, sharing equally the religious merit or demerit.[7] The half of the body of her husband falls if she takes spirituous liquor.[8] The woman as wife protects the society from chaotic conditions.[9] The wife

1. Bṛh. Upan. 1. 4. 3. Cp. 17. 2. Tait Saṃh., vi. 1. 8. 5. p. 148, Vol. 2, Weber. 3. Śat. Brāh., V. 2. 1. 10. p. 434, Weber's ed. cp. also viii 7. 2. 5. 4. Bṛh. Upan. 1. 3. 4.

5. Op. cit., 1. 4. 17. Ait. Āran., 1. 3. 4.

6. Manu., iv, 184, ix, 45. 7. Bṛh., XXV, 46. Cp. the following verses: also XXIX. II.

8. Vaś. DhS., XXI, 16. p. 222, 1. 2. (ASS) पतत्यर्धं शरीरस्य यस्य भार्यां सुरां पिवेत् 9. MBh. 1. 128; cp. also to 76. 28.

makes the husband holy.[1] She opens the gateway to truth for her husband.[2] The wife is the home[3] and as such, she protects all the four stages of life by her munificence and gracious help.

It is no wonder then that the wife and the husband, from birth to birth, are reborn in the same *yoni* be it human or some other. The Śruti says when the female half of Prajāpati became a cow, the male half became a bull; when the former became a mare, the latter became a stallion; when the former a she-ass, the latter a he-ass.[4] As they are two equal halves, in some births the wife becomes the husband and in some others the husband becomes the wife. He who performs the cremation of his wife with the Agnihotra becomes the wife and his wife becomes the husband in the following birth; if a respectable wife dies before the husband as a consequence of the insults done her by the latter, she becomes the husband and he the wife for three lives to follow.[5] King Purañjana was capable of transforming himself into Vaidarbhī by virtue of his deep devotion to his wife.[6] The view of the wife and the husband being one person and

1. Tait Brāh. 2. 2. 2. 6, अयज्ञियो वा एष योऽपत्नीकः ।

3. RV. X. 85. 24, तस्य योनौ सुकृतस्य लोके ।

4. Bṛh. Upan., 1. 4. 4, सा गौरभवदृषभ इतरः, etc.

5. Gobh. Smṛ., III, 13, मान्या चेन्म्रियते पूर्वं भार्या पतिविमानिता । त्रीणि जन्मानि सा पुंस्त्वं पुरुषः स्त्रीत्वमर्हति ॥

6. Bha. Pur., iv. 26. 22.

two equal halves with equal rights is also upheld by the principles laid in the Śrāddha ceremonies, particularly, the Sapiṇḍīkaraṇa.

As against the above passages, Aitiśāyana[1] goes so far as to say that the woman, far from having equal right with man, has no right (Adhikāra)[2] at all to sacrifices. He says, the word स्वर्ग-कामः in the श्रुति text दर्श-पूर्णमासाभ्यां स्वर्ग-कामो यजेत refers to a man only; the woman is, therefore, excluded. Moreover, the wife is "nirdhanā—without any property;" so she cannot have any right over the sacrificial staff required for the proper performance of the sacrifice. The wife is herself a property as she is sold by the father and purchased by her husband. Whatever she may earn by means of spinning, etc., belongs to her husband; as she is dependent, she cannot independently work for herself and acquire property thereby. A property cannot be said to have possession of other property; so as she has no possession over the sacrificial materials, *viz.*, the wheat, the rice, etc., she cannot have any right to offer sacrifices.

But this view is not tenable, as the masculine gender in स्वर्ग-काम is not, however, intended to designate males only,

1. Jaim. NMV. on Jaim. NM., 6. 1. 6. p. 303, ASS. Vol. 24, Poona, 1823. Cp. Jaim. NMV. (iv. 1. 3) of Mādhavācārya, ed by Goldstuecker and Cowell, London (Truebner & Co.), 1886, p. 252. Jaimini, लिङ्गविशेषनिर्देशात् पुंयुक्तमैतिशायनः।

2. तत्र दर्श-पूर्णमासादौ यागनिष्पादकत्वं कर्तृत्वम्। फलभोक्तृतया स्वामित्वमधिकारः—Mādhavācārya,

the class Man being indicated. It means "यः स्वर्गकामः स यजेत —one who aspires to Heaven should sacrifice." As a woman certainly longs for heaven, she is also entitled to offer the sacrifice.[1]

According to Jaimini, the wife cannot be said to have any claims to property; she does not possess riches, as she does not want to; but whenever necessary, she may justly claim her share in the property—फलोत्साहाविशेषात्तु ।[2] When she is married, she is assured that she will never be deprived of her common rights to Religion, Wealth and Love. According to Yājñikadeva, she has certainly the right of possession over the property acquired by means of her personal labour and that awarded by her father, brother, etc.; and the property earned by her husband is the common property of the wife also.

It is not right that the wife is sold and purchased like a chattel. The selling of a daughter is severely condemned in Brahmanic Literature. The passages, *viz.* दुहितृमते दद्यात्,[3] आर्षं गोमिथुनम्[4] etc., which Aitisāyana seems to refer

1. Cf. Jaimini 6-1-7, Nyāyamālā on Jaim. 6-1-6 ff. "अस्ति स्त्रियाः कर्माधिकारः। कुतः—पुंलिङ्गस्याविवक्षितत्वात् ।......तस्माल्लिङ्गस्य प्रकृत्यर्थत्वाभावादुद्देश्यगतत्वेनाविवक्षितत्वाच्च स्त्रिया अप्यधिकारः ॥" See pp. 304-305 and ed.. Ānandāśrama ed,, 1916. See also Mimāṃsā-darśana, Ānandāśrama ed., 1932, p. 1357 f. 2. Jaimini 6. 1. 13; see also Mimāṃsā-darśana, op. cit., p. 1360. 3. SāṅkSS. 1. 14. 16.

4. VasDhS. 1. 32. Cf. ĀśvŚS, 1. 6. 1. Baudh. DhS. 1. 20. 4, etc.

to, do not refer to the selling of the daughter or the purchase of the wife. The price of objects for sale always varies; it can never be permanently fixed, but in the passages mentioned above the price, if it be price at all, is always the same, be the girl qualified or not, beautiful or ugly. As regards the first passage, Gārgya Nārāyaṇa says the direction would apply only in those cases where the girl has no brother. The second passage refers to a particular kind of marriage and can therefore never be a general rule. And so on. There are direct statements in scriptures regarding the possession of the wife over property.[1]

By means of love she offers the sacrifice; she has her prowess in Love; by means of Love she takes possession of the wealth in her husband's house.

Kātyāyana[2] also says, स्त्री चाविशेषात् i.e. the woman also has the right to sacrifice because there is no particularisation. Karkācārya,[3] commenting upon the सूत्र, says स्वर्गकामः in स्वर्गकामो यजेत is an uddiśyamāna viśeṣaṇa; and because of viddhisaṃsparśābhāva, the number and gender are not significant (avivakṣita).[4] Yājñikadeva[5] also argues in the same way as Karka and comes to the same conclusion *viz.*, the

1. Compare the Commentaries on KātSS. 1. 1. 7. For DhS. ĀpDhS. 11. 14. 9; Gau DhS 18, 21. etc. 2. Śrauta-sūtra, 1. 1, 7. 5. 3. See p. 5, Chowkhamba edition.

4. For the vivakṣā in the number and the gender, compare the dictum "Paśum ālabheta." 5. P. 8, Weber's edition of KātSS.

woman has every right to perform sacrifices. He gives an alternative explanation to say that अविशेषात् in Kātyāyana's सूत्र may mean स्वर्गकामत्वाविशेषात् as there is no difference in longing for heaven, i.e., as both of them equally desire for heaven."[1] The conclusion is that the woman is also entitled to perform sacrifices.

The right of the wife to offer sacrifices for the acquirement of religious merit is also established by scriptures. "(He) initiates the sacrificer with the girdle (mekhalā), the wife with the tie of the yoke of a plough,[2] "the wife in the iron,[3] "the wife in the Gārhapatya silently"[4] etc., show what particular rites the wife has to observe and with what ends.

The wife is entitled to offer sacrifices, but can she offer them in her exclusive personal rights? A woman is entitled to perform sacrifices alone so long as she is alone. Thus, a maiden walks round the sacred fire in the Sākamedha for having a suitable husband. When the Phālguna Full-moon enters Uttaraphālgunī, she offers a furnished bed to a Brāhmaṇa for having a suitable husband.[5] In the Horse-

1. Compare in this connection Jaimini's Sūtra फलोत्साहाविशेषात्तु।

2. See sections on the Dikṣā. Tait Saṃh. 6. 1. 3 मेखलया यजमानं दीक्षयति, योक्त्रेण पत्नीम्। See also KātŚS. 1. 1.8—दर्शनात् ॥

3. Patnī Lohe—KātŚS. 7. 4. 34.

4. Patnī ca Gārhapatye tuṣṇīm, op. cit., 5. 5. 36. · See also 2 7. 4.

5. Viṣṇu, XC, 7-8, Unav. Saṃh., p. 110.

sacrifice she puts pearls into the manes of the horse.[1] Yearning for Nārāyaṇa, Vedavatī devotes herself to dreadful ascetic vows and in her later birth nets him.[2] Satī, daughter of Dakṣa, undergoes penances for Śiva, goes to Himavatpura and advises Haimavatī to worship Śiva.[3] Rukmiṇī worships Umā in her maidenhood; Kṛṣṇa abducts her while she is returning from her place of worship.[4] A widow can also perform some rites as we have shown in our section on the widow.

The brahmavādinīs who do not even marry for observing religious practices are certainly entitled to offer sacrifices.[5]

The wife is not, however, entitled to do so. The wife and the husband are mutually dependent in sacrificial matters; in the same rite the husband is to perform some part, the wife the corresponding counterpart. Thus, in the Darśapūrṇamāsa while she looks at the sacrificial ghee, he is to bind together kuśa grasses. Now, if the wife or the husband intends to celebrate the sacrifice individually, the sacrifice cannot be properly performed as the absence of

1. SatŚS Vol. V. p. 238, 1. 1-2, Cf. ĀpŚS, XX. 15, Vol. III, p. 159. 2. Rāmāyaṇa 7th Book (Uttarakāṇḍa), 17th Sarga.

3. The Pauranic legend, as given in Kāl P. 1. 8. Cp. Mahāśvetā etc. practising austere penances. 4. The famous story of the Har V. 5. Saṃs-RM. Vol. I, p. 166, 1. 6. Cp. the appelations Kaṭhīs, Bahvṛcis, etc. referred to above.

either of them would involve in the sacrifice an improper procedure. Neither the wife nor the husband should try to have the other's part of the sacrifice performed by selecting a substitute. The performer of the sacrifice reserves this power of selection; he may select a Hotṛ, Udgātṛ, Brahmā, Adhvaryu or any other person in connection with the sacrifice. But no selection in the case of the wife and the husband is possible. The husband is to be the Yajñasvāmin while his wife the Yajñasvāminī. The dictum स्वर्गकामो यजेत also shows that the wife and the husband are to offer together. By saying अग्नीषोमौ देवता it is meant that both Agni and Soma are to be worshipped but as their attribute godliness "Devatātva" is common, "Devatā" is purposely kept in the singular; similarly by saying स्वर्गकामो यजेत, it is meant that both the wife and the husband are to offer the sacrifice together as they have a common right. Again at the time of their marriage, their common possession of property is declared. The expenses to be incurred in the sacrifice must be borne by both of them. In no circumstances is the husband or the wife entitled to divide property; so no occasion for celebrating a sacrifice separately should really arise. The scriptures directly declare that the wife should not be deprived of her rights regarding Religion, Wealth and Love.

The Scriptures furnish us copious evidence regarding the joint sacrifice of the husband and the wife. They perform sacrifices together and pray to their gods so that they may, with their daughters and sons by their side, reach the full extent of life.[1] They with one heart and soul offer oblation to and worship their beneficent god Agni.[2] They with uplifted ladle serve together their God Indra and the latter in his turn profusely blesses them.[3] They together pour their presents to Indra in order to win a stall of kine.[4] They with their hearts knitted together with the thread of love wax old in their devotion to seek Agnl.[5] They of one accord press out and wash the Soma juice*and invoke their god to approach them.[6]

The Sampatnīya prayer declares that the wife and the husband acquire religious merit in common and enjoy together undecaying light in heaven.[7] Kātyāyana[8] also recognises their common acquirement of religious merit when he says, अनुचरीर्वा फलाधिकारात् or only the attendants (are to be

*See also Manu 5, 53, नास्ति स्त्रीणां पृथग्यज्ञो न व्रतं नाप्युपोषणं See Pāṇini 4. 1. 133 "पत्युर्नो यज्ञसंयोगे". KātŚS. Sūtra 103 Chow.ed., p. 47. Not to speak of the life-time of the wife, even after her death the widower cannot appoint a substitute for her; for detailed information: Karka's commentary on the above.

1. RV. VIII. 31, 8. 2. RV. I, 72, 5. 3 RV. I, 83, 3. 4. RV. I, 131, 3. 5. RV. V, 43, 15. 6. RV. VIII, 31. 7. Mait Saṃh., 1. 4. 3 (p. 51. 4). Cp. 1. 4. 8 (p. 56, 10). Kath Saṃh., 5. 4 (p. 46). Tait. Brah., 3. 7. 5. 11. ApŚS., 1. 3. 5. 5. 7. 8. KātŚS. 20. 8. 24: उदवसानीयान्ते भार्या ददाति । 20. 8. 26: कुमारीं पालागलीं चाध्वर्यवे । 20. 8. 26: चतुरीर्वा अफलाधिकारादितरासाम् । 20. 8. 27: अनारभ्यत्वाच्च ।

awarded as sacrificial fee in the Aśvamedha sacrifice after Udavasānīya) as others (i.e., wives and the maiden daughter) obtain religious merit. Karka says that the wife cannot give the husband as sacrificial fee; so the sacrificer also cannot give his wife away: their possession, gift and acquirement of merit are in common and nobody is entitled to give the other away as sacrificial fee.

When the match-makers come in to select a girl, they say expressly that the hand of the girl is sought by them for such and such of such and such family in order that he may have children by her and offer sacrifices with her.[1] The Vedas, as cited by Manu, deelared that the religious rites are to be performed by the husband together with the wife.[2] In commenting upon the Prājāpatya form of marriage which ordains that the husband and the wife are to perform religious duties together[3], Haradatta commenting on AsvGS.[4] points out that in all other forms of marriage too such duties are to be performed together, but here the emphasis lies on the fact that those who are married according to the Prājāpatya form are to lead household life up to

1. Winternitz, Altindische Hochzeitsrituell, p. 40.

2. IX. 36. Baudh. Dhs 1. 7. 15. 10 and Govinda's commentary.

3. Cf. Gau. DhS. IV. 7. Nar. DhS. XII. 40. Man. DhS. III. 30. Yajn., I, 60. In connection with Brahma form, Ap. DhS. II. 11. 17. 4. Trivandrum ed., p. 21, sūtra 15.

the end of their life.[1] In enumerating the forty sacraments, Gautama[2] uses the following words instead of the word Vivāha or any of its synonyms—"The taking of a help-mate for the fulfilment of the religious duties." The word "Sahadharmiṇī" is extremly significant in this connection.

Viṣṇu[3] says the wife should observe the same vows as her husband. Manu,[4] Viṣṇu,[5] and the Bṛhaddharmapurāṇa[6] have the same couplet saying that the wife should not perform sacrifices, observe vows and fast separately. They[7] think her highest duty is to act according to his directions and should not, therefore, observe vows, etc. (against his will).

Similarly, the husband too cannot perform any sacrifices or observe vows without the wife. In all the religious observances the wife sits on the right of her husband except in the consecration (abhiṣeka) and the washing of Brāhmaṇa's feet in which she remains on the left—says

1. यद्यप्यन्येष्वपि विवाहेषु सहधर्मचरणमस्ति तथाप्यत्र यावज्जीवनं सहधर्मचरणमेव न मध्ये आश्रमान्तप्राप्तिरिति विशेषः ॥ 2. DhS. VIII. 16.

3. Ch. XXV. 2. Unav. Saṃh. p. 63. Vyāsa, Ch. III. "Samānavratavṛttiḥ" 4. v. 66. (Nir. Ed., p. 203, 1. 30—31).

5. Ch. XXV, 15. UnavSaṃh., p. 66. 10.

6. Bṛhad DhP. p. 317. 81. 1. 7. Viṣṇu, op. cit., sl. 16. Cf.: Brahma V. P. Śrikṛṣṇajanmakhaṇḍa, M. Tarkaratna's ed., p. 153. 1. 6-7. Atri. sl. 137. Smṛ. Samu., p. 15. 1. 5-6.

Bhaṭṭa Gopīnātha[1]: Kātyāyana[2] says both the husband and the wife should sit on the west of the fire, the wife being on the right of the husband. According to Atri[3] also the wife should be on the right of the husband in Śrāddhas, sacrifices and marriage. Vṛddhahārīta[4] says the wife is the mantra; so it is certain that as without the mantra, so without the wife the sacrifice cannot be performed. Even after her death the husband is required to make an image of her with kusa grasses in order that he may offer in the fire raised from the previous fire with which she was cremated, the Agnihotra and Pañcayajñas as before.[5] Sāyaṇa in his Commentary on Ait. Brā. interprets the passage recommending the performance of Agnihotra by a widower[6] in the above light and refers to the rule of three debts. Kātyāyana[7] refers to the substitution of the golden image of Sītā by Rāma for his exiled wife and makes the rule that a widower should have his wife's substitute in order that he may perform the Vedic sacrifices. So, alive or dead, the wife is always with her husband during the performance of their sacrifices.

1. Upod., p. 40, 1. 48; also p. 64, 1. 1. 1-2 see also his SamsRM., p. 13, 1. 1. 1-2. 2. Śrautasūtra, 193.

3. Sl. 138 Smr., Sam., p. 15, 1. 8.

4. Smr. Sam., p. 325. sl. 15, मन्त्राः पत्न्यः प्रकीर्तिताः ॥

5. Vṛddhahārīta XI, 113-115. Smr. Sam., p 349. Otherwise the husband is to become a monk or to marry again.

6. VII. 9. Kaus-Br., XXXII. 8. 7. ChandP. III, 9.

The Padmapurāna[8] says the sacrifices of a person having no wife are useless. The wife is the highest religion and in the three worlds there is no other Dharma like her for the husband. Kṛkala, otherwise an ideal religious Personality, is abused by Dharma (Religion personified) as narādhama (worst among men) and caura (thief) because he was not accompanied by his wife Sukalā during the Śrāddha offered by him to his parents. The wife is the head of domestic religion. Without her there can be no religion at all.

8. Bhūmikhaṇḍa, p. 221, 1. 11 f; pp. 243-244 of the ĀSS. ed. नास्ति भार्यासमं तीर्थं धर्मसाधनहेतवे। शृणुष्व त्वं गृहस्थस्य नान्यो धर्मो जगत्त्रये॥ यत्र भार्या गृहं तत्र पुरुषस्यापि नान्यथा। ग्रामे वाप्यथवाऽरण्ये सर्वधर्मस्य साधनम्॥ नास्ति भार्यासम तीर्थं नास्ति भार्यासमं सुखम्। नास्ति भार्यासमं पुण्यं तारणाय हिताय च॥ गृहस्थस्य च धर्मस्य भार्या भवति स्वामिनी। तस्माद्भार्यां विना धर्मः पुरुषस्य न सिध्यति॥

Appendix C

Additional Note on the Chief Wife

If the fire goes out, it is the first wife who is to rekindle it. She should on the preceding day take her food in the day time,[1] observe brahmacarya and silence, wear silken garments[2] and towards sunset enter the Gārhapatya house from the south and seat herself to the right of her husband, both facing the east. At the beginning of the sacrifice, when the Adhvaryu offers both the Araṇis to the sacrificer, he places the upper one on his own lap and hands over the lower one to her which she similarly places on her own lap.[3] During the night she keeps awake with her husband to keep up the fires.[4]

If a co-wife is left at home, the wife may leave the fires in charge of her, but that would mean that the co-wife would be simply a representative of the wife and nothing more than that. Certainly the wife should take away the fires with her[5] if it is not simply impossible for her to do so.

1. Śat. Br., II. 1, 4, 1. 2. Sat. ŚS, vol. II. p. 528, I. 27.

3. Kat. ŚS., Chow. Ed,, p. 298 Sūtras 307-308; Sat ŚS., vol. II, p. 535, I 5. 4. Śat. Br. II, 1, 4, 7.

5. Sat. ŚS., vol. I, p. 358, 1. 11, ff.; note particularly the remark of the Scholiast "Bahubhāryasya ekayā saha bhāve'pi na doṣaḥ"; also vol. II, p. 544 "Bahubhāryasya ekasyā api sannidhau na dosaḥ., The words "na doṣaḥ" in these texts cannot mean otherwise than this, that the (first) wife is the proper person to attend, but in her absence, some othe wife might be allowed to do so (but never a Śūdrā wife), and thus be a representative for her.

BIBLIOGRAPHY.

Ācārādarśa.—By Śrīdattopādhyāya, Bombay, 1884. Oblong.

Ādityadarśana:—Author of the Vivaraṇa on the Kāṭhaka Gṛhya Sūtra. See Kāṭhaka Gṛhya Sūtra.

Agnipurāṇa.—Prose Eng. Trans. by M.N. Datta, 2, Vols., Calcuṭṭa, 1903.

Aitareya Āraṇyaka of the Ṛgveda with commentary of Sāyaṇa. Ed. by R. Mitra, Bib. Ind., N.S., Vol. 134, 1895, etc. trans. by Martin Haug, Bombay, 1863 and A.B. Keith, H.O.S., Vol, 25. Cambridge, Massachusetts, 1920.

Aitareya Upaniṣad.—Ed. by E. Roer, Bib. Ind., N.S., Vol.6.

Amarakoṣa.—Ed. by Gurunātha Vidyānidhi, Calcutta, 1907.

Anton Nomilov:—The Boilogical Tragedy of Women, London, 1932.

Antyeṣṭipaddhati of Nārāyaṇa Bhaṭṭa;—published by Tukaram Javaji from the Nirnaya Sagara Press, Bombay, together with the Author's Prayogaratna in the same volume; Bombay, 1915.

Antyeṣṭipaddhati of Bhaṭṭa Harihara, Ms. 1974, Egg. p. 105, I·O.L.

Āpastamba Dharma Sūtra, Ed.—by Dr. G. Buehler, Second Edition; Bombay Sans. Ṣeries, Nos. xliv and 1, 1892-

1894; trans. by the same author in S.B.E. Vol. II, Oxford, 1897.

Āastamba Gṛhya Sūtra.—Ed, by A.M. Sastri, M.G.O.L.S., No. 1, 1893; Sutras only trans. by Herman Oldenberg, S.B.E., Vol. XXX, Oxford, 1892.

Āpastamba Srauta Sūtra with commentary of Rudradatta, Ed.,—by R. Garbe, Bib. Ind., N.S., Vol. 92, 1882, etc.; German trans. by W. Caland, Goettingen. Amsterdam, 1921-24.

Aṣṭāvakra:—See Mānava Gṛhya Sūtra.

Āśvalayāna Gṛhya Kārikā of Kumārila Bhaṭṭa:—pp. 263-326 of Āsvalayana Gṛhya Sūtra, Bombay Edition.

Āśvalāyana Gṛhya Pariśiṣṭa:—pp. 201-262 of the Bombay Edition of the Āśvalāyana Gṛhya Sūtra.

Āśvalāyana Gṛhya Sūtra with the commentary of Haradattācārya,—Ed. by T.G. Shastri, S.S. No. 78, Trivandrum, 1923; and with the commentary of Gārgya Nārāyaṇa, Ed. by J. Mukundaji. 2nd Edition, Bombay, 1909; Bib. Ind. Edition, 1869; Sutras only trans., S.B.E., Vol. XXIX.

Āśvalāyana Śrauta Sūtra with the commentary of Gārgya Nārāyaṇa, A.S.S., No. 61, Poona, 1917; R. Vidyaratna's Edition in Bib. Ind., 1874.

Aśvalāyana Yājñika Paddhati:—Ms., Buehler 15, Keith's Catalogue, Vol. I, p. 171, I.O.L.

Atharvaveda.—Ed. by Shankar Pandurang Pandit, Bombay, 1895, etc., trans. by W.D. Whitney, H.O.S., Vols.

7-8 (1905); R.T.H. Griffith, Banaras, 1895-96; M. Bloomfield, S.B.E., Vol. XLII.

Aufrecht, T.: —Die Hymnen des Ṛgveda, 1st part (m. i-vi), 2nd part (m. vii-10) Bonn, 1877. The 2nd Vol. includes Khilas 672-88.

Aurdhvadehika-prayoga by Kṛṣṇadīkṣita—Ms. 1270a, Eggeling's Catalogue, p., I.O.L.

Bālamanoramā, the: —2 Vols. (1910-12), Ed. by S. C. Sastrigal, Teppakulam, Trichinopoly.

Barnett, L.D.; – Antiquities of India, London, 1913.

Baudhāyana Dharma Sūtra with the commentary of Govindasvāmin,—Ed. by L. Śrīnivāsācārya, M.G.O.L.S., No. 34, Mysore, 1907.

Baudhāyana Gṛhya Sūtra,—Ed. by M.U.O.L.P., S.S.. 32 and 55.

Baudhāyanapaddhati of Keśavasvāmin: —Ms. 604, Eggeling's Catalogue, p. 52.

Baudhāyana Pitṛmedha Sūtra: —published in the same Vol. as Baudhāyana Gṛhya Sūtra.

Baudhāyana Śrauta Sūtra.—Ed. by W. Caland, Bib. Ind., 1904-1924.

Bhababhūti: —Uttaracarita, Ed. and trans. by S. Roy, Calcutta, 1923.

Bhāradvāja Gṛhya Sūtra.—Ed. by H.J.W. Solomens, London, 1913.

Bhaṭṭa Harihara: —See Antyeṣṭipaddhati.

Bhūmikhaṇḍa of Padmapurāṇa,—Ed. by P. Tarkaranta, Calcutta 1914-15.

Blagden, C.O.:—Malayan Sociology (for details see Thesis, P. 317), London, 1926.

Bloomfield, M,:—See Kauśika Sūtra.

Brāhmanṇs:—See

(1) Aitareya Brāhmaṇa
(2) Jaiminīya Brāhmaṇa.
(3) Kauṣītaki Brāhmaṇa
(4) Śatapatha Brāhmaṇa
(5) Taittirīya Brāhmaṇa

Brāhmaṇabala:—Padhatikāra on the Kāṭhaka Gṛhya Sūtra, See Kāthaka Gṛhya Sūtra and Paddhati.

Brahmāṇḍapurāṇa:—Ed. by T. Kavyatīrtha, Calcutta, 1908.

Brahmavivartapurāṇa:—Ed. by T. Kavyatīrtha, Calcatta, 1909.

Bṛhadāraṇyaka Upaniṣad:—S.B.E., Vol. XV (pp. 43-230), Oxford, 1900.

Bṛhaddevatā:—Ed. by R. Mitra, Bib. Ind., Vol. 127.

Bṛhaddharmapurāṇa:—Ed. by Pañcānana Tarkaratna, Calcutta, 1907-1908.

Bṛhaspati-Smṛti:—Ed. by M.N. Datta, Calcutta, 1906-1909.

Caland, W.:—

(1) Die Altindischen Todten und Bestattungage-brauche, Amsterdam. 1896.

(2) Pitāmedhasūtras, z. D.M.G., X, No: 3.

(3) Das Vaitānasūtra des Atharvaveda, Amsterdam, 1910.

(4) Vaikhānasasmārtasūtra, Bib. Ind., 1927.

(5) See also Āpastamba Śrauta Sūtra, Baudhāyana Śrauta Sūtra, Jaminīya Gṛhya Sūtra, and Kapiṣṭhala-Kaṭha-Saṃhitā.

Candrakānta Tarkālaṅkāra:—See

(1) Gobhila Gṛhya Sūtra.

(2) Gobhila Pariśista.

(3) Karmapradīpa.

Caturvargacintāmaṇi of Hemādri:—Bib. Ind. Edition complete 7 vols.

Chandogapariśiṣṭa of Kātyāyana:—Bib. Ind. Edition, vol. 178, not yet complete; see Karmapradīpa.

Chāndogya Upaniṣad:—trans. by R. E. Hume in his Thirteen Principal Upanisads, Oxford, 1921.

Colebrooke:—Miscellaneous Essays (reprinted by his son T. E. Colebrooke, London, 1913.

Cook, Arthur Bernard:—Zeus (a study in ancient religion), University Press, Cambridge, 1914.

Dakṣa Smṛti:—Smṛtīnāṃ Samuccayaḥ, pp. 77-84.

Delbrueck:—Die Indogermanischen Verwandschaftsnamen, Leipzig, 1889. (Abhandlungen der phil. -hist. cl. der k. Sachs. Ges. Wissensch. XI. Bd. No. 5).

Devannabhatta:—See Smṛticandrikā and Śrāddhakāṇda.

Devapāla:—Scholiast on Kāṭhaka Gṛhya Sūtra, See Kāṭhaka Gṛhya Sūtra.

Devayajvan:—See Kātyāyana Śrauta Sūtra, ed. by Weber.

Dhātupradīpa of Maitreya Rakṣita, ed. by S. C. Chakravarti, Rajsahi, 1919.

Drāhyāyana Gṛhya Sūtra, A. S. S., No. 74, Poona, 1914.

Drāhyāyana Śrauta Sūtra:—as available in Quotations from Lātyāyana Śrauta Sūtra.

Durga:—See Ṛjvartha on Nirukta (Bhadkamkar's Edition)i

Frazer, Sir J. G.:—Taboo, being part 2 of his Golden Bough, which is complete in 12 volumes.

Gadādhara:—see Pāraskara Gṛhya Sūtra.

Gautama Dharma Sūtra:—A. S. S., No. 61, Poona, 1910.

Geiger, W.:—Ostiranische Kultur im Altertum, Eslanger, 1882.

Gobhila Gṛhya Sūtra:—Ed. with Bhāṣya by C. K. Tarkālaṅkāra, 2nd Edition Bib. Ind., N. S., Vol. 175, Calcutta, 1908; aphorisms only translated into German by Dr. F. Knauer. Dorpat, 1884.

Gobhilapariśiṣṭa:—Ed. with Bhāṣya by C. K. Tarkālaṅkāra, Bib. Ind., N. S., Vol. P82, Calcutta, 1909, It contains, besides other Sūtras, the Śrāddhakalpa and Śrāddhakalpapariśiṣṭa Sūtras.

Gopīnātha Bhaṭṭa. See (1) Jyotsnā; (2) Saṃskāra-ratnamālā; (3) Upodghāta.

Gṛhyakārikā:—See (1) Kumārila.

(2) Śaunaka.

(3) Reṇukārya.

Gṛhyā-saṃgraha of Gobhilaputra:—Ed. by S. Samasrami in the Ūṣā, Vol. I, No. X, and by C. K. Tarkalankara, Bib. Ind., Vol, 186.

Grotten:—Christian Eucharist, Philadelphia, 1913.

Haradatta:—see Aśvalāyana Gṛhya Sūtra.

Harihara:—see Pāraskara Gṛhya Sūtra.

Hemādri:—See Caturvargacintāmaṇi.

Hillebrandt, Alfred:—

(1) Ritualliteratur, Vedische Opfer und Zauber, Strassburg, 1897.

(2) Śāṅkhāyana Śrauta Sūtra in Bib. Ind., 3 vols.

Hiraṇyakeśi Gṛhya Sūtra:—Ed. by T. Kirste, Vienna, 1819; Sūtras only trans., S. B. E., Vol. XXX. See Satyāṣāḍha Gṛhya Sūtra.

Indische Studien:—a long series consisting of 18 vols., Edited by A. Weber, Berlin, 1850-65, Leipzig, 1868-98.

Jaiminīya Brāhmaṇa:—Ed. by Pandita Ramadev, Lahore, 1921; selected texts trans. into German by W. Caland, Verhandlingen der Kon. Akad. vin Wetenschappen to Amsterdam, Deel I, N. R. D. XIX, No. 4.

Jaiminīya Gṛhya Sūtra:—Ed. by W. Caland, P.S.S., No. 2; Lahore, 1922.

Jaiminīyamīmāṃsādarśana, together with Nyāyamālā, A.S.S. Vol. 24, Poona, 1892.

Jaiminīyanyāyamālāvistara of Mādhavācārya, Ed. by Goldstucker and Cowell, London, 1878.

Jātakas, the:—tran. in 6 vols. by various hands under the editorship of Prof. E. B. Cowell, Cambridge Univ. Press, 1896-1907.

Jayarāma—See Pāraskara Gṛhya Sūtra.

Jolly, J. ; Recht und Sitte. Strassburg, 1896.

Journals:

(1) Fraser's Magazine, London.

(2) Journal of the American Oriental Society. Boston, Mass.

(3) Journal of the Royal Asiatic Society. London.

(4) Sitzungsberichte der Berliner Akadamie. Berlin.

(5) The Usa. Calcutta.

(6) Zeitschrift der Deutsch. Morgenl. Gesellschaft.

Jyotsnā. See Satyāṣāḍha-Śrauta Sūtra.

Kaegi:—Der Ṛgveda, die alteste Literatur der Inder, Leipzig, 1881, (trans. by Arrowsmith, Boston, 1886).

Kalesi:—Paddhati (Ṛgvedic School), Serampore Edition, 1898.

Kapiṣṭhala Saṃhitā:—Ed. by Dr. W. Caland and Prof. Raghu Vira, Lahore, 1952. Ist quarter 1933 I. O. L. Punjab.

Karkācārya:—See

(1) Pāraskara Gṛhya Sūtra.
(2) Kātyāyana Śrauta Sūtra.

Karmakāṇḍapradīpa, belonging to the White Yajurvedic Ritual:—Ed. by Vare Anna Sastri Atyaji; Bombay, 1921. Grantha size. First Edition.

Karmapradīpa:—Ed. by C. K. Tarkalankara, Bib. Ind., Vol. 178.

Kāśīkhaṇḍa:—See Skanda Purāṇa.

Kāṭhaka Gṛhya Sūtra:—Ed, by W. Caland, with extracts from the Commentary of Devapāla, Paddhati of Brāhmaṇabala and the Vivaraṇa of Ādityadarśana; Lahore, 1925. Dayanada Mahavidyalaya Sanskrit Series, No. 9.

Kāṭhaka Saṃhitā:—Ed. by Leopol Von Schroeder, Leipzig, 1912; Index by R. Simon, 1912.

Kātyāyna Śrauta Sūtra:—Ed. by M. Pathaka in the Chowkhamba Sanskrit Series, Nos. 68,69, etc; Banares, 1908; also Ed. by Weber (The White Yajurveda, Teil. III) with extracts from the commentaries of Karka and Yājnikadeva; Berlin, 1859.

Kauśika Sūtra: Ed. by Bloomfield in J. A. O. S., Vol. XIV.

Kauṣītaki Brāhmaṇa:—Ed. by G.V. Chhaya, A.S.S., Poona, 1911; trans. by A.B. Keith in H.O.S., Vol. 25.

Kauṣītaki Gṛhya Sūtra:—Ed. by Ratnagopāla Bhaṭṭa, 1908.

Kauṣītaki Upaniṣad:—trans. by Max Muller in S.B.E., Vol. 1,1900.

Keith: (1) Vedic Index, London, 1912.

(2) Kauṣītakī Brāhmaṇa
(3) Taittirīya Saṃhitā.

Khādira Gṛhya Sūtra: —with the Commentary of Rudraskanda, Ed. by A. Mahadeva Sastri, M.G.O.L.S., No. 41; Sutras trans, by H. Oldenberg, S.B.E., Vol. XXIX.

Kṛṣṇamiśra: —See Srāddhakāśikā

Kulluka—See Manu Saṃhitā.

Kumārila Bhaṭṭa: —See Āśvalāyana Gṛhya Kārikā.

Kunāla Jātaka: —See Jātakas.

Lanman, C.R: —Sanskrit Reader, Boston, U.S.A., 1888.

Lāṭyāyana Śrauta Sūtra, with the commentary of Agnisvāmin; Ed. by A. Vedantavagisa, Bib. Ind., N. S., Vol. 63, Calcutta, 1870-72.

Leist: —Alterisches Jus Gentium, Jena, 1889,

Ludwig, A: —Ṛgveda.

Macdonell: —

(1) A History of Sanskrit Literature, London, 1900.
(2) Vedic Index, London, 1912.

Madanapārijāta: —Bib. Ind., Ed.

Mahābhārata, the: =Hitavadi Edition, Calcutta, 1895.

Mahānirvānatantra: —Ed. by Maheśacandra Pāla. Calcutta.

Mahīdhara: —See Vedadīpa.

Maitrāyaṇī Saṃhitā: —Ed. by L.von Schroeder, Leipzig, 1881; numerous passages trans. into German by the same author in his Indiens Literatur und Cultur, pp. 110-162, Leipzig, 1887.

Mānava Gṛhya Sūtra of the Maitrāyaṇīya Śākhā with the commentary of Aṣṭāvakra, Gaekwad's Oriental Series, No. XXXV, Baroda, 1926.

Mānava Śrauta Sūtra of the Maitrayaṇīya Śākhā :—Ed. by Dr. Friedrich Canuer, St. Petersburg, 1900.

Mantrabrāhmaṇa :—Ed. with a commentary in the Journal Usa, Vol. 1, Part 3, by Pandit Satyavrata Samasrami, 1872.

Manu :—Text Nirnaya Sagar Edition, 1929; translation:. Buehler, S. B. E., Vol, XXV.

Manuscripts : —

(1) Ādityadarśana's Vivaraṇa : Bombay Govt. MS. No. 14.

(2) Antyeṣṭipapdhati of Bhaṭṭa Harihara, belonging to B. YV. See under the Title.

(3) Āśvalāyanayājnikapaddhati, belonging to RV. see under the Title.

(4) Aurddhvadehikaprayoga of Kṛṣṇa Dīkṣita, be. longing to SV. See under the Title.

(5) Baudhāyanapaddhati of Keśavasvāmin, belonging to B. YV. See under the Title.

(6) Brāhmaṇabala's Paddhati, belonging to B. YV. Bombay Govt. MS. No. 13.

(7) Devapāla's Commentary on the Kāṭhaka Gṛhya Sūtra, belonging to B. YV. Bombay Govt. MS. No. 12.

(8) Mārkaṇḍeya Purāṇa:
(9) Reṇukārya's Gṛhyakārikā, belonging to W. YV. See under Reṇukārya.
(10) Śaunaka-Kārikā, belonging to RV. See under Śaunaka.

Mārkaṇḍeya Purāṇa:—Ed. by Dr. Sastri in Bib. Ind., Calcutta, 1909; see also under Manuscripts.

Mason:—Woman's Share in Primitive Culture, London, 1895.

Matsyapurāṇa:—Hitavādi ed. Calcutta.

Max Mueller:—Ṛgveda.

Mayr Aurel:—Das Indische Erbrecht, Wien, 1873.

Monier-Williams:—Brahmanism and Hinduism, 4th Ed., London, 1891.

Nārada Smṛti:—Ed. by R. Chattopādhyāya 2nd Edition, Calcutta, 1915.

Nārāyaṇa:—See Āśvalāyana Gṛhya and Śrauta Sūtras.

Nārāyaṇa Bhaṭṭa:—See Prayogaratna.

Nirukta:—Ed. by Pandit Satyavarata Sāmaśrami, Bib. Ind., 4 vols; trans. by L. Sarup, Oxford Univ. Press., 1921. With Durga's commentary, Ed. by Bhadkamkar, Bombay, 1913; Ed. by L. Sarup, Lahore, 1929; Indices and Appendix to Nirukta by L. Sarup, Lahore, 1929; Commentaries of Skandasvāmin and Maheśvara on Nirukta, Ed. by L. Sarup in 2 volumes; Lahore 1927 (vol. 1) and 1931 (vol. 2).

Nṛsiṃhatāpaniyopaniṣad:—A.S.S., Vol, 31, Poona, 19.

Oldenberg: —Religion des Veda.

Paddhatis: —

(1) Baudhāyana Paddhati of Keśavasvāmin (B.YV.).

(2) Bhavadeva Paddhati (SV).

(3) Bīreśvara's Paddhati (S.V.)

(4) Brāhmaṇabala's Paddhati (B.YV.)

(5) Kālesi Paddhati (V RV).

(6) Paddhatis given in the Bombay Edition of the Pāraskara Gṛhya Sūtra (W.YV.).

(7) Samskārapaddhati (B. YV).

(8) Trivedīyakriyākāṇḍapaddhati.

(9) Yānikadeva's Paddhati.

Padmapurāṇa: —Ed. by T. Kāvyatīrtha, Calcutta, 1914-19.

Pañcaviṃśa Brāhmaṇa: —Ed. by Ānāndacandra Vedāntavāgīśa, Y Bib. Ind., Vol. 62, Calcutta, 1870-74.

Pāṇini: Aṣṭādhyāyī:—Ed. by Pandita Devendranath Sarma with the commentary Prabha, Calcutta, 1920. See also Siddhāntakaumudī and Bālamanoramā.

Pāraskara Gṛhy Sūtra: —Ed. by Mukundapanta, Kasi Sanskrit Series, Vo. 2, Banaras, 1920; also Ed. by Mahadeva Gangadhara Bakra with the commentaries of Karka, Jayarāma, Harihara, Gadādhara, and Viśvanātha, and with several Appendices variously named. Bombay, 1918; also by several Benares Pandits with the four commentaries. Benares, 1903; Sutras transl, S. B. E., Vol. XXIX (several sections have been omitted in the translation).

Parāśara-Smṛti:—Bombay Sanskrit Series, Vol. 2, Part I, Bombay, 1901.

Pariśeṣakhaṇḍa—Vol. VI of Hemādri's Caturvargacintāmaṇi, Bib. Ind., Ed.

Patañjali:—Mahābhāṣya. Benaras Edition, 1910.

Pischel & Geldner:—Indische Studien (see Geldner), 3 vols., Stuttgart, 1889, etc.

Prajāpati-Smṛti:—Smṛtīnāṃ Samuccayaḥ, pp. 80-98.

Prayogaratna of Nārāyaṇa Bhaṭṭa:—Nirṇayasāgara Edition, Bombay, 1915.

Raghunandana—Tattvas. Serampore Edition, 1908.

Rāmāyaṇa, the:—Hitavādi edition, Calcutta, 1912.

Reṇukārya's Gṛhyakārikā (W. YV):—MB,, also known as Kātīya Gṛhya Sūtraprayogavṛtti: Egg. 361, I.O.L.

Ṛgveda:—Max Mueller's Edition, 6 vols.: translations by Griffith (Benares, 1896), Wilson (London, 1888), etc.

Rudraskanda:—See Khādira Gṛhya Sūtra.

Sāmaveda, the:—ed. Rāmasvarūpa Śarman. Moradabad, 1927.

Sāmavidhānabrāhmaṇa:—Ed. by Pandita S. Sāmaśrami in the Journal Usa, Vol. 5, Benares, 1867; also Ed. by A.C. Burnell with English transliteratiod, London, 1873.

Saṃhitās (Vedic):—

(1) Atharvaveda.
(2) Kāthaka Saṃhitā.
(3) Kapiṣṭhala Saṃhitā.
(4) Maitrāyaṇī Saṃhitā.
(5) Ṛgveda.

(6) Sāmaveda.
(7) Taittirīya Saṃhitā.
(8) Vājasaneyi Saṃhitā.

Saṃskāramayūkha:—Ed. by N. Shastri Shende, Bombay, 1913.

Saṃskārapaddhati of Bhāskara Śāstri:—A. S. S., Vol. 94, Poona, 1924.

Saṃskāraratnamālā of Bhaṭṭa Gopīnātha:—A.S.S., No. 39, 2 vols., Poona, 189/.

Śaṅkha Smṛti:—Smṛtīnāṃ Samuccayaḥ, pp. 374-395, and Unaviṁśati Saṃhitā, pp. 406-427.

Śāṅkhāyana Āraṇyaka:—Ed. by S. Pathaka, A.S.S., No. 90.

Sāṅkhāyana Brāhmaṇa:—See Kauṣītaki Brāhmaṇa.

Sāṅkhāyana Gṛhya Saṃgraha of Paṇḍit Vāsudeva:—Ed. by Somanāthopādhyāya; Benares, 1908.

Sāṅkhāyana Gṛhya Sūtra with extracts from the commentaries of Nārāyaṇa and the Paddhati of Rāmacandra:—Ed. by H. Oldenberg, Ind. St., Vol. XV; Sūtras only trans. into English by the same author in S.B.E., Vol. XXIX. See also Kauṣītaki Gṛhya Sūtra.

Śāṇkhāyana Śrauta Sūtra, together with the commentaries of Anartīya, son of Varadatta:—Ed. by A Hillebrandt in Bib. Ind., 1888ff.

Sarvānukramaṇī of Kātyāyana:—Ed. by Pandit Y. Pathaka, Benares 1893, etc.

Śatapatha Brāhmaṇ:—Ed. by Paṇḍita S. Sāmasrami, Bib. Ind., N. S. Vol. 145, 1900, etc.; also by Weber with

Sāyaṇa's commentary, The White Yajurveda, Vol. 2, Berlin, 1859; trans. by J. Eggeling in S.B.E. Vols. XII, XXVI, XLI, XLIII and XLIV.

Satyāṣāḍha Gṛhya Sūtra, with the commentary of Mātṛdatta: Vol. VII of Satyāṣāḍha Śrauta Sūtra.

Satyāṣāḍha Śrauta Sūtra: —A.S.S., No. 53, 10 vols. Vol. I: First three Praśnas with the Vaijayantī of Mahādeva. Vol. II: Praśnas IV-VI with the Vaijayantī of Mahādeva. Vol. III: Praśnas VII-VIII with the Jyotsnā of Gopīnātha Bhaṭṭa.

Śaunakakārikā: —MS. No. 4785, Buehler 61, I.O.L.

Schrader: —

(1) Prehistoric Antiquities of the Aryan Peoples, London, 1890. (trans. into English by F. B. Jevons from the author's original "Sprachvergleichung and Wigeschichte").

(2) Reallexicon der Indogermanischen Altertumskunde, Strassburg, 1901.

Schroeder: —

(1) Ind. Literatur Und Kultur, Leipzig, 1887.

(2) see Kāṭhaka Saṃhitā and Kapiṣṭhala Saṃhitā.

Siddhāntakaumudī: —Bālamanoramā Edition.

Skandapurāṇa: —Bangavasi Edition in 7 vols. Calcutt, 1911.

Smṛticandrikā of Devanabhaṭṭa: —Mysore Edition, 4 vols., G. O. L. S., No. 52, Mysore, 1914.

Smṛtīnāṃ Samuccayaḥ:—A.S.S., Vol. 48, Poona, 1905.
Smṛtyarthasāra:—A.S.S., Vol. 70, Poona, 19.
Śrāddhagranthas:—

(1) Śrāddhakalpa: see Gobhilapariśiṣṭa.
(2) Śrāddhakalpa L. Vol. VII of Hemādri's Caturvargacintāmaṇi, Bib. Ind.
(3) Śrāddhakāṇḍa: Vol. IV of Smṛticandrikā, see Smṛticandrikā.
(4) Śrāddhakāśikā of Kṛṣṇa Miśra, published in the Bombay Edition of the Pāraskara Gṛhya Sūtra. See Pāraskara Gṛhya Sūtra.
(5) Śrāddhakriyākaumudī of Govindānanda, Ed. by Paṇḍita Kamalakṛṣṇa Smṛtibhūṣaṇa: Bib. Ind., N.S. Vol. 157; Calcutta, 1904.
(6) Śrāddhamañjarī by Vāpubhatta Mahādeva Kelkar, A.S.S., Vol. 59, Poona, 1907.
(7) Śrāddhamayūkha of Nīlakaṇṭhamīmāṃsaka Bhaṭṭa: Ed. by J. R. Gharpure, Collection of Hindu Law Book, Vol. XVIII, Bombay, 19.
(8) Śrāddha Sūtra of Pāraskara: with Karka's Commentary: Bombay Edition of Pāraskara's Gṛhya Sūtra.
(9) Śrāddhasūtrakaṇḍikā: published in the Bombay Edition of Pāraskara Gṛhya Sūtra.
(10) Śrāddhasūtrapaddhati of Gadādhara Dīkṣita: published in the Bombay Edition of Pāraskara Gṛhya Sūtra.

Sraddhagranthas, contd

(11) Śrāddhatattva: Serampore Edition of Raghunandana's Aṣṭāviṃśatititattva; also separately Ed. by Pandit Hrisikesa Sastri, Calcutta, 1909-10.

(12) Srāddhaviveka of Rudradhara Mahopādhyāya: Bombay, 18, Oblong.

(13) Śrāddhavivekasaṃgraha of Sūlapāṇi, Calcutta, 1880.

Stenzler, A. F.:—Gṛhyasūtrāṇi (Indische Hausregeln), Z. D. M. G., Ed. III-IV.

Śūlapāṇi:—See Srāddhavivekasaṃgraha.

Sūtras:—

(a) for Dharmao, see

(1) Āpastamba Dharma Sūtra.

(2) Baudhāyana Dharma Sūtra.

(3) Gautama Dharma Sūtra.

(4) Vaśiṣṭha Dharma Sūtra.

(b) For Gṛhyao, see

(1) Āpastamba Gṛhya Sūtra.

(2) Āśvalāyana Gṛhya Sūtra.

(3) Baudhāyana Gṛhya Sūtra.

(4) Bhāradvāja Gṛhya Sūtra.

(5) Drāhyāyana Gṛhya Sūtra (same as Khādira Gṛhya Sūtra).

Sūtras: —Contd.

(6) Gobhila Gṛhya Sūtra.
(7) Hiraṇyakeśi Gṛhya Sūtra (same as Satyāṣāḍha Gṛhya Sūtra).
(8) Jaiminīya Gṛhya Sūtra.
(9) Kāṭhaka Gṛhya Sūtra.
(10) Kauśika Sūtra.
(11) Kauṣītaki Gṛhya Sūtra (same as Sāṅkhāyana Gṛhya Sūtra).
(12) Khādira Gṛhya Sūtra (same as Drāhyāyana Gṛhya Sūtra).
(13) Mānava Gṛhya Sūtra.
(14) Pāraskara Gṛhya Sūtra.
(15) Śāṅkhyāna Gṛhya Sūtra (same as Kauṣītakī Gṛhya Sūtra).
(16) Satyāṣāḍha Gṛhya Sūtra (same as Hiraṇyakeśi Gṛhya Sūtra).
(17) Vaijavāpa Gṛhya Sūtra (a few quotations only available).
(18) Vaikhānasa Gṛhya Sūtra.
(19) Varāha Gṛhya Sūtra.
(20) Also, various Gṛhya Saṃgrahas and Pariśiṣṭas.

(c) For Srauta°, see

(1) Āpastamba Śrauta Sūtra.
(2) Āśvalāyana Śrauta Sūtra.
(3) Baudhāyana Śrauta Sūtra.

Sutras Cont.

(4) Drāhyāyana Śrauta Sūtra (as available in quotations in the printed Edition of Lātyāyana Śrauta Sūtra).

(5) Kāṭhaka Śrauta Śutra (a few quotations only available in Weber's Edition of Kātyāyana Srauta Sutra).

(6) Kātyāyana Śrauta Sūtra.

(7) Lātyāyana Śrauta Sūtra.

(8) Mānava Śrauta Sūtra.

(9) Sāṇkhāyana Srauta Sūtra.

(10) Satyāṣāḍha Śrauta Sūtra.

(11) Vaitānā Sūtra.

Taittirīya Āraṇyaka: —Ed. by R. Mitra, Bib. Ind., N. S., Vol. 52, 1864-72.

Taittirīya Brāhmaṇa: —Ed. by R. Mitra, Bib. Ind. O. S., Vol. 31, 1855-70; also the Mysore Edition.

Taittirīya Saṃhitā: —Ed. with Sayana's commentary in Bib. Ind., 1860-1899; trans. into English by A. B. Keith, H. O. S., Vols, 18, 19; 1914.

Talavakāropaniṣad: —S. B. E., Vol. 1.

Tāṇḍyamahābrāhmaṇa (see Pañcaviṃśa Brāhmaṇa).

Trivedīyakriyākāṇḍapaddhati: —Ed. by Syāmācaraṇa Kaviratna, Calcutta, 1887.

Ūnaviṁsāti Saṃhitā: —Ed. by Pañcānana Tarkaratna, Calcutta. 1903.

Upodghāta of Bhaṭṭa Gopīnātha:—A. S. S., Vol. 94, Poona, 1924.

Vaijavāpa Gṛhya Sūtra:—(see under Sūtras 'Gṛhya').

Vaikhānasasmārtasūtra:—consisting of the Gṛhya and Dharma Sūtras:—Ed. by Dr. W. Caland, Bib. Ind., 1929.

Vaitāna Sūtra:—Ed. and trans. into German by R. Garbe in two separate vols., London-Strassburg, 1878; also trans. into German by W. Caland, Amsterdam, 1910.

Vājasaneyī Saṃhitā:—Ed. by A. Weber, with the commentary Vedadīpa of Mahīdhara, Berlin-London, 1852.

Vārāha Gṛhya Sūtra:—Ed. by R. Samasastri, G. O. S., No. 18, Baroda, 1921; also by Prof. Raghu Vīra, Lahore, 1932.

Vaśiṣṭha Dharma Sūtra:—trans. by G. Buehler, S. B. R., Vol. XIV.

Vātsyāyana Kāma Sūtra:—Calcutta Edition, 1893; Niraṇyasāgara Edition, with Yaśodharā's commentary, Bombay, 1891.

Vedadīpa of Mahīdhara:—Commentary on the White Yajurveda. See Vājasaneyī Saṃhitā.

Vedische Studien:—see Pischel.

Viṣṇusmṛti:—A. S. S., No. 48, Poona, 1905.

Viṣvanātha:—See Pāraskara Gṛhya Sūtra.

Vṛddhahārita:—A S. S., No. 48, Poona 1905.

Vyāsa Smṛti:—A. S. S., No. 48, Poona, 1905.

ABBREVIATIONS.

AitAran.	= Aitareya Āraṇyaka.
AitBrah.	= Aitareys Brāhmaṇa.
Ap. DhS.	= Āpastamba-Dharma Sūtra.
ApGS.	= Āpastamba Gṛhya Sūtra.
ApGS.	= Āpastamba Śrauta Sūtra.
AsvGK.	= Āśvalāyana Gṛhya Karika.
AsvGP.	= Asvalayana Gṛhya Pariśiṣṭa.
AsvGS.	= Āśvalāyana Gṛhya Sūtra.
AsvSS.	= Āśvalāyana Śrauta Sūtra.
Asv. Yaj. Pad.	= Āśvalāyana Yājñika Paddhati
Atri.	= Atri Saṃhitā.
AV.	= Atharvaveda.
B.PV.	= Black Yajurveda.
Baudh. DhS.	= Baudhāyana Dharma Sūtra.
BaudhGS.	= Baudhāyana Gṛhya Sūtra.
BaudhSS.	= Baudhāyana Śrauta Sūtra.
BhagPur.	= Bhāgavata Purāṇa.
BharGS.	= Bhāradvāja Gṛhya Sūtra.
Bib. Ind.	= Bibliotheca Indica
Brh.	= Bṛhaspati Smṛti
BrhUpan.	= Bṛhadāraṇyaka Upaniṣad.
DhS.	= Dharma Sūtra
DrahGS.	= Drāhyāyana Gṛhya Sūtra.
GautDhS.	= Gautama Dharma Sūtra.
GobhGS.	= Gobhila Gṛhya Sūtra.
GobhSmr.	= Gobhila Smṛti
GS.	= Gṛhya Sūtra

HiranGS. =Hiranyakeśi Gṛhya Sūtra.
Ind. St. =Indische Studien.
J.A.O.S. =Journal of the American Oriental Society.
JaimBrah. =Jaiminīya Brāhmaṇa.
JaimGS. =Jaiminīya Gṛhya Sūtra
JaimUp. =Jaiminīya Upanisad.
J.R.A.S. =Journal of the Royal Asiatic Society.
KapSamh. =Kapiṣṭhala Saṃhitā.
KarmaKP. =Karma Kāṇḍapradīpa
KathGS. =Kāṭhaka Gṛhya Sūtra.
KathSamh. =Kāṭhaka Saṃhitā.
KatSS. =Kātyāyana Śrauta Sūtra.
KausBrah. =Kauśītaki Brāhmaṇa
KausS. =Kauśika Sūtra.
KausUpan. =Kauśītaki Upaniṣad
KhaGS. =Khādira Gṛhya Sūtra
LatySS. =Lātyāyana Śrauto Sūtra
MaitSamh. =Maitrāyaṇī Saṃhitā.
ManDhS, =Mānava Dharma Śāstra.
ManGS. =Mānava Gṛhya Sūtra.
ManSS. =Manava Śrauta Sūtra.
NarDhS. =Nārada Dharma Śāstra.
PancBrah. =Pañcaviṃśa Brāhmaṇa
ParGS. =Pāraskara Gṛhya Sūtra.
RV. =Ṛgveda.
SmsRM. =Saṃskāraratnamālā
SankAran =Śāṅkhāyana Āraṇyaka.

SankGS.	=Śāṇkhāyana Gṛhya Sūtra.
SankSS.	=Śāṇkhāyana Śrauta Sūtra.
SatBrah.	=Śatapatha Brāhmaṇa.
SatGS.	=Satyāṣāḍha Gṛhya Sūtra.
SatSS.	=Satyāṣāḍha Śrauta Sūtra.
S.B.E.	=Sacred Books of the East.
SamrSam.	=Smṛtīnām Samuccayah.
St.Pt.Dict	=St, Petersburg Dictionary.
SV.	=Sāmaveda.
TaitAran.	=Taittirīya Āraṇyaka.
TaitBrah.	=Taittirīya Brāhmaṇa.
TaitSamh.	=Taittirīya Saṃhitā.
TaitUp.	=Taittirīya Upaniṣad.
UnaSamh.	=Ūnaviṃśati Saṃhitā.
VaitS.	=Vaitānasūtra.
VajSamh.	=Vājasaneyī Saṃhitā.
VarGS.	=Vārāha Gṛhya Sūtra.
VasDhS.	=Vaśiṣṭha Dharma Sūtra.
Ved-St.	=Vedische Studien.
Visnu.	=Viṣṇu Smṛti
Vyasa.	=Vyāsa Smṛti
W. YV.	=White Yajurveda.
Yajn.	=Yājñavalkya-Smṛti
YV.	=Yajur Veda
Z. D. M. G.	=Zeitschrift der Deutsch. Morgerland. Gesellschaft.
Zim. Alt. Leben.	Zimmer; Altindisches Leben.

GENERAL INDEX

Thr Arabic figures here refer to pages of this work, No attempt has been made in this Index to record the references to original Sanskrit works that were found too numerous to be included here, Only a few works or authors that have been casually referred to have, however, been included here.

Correction

P. 32, l. 13 For Gārgi, read Kātyāyanī

P. 56 read [4] after Mahābhāṣya in l. 10 and not after cost in l. 9.

P. 131, l. 8 read *before* the former in their turn, etc. and *after* the son of ten fathers : —

Vālī and Sugrīva were born of two husbands living at the same time (Rāmāyaṇa, vii. 42).